T0400004

Teaching Democracy in an Age of Uncertainty

The strength of democracy lies in its ability to self-correct, to solve problems, and adapt to new challenges. However, increased volatility, resulting from multiple crises on multiple fronts—humanitarian, financial, and environmental—is testing this ability. By offering a new framework for democratic education, *Teaching Democracy in an Age of Uncertainty* begins a dialogue with education professionals towards the reconstruction of education and by extension our social, cultural, and political institutions.

This book is the first monograph on philosophy with children to focus on democratic education. The book examines the ways in which education can either perpetuate or disrupt harmful social and political practices and narratives at the classroom level. It is a rethinking of civics and citizenship education as place-responsive learning aimed at understanding and improving human–environment relations to not only face an uncertain world, but also to face the inevitable challenges of democratic disagreement beyond merely promoting pluralism, tolerance, and agreement.

When viewed as a way of life, democracy becomes both a goal and a teaching method for developing civic literacy to enable students to articulate and apprehend more than just the predominant political narrative, but to reshape it. This book will be of interest to scholars of philosophy, political science, education, democratic theory, civics and citizenship studies, and peace education research.

Gilbert Burgh is an Honorary Associate Professor in Philosophy in the School of Historical and Philosophical Inquiry, The University of Queensland, Australia. He has published widely on democratic education, civics and citizenship education, dialogic pedagogy, and the development of the community of inquiry in educational discourse.

Simone Thornton is a Lecturer in Philosophy in the School of Historical and Philosophical Inquiry, The University of Queensland, Australia. Simone's research interests and publications intersect ethics, environmental philosophy, philosophy and education, and social and political philosophy, including environmental education, decolonisation, philosophy in schools, and the philosophy of Albert Camus and Val Plumwood.

Routledge International Studies in the Philosophy of Education

For more information about this series, please visit: https://www.routledge.com/Routledge-International-Studies-in-the-Philosophy-of-Education/book-series/SE0237

Teaching Democracy in an Age of Uncertainty

Place-Responsive Learning

Gilbert Burgh and Simone Thornton

Routledge
Taylor & Francis Group

LONDON AND NEW YORK

First published 2022
by Routledge
2 Park Square, Milton Park, Abingdon, Oxon OX14 4RN

and by Routledge
605 Third Avenue, New York, NY 10158

Routledge is an imprint of the Taylor & Francis Group, an informa business

British Library Cataloguing-in-Publication Data
A catalogue record for this book is available from the British Library

Library of Congress Cataloging-in-Publication Data
A catalog record has been requested for this book

ISBN: 978-0-367-56509-1 (hbk)
ISBN: 978-0-367-56510-7 (pbk)
ISBN: 978-1-003-09808-9 (ebk)

DOI: 10.4324/9781003098089

Typeset in Galliard
by SPi Technologies India Pvt Ltd (Straive)

We acknowledge the Turrbal and Jagara people as the First Nations custodians of the unceded lands on which The University of Queensland is situated. We also pay respect to their Elders, Law, lore, customs, and creation spirits. We do so to recognise that these lands have always been places of teaching, research, and learning long before The University of Queensland was built. And we acknowledge the important role that Aboriginal and Torres Strait Islander peoples continue to have within The University of Queensland community and, therefore, in the reconciliation process toward building new relationships between Indigenous and non-Indigenous people.

Contents

Acknowledgements

There are many people who contributed to the evolution of this book. Chronologically, first thanks go to Angeles Alvarez, Richard Anthone, Hrannar Baldursson, Hannu Juuso, Walter Kohan, John Portelli, Tim Sprod, Wendy Turgeon, Mark Weinstein, and Steve Williams for sharing their ideas on the philosophy for children internet discussion group all those years ago, sometime in the 1990s. The ideas that grew out of those conversations initially appeared in Burgh (2003a) and were later modified in Burgh (2003b). The ideas were modified again and appeared as part of a larger argument on education for deliberative democracy in Burgh, Field and Freakley (2006, Ch. 5). They were again explored in relation to politics, power, and group dynamics in Burgh and Yorshansky (2011; published early on-line in 2008). Significant amendments were made in terms of a discussion in the context of citizenship, and focus on different approaches to classroom practice, in Burgh (2010). These ideas were again revised in Burgh (2014). Thanks, therefore, must go to Terri Field, Mark Freakley, and Mor Yorshansky for lending their ears, as well as the anonymous reviewers. We have since re-examined these ideas and developed them further for inclusion in Chapter 3.

Other key ideas presented here initially appeared scattered through our previous publications: Burgh (2005, 2009), Burgh and Thornton (2016a, 2016b, 2017, 2019b), Thornton (2019), Thornton and Burgh (2017). We have extended on our original thoughts, resulting in extensive revisions or reorganisation of our ideas, which now appear throughout the book in the new context of democratic education as presented here.

Since 2016, we have collaborated with Mary Graham, a Kombumerri person (Gold Coast) through her father's heritage and affiliated with Wakka Wakka (South Burnett) through her mother's people. We cannot thank Mary enough for her endless hours of dialogue, conversation, and yarning on so many topics, especially on *Place*, that permeates throughout the book. We are very grateful to her for allowing us to include some of these ideas in Chapter 6, together with the excerpts we have extracted from Thornton, Graham and Burgh (2019, 2021).

Our conversations with Mary were also part of our regularly held meetings of the recently formed group, the Australian Philosophy Research Group (APRG), initiated by her to introduce the idea of an Australian philosophy to create a dialogue, emerging out of place, between Indigenous and non-Indigenous scholars. We would like to show our appreciation to our colleague and other founding member of the group, Michelle Boulous Walker, for her commitment and collaborative contributions to these conversations.

We wish to also express our thanks to the following colleagues who, over the years, have engaged in conversation with either or both of us on topics that have made their way into the book or read drafts or excerpts (in alphabetical order): Jennifer Bleazby, Philip Cam, Liz Fynes-Clinton, Sarah Davey Chesters, Eugenio Echeverria, Jennifer Glaser, Clinton Golding, Maughn Gregory, Joanna Haynes, Lynne Hinton, David Kennedy, Megan Laverty, Ching-Ching Lin, Karen Martin, Freya Mathews, Richard 'Mort' Morehouse, Karin Murris, Kim Nichols, Kei Nishiyama, Rosie Scholl, Lavina Sequeira, Laurance Splitter, Merle Thornton (AO), Tom Wartenberg, and Susan Wilks.

A special thank you to the late Matthew Lipman and Ann Margaret Sharp not only for their dedication but also for their generosity in giving their time for discussion on many of the topics raised here.

Preface

A telephone conversation about the *School Strikes 4 Climate*, in the wake of the 2019 Australian bushfires, settled our doubt on the idea of writing a book together. The conversation meandered around related topics including the social, political, and psychological reactions to the widespread devastation to humans, wildlife, property, and ecosystems. We touched on the various climate change denial positions; from staunch deniers who believe the established science is not real and part of a global conspiracy, to those who seem to absorb the extent of the acceleration of the problem but deny human involvement. We covered the wide range of emotional reactions displayed by those who acknowledge climate change is a pressing human problem, including displays of angst, terror, indifference, and outrage, all of which elicit diverse responses, such as anxious resignation, climate change or apocalypse fatigue, disaster-preparedness planning, moral or civic pride for taking individual responsibility to reduce emission or waste, and ongoing local political activism and civic disobedience. We also covered the stark inequality driven by climate change and the increasingly apparent ineffectiveness of Western-style democracies to reconcile economic and environmental interests and develop effective national and international policies. Ensuing conversations sparked the formulation of a broader question beyond climate change; a question guided by our observations of a world in which people are trying to navigate their experiences of uncertainty when confronted by the absence of a unifying narrative over global issues that impact on their lives. It became the question that lies at the heart of this book: How can education in a democracy best develop civic literacy that increases civic participation and engagement in public affairs?

Subsequently, we reviewed our previously published papers in academic journals and edited collections, as well as research we had started, both in-progress and archived, and set out a tentative structure to re-think and reconstruct our previously held positions in light of current world problems. This experience generated new ideas, which were integrated with some of our previous and current thoughts or became catalysts for rejecting or modifying others. The result is this book, a pragmatist reconstruction of our research to date on education in a democracy: a pedagogical framework we call place-responsive democratic education.

Introduction

Educating democracy

Like it or not, we live in an age of digitalisation that has seen the rise of social media. With the increase in mobile devices, over 2.6 billion people now use social networking platforms and apps. Easily the largest social networking site currently is Facebook, but, along with others, like Twitter, Reddit, Instagram, WhatsApp, WeChat, and QZone, these sites have become part of politics around the globe. The spread of social media, or more accurately, its entanglement with politics has raised concerns over hate speech, fake news, emboldened fascism, undemocratic governance, and market-driven political campaigns, to name but a few. All these raise questions regarding liberal-democracy, the predominant political system globally, and its survival in an age of technology. Because liberal-democratic nation-states, also known as 'Western-style democracies',[1] rely variously on voting to select political representatives, an active and informed citizenry is vital to the effectiveness of democracy—that is, if we understand that, by definition, democracy means 'people rule', or as Abraham Lincoln defined it, government of the people, by the people, for the people. Inevitably, political conversations and scholarly discussions have questioned partisan competition, preference aggregation through voting, and political representation as effective means for political decision-making.

Increasingly, worsening global social and political issues, such as the ecological and climate change crisis, violence, poverty, malnourishment and hunger, human rights, Indigenous sovereignty, and economic and environmental inequality, are drawing attention to liberal-democracy's failure to adequately respond to these issues. In fact, the environmental problems we are now facing are so severe that

> [t]he entire Earth system is threatened by further destruction of biodiversity, the degrading of our land, forests and oceans, polluting air and water, destabilizing the climate and general devastation of our natural capital. Together they can undermine or destroy the basis for our livelihoods, where and how we can live—indeed, whether many can survive. If these forces are not managed much better, if we do not find better

DOI: 10.4324/9781003098089-1

ways of producing and consuming, integrating adaptive capacity and flexibility—that is, resilience—in our social and environmental fabric, the consequences could be catastrophic, with widespread loss of life, great movements of people and the likelihood of severe and extended conflict. We are all threatened, but it is the poorest who are hit earliest and hardest.

(Rockström & Stern, 2020, pp. 3–4)

Responding to such widespread and potentially catastrophic challenges will require a concerted effort by global governmental and citizens.

Emphasis on active and informed citizenship ties politics together with education. The recent rise in 'school activism' and the global school strikes on climate change, started by Swedish teenage activist Greta Thunberg, point to both the successes and failures of the role education plays and has played in a democracy. The strikes can be viewed as a sign that whatever limited citizenship and environmental education there has been, has produced some active and aware citizens, such as those who joined in the school strikes. But overwhelmingly, the climate strikes are an indication that democracy has not only failed education, but that education has also failed democracy, and together they have failed its citizens. As Thunberg said in her address to the United Nations COP24 Climate Summit in Poland in December 2018:

Since our leaders are behaving like children, we will have to take the responsibility they should have taken long ago. We have to understand what the older generation has dealt to us, what mess they have created that we have to clean up and live with. We have to make our voices heard.

(UN News, 2018, n.p.)

Later, in a speech at a climate protest in Hamburg, Germany, on 1 March 2019, she said: 'We are striking because we have done our homework, and they have not' (BBC, 2019, n.p.). And at the U.N. Climate Summit in New York on 23 September 2019: 'The eyes of all future generations are upon you. And if you choose to fail us, I say—we will never forgive you' (BBC, 2019, n.p.). Put another way, successive governments have failed to educate children to become active and informed adult citizens, who, then, elect governments that have failed children by their lack of concern for their future.

Thunberg's actions in a situation of *deafening silence*—when something ought to be said but is not—disrupted a perilous mood of increasing complacency, apathy, and indifference to politics. In the rebellious act of skipping school, she demonstrated that she did not want to make the error Edmund Burke[2] wanted us to avoid—she did whatever she could despite the millions who did nothing because they thought doing little not worthwhile. In doing so, she facilitated the global potential for democracy as a *corrective social and political institution*. Even if nothing further were to come of her actions, and the deafening silence eventually returns, Thunberg's dissenting voice epitomises the citizen who is active and informed; the kind of citizen that is crucial for cultivating collective action and, therefore, vital to a functioning democracy. Indeed, she has been applauded in some radical circles for her traitorous character—someone, in her case a teenager legally not a citizen, who belongs to the predominant national culture yet resists its expected assumptions and orientations, and consequently has influenced countless children and adolescents, as well as adults, to the chagrin of multinational corporations, climate change deniers, 'shock jocks', and governments. No-one is more surprised than Thunberg that her decision in August 2018 to skip school on Fridays to protest outside the Swedish Parliament would lead to a global movement for which she is seen as an influential figurehead and voice for youth climate angst and activism. Ironically, she did more for civic literacy than the civics and citizenship education of her country and other liberal-democratic nation-states around the globe.

But what is civic literacy? And why is it important? American political theorist and author of *Strong Democracy*, Benjamin Barber characterises *civic literacy* as 'the competence to participate in democratic communities, the ability to think critically and act with deliberation in a pluralistic world, and the empathy to identify sufficiently with others to live with them despite conflicts of interest and differences in character' (in Westbrook, 1996, p. 125). This immediately raises the question of the purpose and aims of education consistent with democracy. At first glance, it seems straightforward. Education can provide a service to liberal-democratic nation-states through a system of schooling in which teachers, through curriculum, teaching methods, and assessment inculcate the appropriate cognitive and normative skills and virtues for citizens to participate in democratic communal life. However, there is a political undercurrent in the inherent tension between civics and citizenship education and liberal-democratic statehood. If education is to be effective in developing civic literacy, deliberative competence is essential for dealing with conflicting worldviews at a time of accelerating globalisation and demands for cultural, epistemic, and ontological pluralism by marginalised groups. Nation-states, on the other hand, are primarily concerned with the transmission of the normative privileges that maintain the predominant cultural views and institutional practices.

To reconcile this tension would require persuading politicians that a critical citizenry is in their best interests. Alas, this is easier said than done. Formal education is an agent of socialisation that can impress social norms upon an individual. Indeed, the school is the most important formal learning institution in the lives of children and adolescents. Schooling has a primary role in identity formation, including the process of national identity building, which is reflected in education policies and national curriculum, as well as the hidden curriculum (Anyon, 2006). The hidden curriculum is a 'side effect' of formal education, as it is not openly intended but, rather, unavoidable as teachers, through their actions and behaviour and the institutional practices in which they themselves are inculcated, transmit the values they personally hold to their students (Martin, 1983). The social transmission of values—stable long-lasting beliefs about what people, groups, communities, or societies consider important—facilitates the reproduction of social norms, moral standards, and cultural practices that sustain a common public culture. Successive governments, both conservative and progressive, will, therefore, closely guard education as an institution for their own political agendas and inculcation of values.

Not surprisingly, there is a tendency among policy makers who profess a commitment to the goals of lifelong learning to see education as providing a means for enabling individuals, organisations and nations to meet the challenges of an increasingly competitive world to the neglect of involving people in a continuing process of education aimed at self-actualisation and a learning society. For example, in Australia, many of the reforms that manifest in the curriculum have their origins in the Education Revolution initiative of the Rudd-Gillard Labor government of 2008, which put education at the centre of the 'productivity agenda'. While Prime Minister Julia Gillard expressed a desire to reduce inequity, her primary motivating vision was for 'Australia to become the most educated country, the most skilled economy and the best trained workforce in the world' (in Gorur, 2016).

What this example demonstrates is the irony of government attitudes to education. There 'is the tendency to engage in large scale policy dreaming about knowledgeable nations, about smarter states, about intellectual isles, and so forth—while it continues to invest in inward looking, compilationist approaches to curriculum and pedagogy' (Luke, 2018, p. 149). These charges have serious implications for contemporary democratic societies and attitudes toward education. Schools are institutions that produce a product, which is sold to parents as education, rather than places of opportunity which are integrated with work and the rest of life to prepare and direct children and adolescents toward becoming an integral part of a well-informed and active democratic citizenry. Our concern, therefore, is how best to facilitate the latter in light of the former, and on this score, we favour the view of American philosopher, psychologist, and educational reformer John Dewey, who asserted that education is not merely preparation for future life but life itself. The sole purpose of public schooling should not be to equip students with the skills needed to obtain employment, nor should it be to create knowledgeable consumers. In addition to teaching core curriculum subjects, public schools must be constitutive of a public; to create generations of citizens. To this end, the function of civics and citizenship education should be to *create a public*, which necessitates more than civic knowledge but also civic participation, hence Barber's emphasis on civic literacy.

Traditional approaches to civics and citizenship education have been marginalised and have had negligible impact on the core curriculum. An alternative curricular strategy, which we will pursue, is to explicitly address civic and democratic engagement through a critical but experiential approach to civic literacy that has the potential to put democracy and citizenship at the centre of the educational process. This strategy provides a critical interface between cultural transformation and transmission that can facilitate the educational task of identity formation by moving away from dominant liberal individual conceptions of citizenship and national identity and towards pluralistic, intercultural conceptions of citizenship and lesser state-centrism. This is especially important, as in modern liberal-democratic nation-states, national identity is not, to varying degrees, inclusive of all the state's citizens and is structurally (i.e., institutionally) privileging of members of the dominant group and culture and, therefore, unable to meet Indigenous peoples' and other marginalised groups' needs for individual and communal identity reproduction, including ways of knowing, being, and doing.

With the benefits of hindsight, and thanks to the tremendous efforts of multi-generational resistance, the ways in which groups have historically been marginalised have, to some extent, become understood and unacceptable. However, new forms of marginalisation have become increasingly obscure and sophisticated, and yet other ways continue to operate uninterrupted. Such insidious forms of domination, particularly those perpetuated against Indigenous peoples and their connection to land, also stem from and involve environmental domination; the instrumental valuation of land also known as capitalism. Resistance against systemic environmental domination has manifested largely in the call for economic and environmental sustainability. For example, Rockström and Stern (2020) note the need for economic policies that 'build resilience rather than build in brittleness', to 'provide for more equitable distribution of well-being, both within and across generations' (p. 5). This need arises from the failure to deliver effective and just social and environmental policies which has its roots in much deeper problems, namely, 'an absence of understanding of how ecosystems work, a short-sighted and narrow view of objectives, and a neglect to address market failure' (p. 5).

These deeper problems are exacerbated by liberal-democratic politics and economics, which are grounded in liberalism and described by Val Plumwood (1995) as an 'historical vehicle of a privileged, property-owning "middle" class' (p. 148). With thanks to liberal-democracy (increasingly influenced by neoliberal laissez-faire economics), 'impoverishment and environmental degradation are produced as twin offspring of the same processes of development' (p. 139). Environmental and economic goods are distributed upwards to those in positions of power, while environmental ills are fostered on those already bereft of power. Nature and those closest to it are objectified, exploited, and backgrounded; that is, nature is viewed simply as a backdrop to human activities and as a means to our individual liberation. This produces a political system lacking in the capacity for correctiveness and, thus, an inability to detect and respond to social, economic, and environmental problems. As Plumwood puts it, blindspots are created by 'an elite-dominated polity' unable and often unwilling to listen to those closest to nature who are the first to witness and understand environmental failures. The resulting system then is marked by 'a dysfunctional rigidity and informational distortion regarding the degradation of nature which render it resistant to an important range of changes, unable to detect or correct its blindspots, as indifferent to gross damage to the surrounding natural world as it is to gross damage to the social world' (p. 137).

In response, this book investigates the potential of democratic education as an educational practice (in which democracy is both a goal and a teaching method) for developing civic literacy to counter the transmission and perpetuation of dominant discourses. Countering such discourses serves to minimise the exclusion or marginalisation of others and increase diversity, as '[d]iversity of stimulation means novelty, and novelty means challenging thought' (Dewey, 1916, p. 85), which is vital for democracy as a communicative practice and a mode of associated living. To this end, we develop a framework for democratic education as experiential, place-based education; a specific kind of peace education that engages students in collaborative philosophical inquiry to explore ecological relationships (i.e., relationships between organisms and their environment, including socio-political, economic, and cultural processes within human–environmental interactions). The framework is both conceptual and practical and, thus, provides a 'guiding document' for educational practice and policy making: (1) broadly, for education as a corrective social and political institution that works hand-in-glove with democratic practices, and (2) specifically, for teachers, teacher-educators and curriculum designers to develop, implement, and evaluate curricula, syllabi, lessons, and other educational activities, with the aim of developing students' capacities to lead socially and civically engaged lives. It is also a radical approach to education that can co-exist as a cross-curriculum priority or general capability within existing curriculum frameworks, insofar as it directly attends to education's unavoidable role in identity formation and national identity building. The focus is on pedagogy as a corrective process and, thus, education as the reconstruction of experience 'which increases ability to direct the course of subsequent experience' (Dewey, 1916, p. 76). As such, it has the potential to mitigate (1) the lack of attention to identity as connections to place, and (2) the reproduction of collective individual identity, including societal, cultural, institutional, and political identities, reflected in education policies, curricula, and the hidden curriculum.

It would be naïve, however, to expect education reform to be an easy task; as mentioned, it is a closely guarded institution, replete with competing moral and political agendas and hidden curricula.

> Those in control of public comprehensive education are always eager to invest it with instruction on certain specific political–moral–ideological worldviews and good life frameworks, but the direction and content of this instruction rarely unfold in predictable patterns or in keeping with directives.
>
> (Strandbrink, 2017, p. v)

Regardless of how well schools fulfil their role as democratic institutions, despite any gallant efforts by scholars and practitioners, including teachers, philosophers of education, teacher-educators, policy makers, administrators, as well as parents and community groups, dissension and confrontation will persist in a democratic society. It is unlikely that people will be completely happy with their social, economic, and political status, because even so-called reasonable people disagree on solutions or the formulation of problems. There is no unifying narrative to provide us with security or certainty over the future. The future has never been certain or secure; as in the past, there will always be multiple narratives. Conflict is inevitable because people bring different frames of reference, including prejudices, epistemic assumptions and other things we do not think to question, to specific situations, thereby deriving different solutions and policy decisions.

The success of efforts to deal with the resulting problems arising from such conflict will hinge on the shared commitments of citizens, which will provide a context for deliberation and decision-making. In schools, such commitment can be brought about by helping students understand the complexity of epistemic relations between societal beliefs, values, and attitudes and those of their own to bring about self- and peer-correction in the democratic microcosm of the classroom. We strive to answer the question of how to facilitate sustained dialogue in an age of uncertainty, in which the philosophical imaginary of the age of enlightenment, expressed in contemporary times as a yearning for certainty and security, still has a foothold. Rather than rely on political decision-makers who try to sell simplistic solutions or fall back on the past, we need to learn to navigate complexity amidst uncertainty. How, and in what way, this might be achieved is the topic of this book.

About this book

The book concentrates on the epistemic and pedagogic dimensions of education in a democracy. The title is a play on words. To *teach democracy* is both to teach existing Western-style democracies where they have erred regarding democratic and ecological flourishing and to teach students to be collectively self-correcting so that democracy rests with citizens. To live in an *age of uncertainty* also has a twofold meaning: due to the increasingly volatile state of the world, we face an uncertain future, but also if universal truths allude us, then we have only uncertainty, and if this dual uncertainty is so, then we need to find justification for our collective decision-making within uncertainty. This might not satisfy anyone who seeks certainty in the shape of absolute truth or reality, but until such truths are forthcoming and make themselves known as self-evident, we must learn to live with doubt. But this should not be interpreted as an 'anything goes' epistemology or as an endorsement of relativism. It is a pragmatic approach to deliberative decision-making by the demos who rely on each other to collectively move from a state of doubt to reflective equilibrium, which provides justification for democracy as an ongoing self-corrective process in which the knowledge that informs decisions is provisional as this process is in a constant state of flux, shaped and complicated by changing demographics.

We propose a theoretical framework for *place-responsive democratic education* that contains pedagogical principles and guidelines for classroom practice, whereby students *practice* deliberative self-corrective citizenship to develop an experiential understanding of civic participation and engagement. It is also a form of peace education, a method of experiencing conflict as collaborative philosophical inquiry rather than as adversarial debate and, thus, an educative process for deliberative democracy. In this way democratic education provides guidelines for civics and citizenship education conceived of as a way in which school-aged students develop the social and intellectual capacities and dispositions for active and informed citizenship to not only face an uncertain world, but also to face the inevitable challenges of democratic disagreement beyond merely promoting pluralism, tolerance, and disagreement. The importance of place-responsive citizenship cannot be overstated as citizens belong to land and country, so democracy needs to *find its place* by paying attention to the past narratives and future imaginings that are embedded in the features of its landscape (historical, social, political, cultural, and spiritual). Democratic education needs to be both sensitive and responsive to democracy otherwise it will be an obstacle to itself. *Place-responsive democratic education*, we argue, provides a theoretic framework for education professionals to begin communication to reconstruct education. What follows is a chapter-by-chapter summary of the arguments we present in the book.

Our first task is to foreground the problems facing liberal-democracy in a world of uncertainty that requires the attention of education. Focusing on the relationship between democracy, citizenship, and identity formation, Chapter 1 presents objections to liberal citizenship and its ideological commitments to individualism, independence, and rationality and offers an alternative radical theory of democracy and democratic citizenship. To mitigate the rigidities that hinder the democratic correction of social institutions in liberal-democratic nation-states, we argue requires a new understanding of citizenship as a cultural learning process of ongoing identity reconstruction through collective self-correction.

To address how education can move towards cultural citizenship as a collective learning process, Chapter 2 compares three conceptions of education: teaching as transmission, transaction and transformation. These different conceptions of education indicate a tension between present societies and social aspirations; at one end, the view that education should reflect the composite values of the present society and preserve it from one generation to the next, and at the other, that it must aspire to lead students towards an idealised society, which raises questions of value conflicts and teacher neutrality. We contend that neutrality is an untenable position that can only privilege the dominant ideology. To avoid this, teachers need to engage students in genuine communicative practices through community-centred, inquiry-based pedagogy with the purpose of the continuous reconstruction of experiences that develops students' capacities for active and informed citizenship.

In Chapter 3, we offer a reclassification of educational approaches to teaching democracy centred on the distinction between education for democracy and democratic education. The distinction is intended to provide teachers with a way to recognise the epistemological commitments often unspoken in civics and citizenship pedagogies and practices and to examine the relationship between democracy and education in pedagogical terms along with its application to practice. Our contention is that education can promote democratic practice itself through a conception of democratic education as communication and deliberation, rather than education for democracy which is merely preparation for students to function effectively as future citizens. Whereas education for democracy fails to involve children and adolescents in a continuing process of education aimed at self-actualisation and the creation of a learning society, thereby serving political agendas rather than democracy itself, democratic education places priority on the development of social and intellectual capacities and dispositions for active and informed citizenship, insofar as it recognises democracy as an educational process and not something to educate toward. We place emphasis on Dewey's notion of reconstruction, paying particular attention to the primacy of education as communication and deliberation as the basis for reconceptualising citizenship as a learning process. We conclude that this can be strengthened further by integrating educational philosophy through classroom communities of inquiry.

In Chapter 4, we provide an overview of the theory and practice of the philosophy for children approach to education, including an examination of the inter-relationship between its curriculum and pedagogy of the community of inquiry. To convert the classroom into a community of inquiry, we argue requires an understanding of two different but overlapping conceptions of the community of inquiry. The wide-sense conception must be treated as the organising or regulative principle of scholarly communities of inquiry and as a classroom-wide ideal for the reconstruction of education. This principle also provides the narrow-sense classroom community of inquiry, a specific procedural method of stages of inquiry for fostering philosophical dialogue and critical discourse, with the pedagogical guidelines needed for the wider aim of converting the classroom into a community of inquiry. The teacher takes on the dual role of facilitator and co-inquirer to mediate between the two conceptions. However, an understanding of this dual role makes sense only if it is theoretically underpinned by a reconstructionist and pragmatist interpretation of Dewey's educational theory and practice. Our analysis leads us to conclude that mediating between the two communities of inquiry demands more than connecting students' learning experiences to curriculum materials, it requires experiential education—being immersed in real-world situations. To this end, we argue for the integration of social reconstruction learning, a critical approach to service learning that involves students engaging in communities of inquiry with their local communities to reconstruct real social problems and facilitate democratic citizenship.

Following on, in Chapter 5, we examine the relationship between pedagogy, epistemology, and inquiry. The pragmatist epistemology that shapes the community of inquiry rests on fallibilism. It rejects certainty and absolute conceptions of truth and reality, thereby relying on doubt as the stimulus for communal inquiry in which collaborative dialogue results in the acceptance of theories that are provisional and subject to further investigation and revision. The attention to genuine doubt is an important part of the community of inquiry and offers a way to respond to feminist concerns regarding philosophy as an adversarial pursuit that historically is underpinned by masculine notions of truth, reason, and rationality. However, we argue that philosophy for children has underplayed the importance of doubt as an experiential feature essential for classroom practice, despite its pivotal role in the theoretical literature of the community of inquiry. Genuine doubt is essential for recognising epistemic bias and prejudice which inhibit the fallibility required for open inquiry. Teachers, therefore, need to cultivate collective doubt. To illustrate how the process is enacted in the classroom, we introduce the notion of 'lucid teaching', which is sustained awareness of the tension between fallibility and the desire for certainty. Lucid teaching facilitates the tension between the experiences of genuine doubt and belief; the recognition of the contingent and the comfort of the familiar, thereby providing pedagogical guidelines to inform teachers' understanding of the epistemic dynamics of communal inquiry, and how to mediate between the narrow-sense and wide-sense communities of inquiry. We introduce the concept of epistemic violence, a form of harm that has the potential to impede inquiry, to show that the community of inquiry is a kind of peace education because it develops students' abilities to turn conflict into inquiry, to directly address epistemic violence and improve the quality of epistemic relationships. To this end, lucid teaching requires teachers to cultivate traitorous identities, and by so doing, to resist the epistemic assumptions and institutional practices of their own culture as a way of mitigating epistemic harm caused to marginalised others.

In Chapter 6, we argue that education aimed at social reconstruction needs to reject both the theory/practice and human/nature dualisms. Citizenship is more than being a member of social and political communities, as such communities are not abstracted from place but ecologically embedded, locally, nationally, and globally. Place-based pedagogies must, therefore, be a key feature of democratic education. But place is not neutral, merely somewhere for learning to occur. Students need to experience a 'sense of place' to develop their identity as citizens who are ecologically interdependent—a mode of associated living necessary for sustainable living. We provide a series of narratives to assist teachers to create and implement place-responsive pedagogies: (1) experiences from environmental education centres that illustrate different ways that groups have developed place-responsive pedagogies, (2) an exploration of Aboriginal Land ethics as people belonging to land compared to liberal conceptions of land as property belonging to people, and (3) a case study of an inner-city school that uses experiential learning to implement its environmental and philosophy programs. These examples also point to the importance of critical Indigenous pedagogies of place. We conclude with a brief discussion on some of the bureaucratic and political challenges that education reformers should expect when attempting to implement the kind of radical democratic education we propose.

Notes

1 Western-style liberal-democracies take various constitutional forms: constitutional monarchies, such as Australia, Belgium, Canada, Denmark, Japan, Netherlands, Norway, Spain, and the U.K.; and republics, such as France, Germany, India, Italy, Ireland, and the U.S.A. Nation-states vary also in that they may have a parliamentary system, for example, Australia, Canada, Germany, India, Israel, Ireland, Italy, and the U.K.; a presidential system, for example, Indonesia and the U.S.A.; or a semi-presidential system, for example, France and Romania.

2 The mistake we refer to is captured in a quote attributed to Edmund Burke, an Anglo-Irish philosopher who served as a member of parliament in the House of Commons with the Whig Party (1766–1794): 'Nobody made a greater mistake than he who did nothing because he could do only a little'.

1 Citizenship as an active learning process

Introduction

After more than 40 years of global climate negotiations, ongoing scientific assessments of global warming by the U.N. Intergovernmental Panel on Climate Change (see IPCC, 2018) and other agencies, numerous strikes and protests across the globe demanding action on climate change, and despite scientists from 50 nations who attended the First World Climate Conference (in Geneva 1979) and later in the publication of 'World Scientists' Warning of a Climate Emergency' 11,258 scientist signatories from 153 countries declaring 'clearly and unequivocally that planet Earth is facing a climate emergency' (Ripple et al., 2020, p. 8), countless individuals, corporations, and governments continue to conduct business as usual. It would seem we are not taking this predicament seriously. Indeed, not everyone is convinced that anthropogenic climate change is a threat. The divide between climate science and public opinion appears to be widening due to the efforts of fossil fuel industry advocates, political lobbyists, conservative right-wing think tanks, and media moguls who have for the last few decades had clear strategies, aided by multi-million dollar budgets, to manufacture uncertainty and influence, delay, or block climate policies. To counter the increasing protestor backlash against political inaction, political lobbying has resorted to 'front groups' who present themselves as experts and to 'climate sadism' to mock and ridicule teenage climate protestors influenced by Greta Thunberg perpetuated by climate denial networks. However, the division this creates is largely illusory as globally most people are now concerned about climate change. Nevertheless, the illusory division is enough to drive political inaction.

This scenario would not be unfamiliar to Plato were he alive today. Almost two and a half millennia ago, he warned against democracy, which, he believed, could be subverted into tyranny by opportunistic demagogues who manipulated citizens to 'overmaster democracy'. This was possible, Plato thought, because citizens follow their impulses rather than pursue the common good. They are more concerned with money than justice and, consequently, they do whatever they want in their life without order or priority. This leads to the unravelling of democracy into oligarchy, which Plato

DOI: 10.4324/9781003098089-2

defines as a system of government that distinguishes between the rich and the poor, and eventually tyranny.

In light of Plato's warning, it is difficult to ignore the neoliberal undercurrent and the repercussions of a widening gap between rich and poor today, the powerful and the powerless. With only 1 per cent of the world's population holding over 44 per cent of the world's wealth, and 56.6 per cent of the world's population holding less than 2 per cent (see Credit Suisse Research Institute, 2020), the world's poor are more likely to be hardest hit by the effects of climate change, such as increased frequency and intensity of extreme weather conditions, more frequent disease outbreaks, potential food shortages, and conflict. They are also the most likely to understand the problems and solutions, but unlikely to have the power to effect change. We've already seen that people in poorer countries and communities are suffering more in times of crises, such as cyclones, bushfires, and droughts. The call for climate justice is to hold those most responsible for the climate crisis to account and to redistribute the wealth to invest in sustainable alternative energies. However, this has proved to be a difficult task as liberal-democratic political institutions are unable to *correct* the social, economic, and ecological imbalances. What does this mean for democracy?

In her paper, 'Has democracy failed ecology? An ecofeminist perspective', Val Plumwood (1995) concludes that it is 'not democracy that has failed ecology, but liberal democracy that has failed both democracy and ecology' (p. 134). She argues that 'the escalation of the processes responsible for ecological degradation, despite the great citizen effort that has gone into challenging them in democratic polities, therefore represents an alarming failure' (p. 135) of the current liberal-democratic political systems. Liberal-democracy, she argues, is an authoritarian political system, with its 'military systems organised around protecting privilege which control so much of the planet' (p. 136), and as a result, fails to protect nature. She does not, however, see democracy *per se* as inherently authoritarian.

> The superiority of democracy to other systems in detecting and responding to ecological problems would seem to lie largely, then, in its capacity for adaptation and *correction*. So in order to discover why democracy is failing, we must now ask which political features of democracy contribute to and what forms hinder its capacity for correction?
>
> (p. 137, *italics* added)

For Plumwood, a major obstacle that hinders this capacity is radical inequality, which, she claims, 'is both itself a hindrance to correctiveness and a key indicator of other hindrances to societal correctiveness' (p. 137). She contends that radical inequality, which has become increasingly far-reaching under liberal-democracy, is an indicator of 'the capacity of its privileged groups to distribute social goods upwards and to create rigidities which hinder the democratic correctiveness of social institutions' (p. 134). In the case of liberal-democracy, economic privilege drives this story of *stark separation*; the separation of the ecologically privileged from the ecologically underprivileged, of those deemed close to nature from those thought of as above or superior to nature. It is a separation that generally plays out along the lines of colonial violence and is a continuation of colonisation, as will be explained.[1] The privileged have the means to escape most forms of environmental degradation; 'toxic wastes and occupations can be directed to poorer residential areas (including Third World destinations), and if privileged suburbs, regions or territories become noisy, degraded or polluted, the privileged can buy places in more salubrious environments' (p. 138).

The story of the rich separated from the poor is a familiar one—the 'salubrious environments' of the economically privileged contrast starkly with those of the economically disadvantaged. This privileging is not restricted to economic class but to gender and ethnicity also. Plumwood says of this divide that '[t]he most oppressed and dispossessed people in a society are those who are made closest to the condition of nature, who are made to share the same expendable condition as nature' (p. 139). Anthropocentrism (the belief, derived from bias towards human values and experiences, that humans are the central or most significant entities in the world), androcentrism (the systemic privileging of the male-centred worldview that positions men as the gender-neutral standard), and ethnocentrism (the evaluation of other cultures from the perspective of one's own culture or ethnicity as a frame of reference) all combine to confer privilege in colonial cultures, widespread throughout the Americas, Africa, Asia, and Oceania, colonised by European countries including Spain, Portugal, France, England, Prussia, the Netherlands, and later the U.S. (itself a product of colonisation). Part of this dispossession is the dispossession of the voices of entire groups of people. A political voice is denied to those who are considered 'other' (dehumanisation often plays a pivotal role in ensuring the security of privilege); no political provisions are made for their perspectives, for their knowledge, to be heard in an existentially meaningful way, that is, in a way that leads to a correction of their situation. For all intents and purposes, they are denied full epistemic legitimacy (the denial of knowledge shared by other groups or cultures by the dominant group or mainstream culture—an idea to which we will return in greater detail in Chapter 5) within the dominant mainstream discourse, educationally, culturally, socially, and politically. The silencing of Indigenous peoples and othering of their culture in Australia, both historically and today, is one salient example (see Thornton & Burgh, 2019; Watson, 2011, 2014).

Globally, those in the most disadvantaged positions are the ones most likely to suffer the greatest effects of anthropogenic climate change,[2] social and economic injustice, and other social and ecological ills, while at the same time, having the least political recourse to address such issues. Plumwood argues that the liberal political system suffers from a communication problem that makes ecological and social justice correction difficult, if not impossible. Often those closest to environmental systems, those with the most to gain from their preservation and the greatest understanding of the problems we face, are unable to protect the environment and must resort to means of physical, psychological, and cultural resistance to protect themselves, their lives, and their ways of knowing being and doing. More often than not, this also means a struggle to protect the environment.

Plumwood's cautionary tale of liberal-democracy has repercussions for education, especially civics and citizenship education. As schools are a major influence on the development of national identity in children and adolescents, who become adult citizens who then participate in democratic institutions, formal education has a significant influence on democracy. It is a reciprocal relationship, or as Dewey put it, our habits shape our habitat which goes on to shape our habits. In this sense, education cannot be separated from democracy just like our habits cannot be separated from our habitats. In liberal-democracies, education policy is influenced by liberal theory, especially its reliance on individualism, the predominant view of the self that underpins identity formation and, thus, civic identity, replete with the social, economic, and institutional values of the nation-state. Such reliance we will argue, restricts the facilitation of self-correction in the classroom. The atomistic citizen is ill-equipped to face the twin challenges of climate change and the global injustices that result for climate crises. It is essential for democratic correctiveness and a well-functioning democracy, then, to identify and clear away obstacles to developing self-correction at the level of institutional education.

The argument this book presents is that education can be a powerful process for teaching self-correction, provided the learning environment is conducive for students' continuous growth to help them become effective agents of change. Dewey's conception of schools as miniature communities and embryonic societies—microcosms of the larger democratic society in which students experience democratic ways of living together—is our starting point for developing a theoretical framework to inform classroom practice and teacher education and professional development. But first, as a preliminary to the chapters that follow, we ask the question: What are the problems facing democracy that arise from Plumwood's concerns regarding liberal-democracy and democratic correctiveness? We argue for a new understanding of citizenship as cultural citizenship, a learning process of ongoing reconstruction of identity through collective self-correction, which provides a more effective conception of citizenship to mitigate the rigidities that hinder the democratic correction of social institutions.

Democracy, citizenship, and identity

Historically, democracy is a social and political construction that has been shaped by diverse ideologies under very specific social circumstances. The debate on democracy has been dominated by Western political thought, especially normative political theory, and recently through the contributions of the social sciences. While there is much contention over definitions of democracy, and disagreement over competing models, it could be argued that democracy is characterised by two principles in terms of the power relations in which individuals and institutions stand to each other in society: (1) citizen control over public decision-making, and (2) equality between citizens in the exercising of making decisions. In its current form, Western-style democracies reaffirm majority rule and generally have failed in practice to strengthen these principles, as evidenced by increasing social divisions and the radical inequality that Plumwood refers to. The result is that democracy fails to live up to its own rhetoric, or as Plumwood says, liberal-democracy has failed democracy.

Liberal-democracy rests on the assumption that without representative government, free and fair elections at regular and frequent intervals, and mandate and merit as rationales for governance, there is no democracy. Indeed, '[g]overnment by elected representatives is taught in schools and presented in the media as the natural way of doing things' (Carson & Martin, 1999, p. 1). However, representative systems of democracy all but exclude citizens from direct decision-making and participation in the political process; 'power is concentrated on a small number of politicians and high-level bureaucrats and citizen input into policy is minimal, political accountability is low and elected representatives susceptible to vested interests, misconduct and corruption' (Burgh, Field & Freakley, 2006, p. 91). Informed by the classical tradition of modern liberal thought, citizenship is a legal status, bound up in pre-political notions of an abstract individual, liberty, the private domain, and consumer rights, to the neglect of the public sphere as the location of citizenship. While much contemporary debate on citizenship has focused on a return to the substantive dimension of citizenship, the relationship of citizenship to democracy has not been the focus of discussion in liberal debates. Instead, 'citizenship is reduced to a formalistic relationship to the state as one of rights and duties' (Delanty, 2000, p. 22). Former British Prime Minister Margaret Thatcher's statement in 1987, that 'there is no such thing as society, only individuals', sums up the lack of a substantive dimension to citizenship. With the shift toward neo-liberal politics since the 1970s, an 'emphasis on decentralisation, deregulation, and privatisation, the concept of citizenship has once again become strongly linked to the market' (Burgh, 2010, p. 60), but with even greater emphasis on the atomistic conception of the individual. By denying the social in favour of individual consumers, neo-liberal versions of citizenship have relegated citizenship to the realm of the market or the sphere of the state.

In modern liberal-democracies, popular participation in decision-making is restricted. The power of electors is formally limited to voting, and decision-making restricted to elected representatives. The longer these representative groups stay in power, 'the more their interests become identified with the survival of the state' (Walker, 1992, p. 316). Although it can be argued that regularly held elections enable citizens to participate in decision-making, the outcome is similar to that of the referendum, and there is no significant way that the majority participates in framing policy. The introduction of the citizen initiative as a supplement to regularly held elections, by which the public can force a referendum, seems to be a way of avoiding some of the pitfalls of representative democracy and the impracticability of direct democracy. However, the difficulty facing contemporary liberal theorists is how to reconcile the notion of individual liberty with constitutional constraint on governments elected by the people. Liberal arguments reason from the value of liberty to imposing limitations on the state, whereupon constitutional mechanisms define and delimit the powers, rights, and duties of the executive, other government institutions and the citizens, in order to protect individual liberty.

These factors contribute to rigidities that result from the concentration of power on a small number of politicians and high-level bureaucrats, which not only 'hinder the democratic correctiveness of social institutions' (Plumwood, 1995, p. 134), but protect privilege and drive hyper-separation. We use the term here to describe what Plumwood (1993) calls the 'standpoint of mastery', defined as the separation of humans from the rest of nature, a reason/nature dualism in which the natural world, including women, Indigenous people, and non-humans, is subordinated—a logic which drives our domination of nature and is often used to normalise our ethical failure to respond to environmental crises. Such logic 'backgrounds' nature and gives us a sense of autonomy from the conditions of nature, the very conditions that give rise to life.

The crucial question that modern democratic theorists need to address concerns not so much the extent of popular control but how such control might be exercised. The answer will depend on the practical applicability of competing liberal theories or theories of democracy. Critical to the assessment of competing theories is whether a solution requires a move away from traditional conceptions of liberalism or from liberalism entirely. A viable solution will also hinge on the practical applicability of an educational pedagogy for the teaching and learning of the relevant democratic procedures that is compatible with the arrived upon democratic principles. This brings us to the communitarian conception of citizenship, which emphasises connections between the individual and the community. Communitarian critiques of liberal political philosophy have modified liberalism to produce liberal communitarianism (Delanty, 2000, p. 25).

Communitarian criticisms of liberal citizenship

Unlike the liberal tradition, which appeals to the *individual* as the foundation of civil society, communitarian versions of citizenship locate civil society in *community*. Emphasis is on identity and participation rather than on rights and duties. Communitarians reject what they consider to be liberalism's excessive individualism and undue reliance on individual rights. Therefore, they also reject the conception of society as aggregate individuals in favour of community (Delanty, 2000, p. 24). However, there are also marked differences in the way communitarians treat identity and participation. For conservative communitarianism the focus on identity is allied with the notion of the nation or civil society, and participation with civic responsibility, but identity is specific to a particular community. Like all communitarians, the self as an abstract and universal entity is rejected. However, in its most conservative form, it is replaced by a culturally specific, socially constructed and embedded self that is likely to 'stress family, religion, tradition, nation and what in general might be called cultural consensus' (p. 29), including the values transmitted by the dominant political culture. This position avoids excessive individualism, but replaces it with social conservatism, which itself comes with its own rigidness steeped in community values, structures, and practices that hinder democratic correctivenes.

In response, some communitarians stress the importance of citizenship as open participation and dialogue in a political community. According to Charles Taylor (1994), the fundamental issue is the integration of self and other, which is an essential feature of social life. The encounter between self and other is embedded in a common language, and crucial to this encounter is a discourse of recognition at a public level. This position integrates both liberalism and communitarianism by stressing the reciprocal relation between individual rights and community by mitigating the excesses of individualism and rationalism and encouraging an ethic of responsibility. However, while reconciling the asocial view of self with a socially situated or contextualised self, a commitment to community remains problematic as communities tend to be either exclusionary, linked to common values or identity, or difficult to define as contemporary populations are geographically highly mobile and, therefore, lacking community, at least in the sense of having shared values. Arguably, the notion of citizenship is becoming increasingly borderless and institutionally less connected to nation-states.

Civic republicanism (or republicanism), often associated with communitarianism, is a radical form of liberal individualism that places emphasis on public or civic bonds, rather than on moral communities as is the case with communitarianism in general. Participation in public life occupies a central space and is the essence of the public bond. It is also equivalent to, but far more pronounced than, the emphasis given to identity in communitarian conceptions of politics that integrate or supplement liberalism with communitarianism. Proponents of republicanism include Jean-Jacques Rousseau (1909), Hannah Arendt (1958), and Benjamin Barber (1984). In their theories, and that of other republicans, we find a commitment to public life, in contrast to the liberal formulation that emphasises self-interest or personal autonomy. Any connection to privatism and negative liberty, which are hallmarks of liberalism, is denounced in favour of an explicit political conception of citizenship, positive liberty, and a self-governing political community. Republicanism, therefore, challenges the liberal presupposition that a self-governing community is incompatible with representative democracy. By relocating politics from the state into the public forum, republicanism is an attempt to find a balance between (1) the individual and society, (2) individual autonomy and community interests, and (3) freedom, rights, and duties, and the common good and civic virtue—it is, thus, an attempt to redress democratic correctiveness. However, the liberalism/republicanism debate has tended to frame the discussion in terms of seeking foundations for democracy, whether constitutional safeguards or popular sovereignty can offer an adequate justification for democracy. In other words, on the republican conception of politics, democracy remains subservient to a normative theory of citizenship. We will analyse this when we discuss radical democracy, in which citizens play an active role in the construction of democracy, later in the chapter. We now turn from our communitarian analysis of liberalism to the feminist analysis.

Feminist criticisms of liberal individualism

It will, perhaps, come as little surprise, given the role philosophy has played in the development of liberal-democracy, that Plumwood extends her critique of liberal-democracy to traditional philosophy also on the grounds of a lack of capacity for correctiveness.

> The participants in the great dialogue of western philosophy, which extends now some two and a half thousand years into the past, have been almost entirely male, white and drawn from the privileged sections of society. That they have not seen this as relevant to their philosophical pursuits indicates how much they have spoken of and for one another, and how incompletely they have, despite their pretensions as philosophers to press the ultimate questions, critically examined themselves and their political relationship to the world about them.
>
> (Plumwood, 1993, p. ix)

A major difference between feminist and non-feminist approaches to philosophy is that non-feminist theory pays little, if any, attention to the experiences of women in its analysis or the lack of women's voices in the history of philosophy, as the passage above illustrates. Elizabeth Spelman's (1982) comment that '[w]hat philosophers have had to say about women typically has been nasty, brutish, and short' (p. 109) sums up this tendency to ignore and exclude well. Although critiques of the exclusion of women are ancient, it has only been since the seventeenth century, with the emergence of urban industrialism and the rise of liberalism, as well as socialist politics, that the liberal-feminist movement arose. The focus was on suffrage, with the aim being the opening up of opportunities for women to partake in the existing social structures open, at the time, only to male citizens. The public sphere was the realm of power and decision making, ruled by reason and accessible only to men, while women were thought of as property to be owned by fathers and then husbands and relegated to the private sphere of family life. The distinction between public and private life has been heavily critiqued by feminists since the time of Mary Wollstonecraft, as we shall see.

Wollstonecraft, regarded by many feminists as the founder of the British feminist movement and precursor to first-wave feminism, is an early example of classical liberal-feminism. Her treatise, *A Vindication of the Rights of Woman*, is a literary protest against liberal reformer Rousseau's sexual politics in which she advocates for social and moral equality of the sexes. The exclusion of women from public discussion and the public sphere at the time was addressed by Wollstonecraft, who based her work on Rousseau's idea of education as a means to the production of future social justice as well as a benefit to the youth in the present. However, she also heavily criticised his proposal that women's education must prepare them to serve men by educating girls only up to the age of 8, after which they should be trained in domestic duties at home. Wollstonecraft thought women should be trained in reason just like men, and just like men, women should submit only to reason, rather than to the opposite sex. In her insistence on equality of the sexes through the extension of reason to both, Wollstonecraft's work has been problematised by later feminists, as well shall see.

Contemporary feminist political philosophy continues to challenge what philosophers and political theorists have to say about women—liberal political thought and theories of democracy have been no exception.[3] As Susan Möller Okin (1979) points out, even when women are included in political discourse, they are usually assigned distinct roles according to 'whatever social and economic structure the philosophers favour and [are] defined as whatever best suits her prescribed functions in that society' (p. 10). Most feminists do not deny that social institutions and practices are structured by rules that validate or establish different types of behaviour as appropriate to both men and women. However, they argue that, in many cases, these rules are particularly oppressive to women, as many of these rules are governed by the public/private distinction. In short, the distinction between the public and private spheres has functioned historically in two ways: practically and theoretically. Practically, the private sphere was, and still is, use to denote the personal realm, the home and non-professional contexts, and the public sphere for the realm outside the home, the professional and the political world of decision-making. However, contemporary social life has problematised this dichotomous division, as there is now significant overlap and interaction at many social and political levels, seen, for example, in the 'strong relationship with the development and ubiquity of information and communications technologies such as mobile telephones and the Internet' (Ford, 2010, p. 550). Theoretically, the public/private division is strongly linked to classical liberal theory's delineation of the boundaries between the political and personal dimensions of liberty; the atomistic individual with private interests that are to be protected from the excessive interference from political authority that encroaches on the rights of individuals to exercise their choices. As we shall see, many feminists have problematised social contract theory, which lies at the core of classical liberal theory and politics, by arguing that it 'has functioned to reinforce a gendered dichotomy between public and private spheres that excludes women from full citizenship' (Mackenzie, 2014, p. 601).

To draw attention to these kinds of problems, feminist philosophers have not only challenged the public/private dichotomy but other oppressive (hierarchical) dualisms, such as reason/emotion, objective/subjective, human/nature, and offered feminist reinterpretations of classical texts, evaluated actual situations in order to draw normative conclusions about social life, clarified the traditional usage of key concepts and challenged existing political categories and presuppositions about human nature. Some of these feminists have challenged the patriarchal construction of contemporary political theory by asserting that the personal is political and, thus, under this description, feminist theory becomes an integral part of political theory itself. Nevertheless, the liberal principles of freedom and equality have gained recognition, not only among contemporary liberal-democratic theorists, but among some feminist scholars, who argue that new interpretations of these concepts might provide insight into the oppression of women, and among those who advocate workers self-management and other forms of participatory decision-making. On the other hand, many feminist philosophers have disregarded or rejected the idea of theorising from the paradigmatic liberal perspective of humans as self-ruling, rational individuals. Indeed, some argue that it is the liberal view of the individual, and thus, the very principles that follow (e.g., freedom, equality. and the right to the protection and acquisition of personal property), which has created difficulties for democracy. Not surprisingly, feminist scholars have turned to the past in order to gain an understanding of women's place in history. By critically examining social contract theories, including those of John Locke and Thomas Hobbes, wherein women were usually given marginal status in the production of culture, a growing body of literature has been dedicated to the construction of alternative women's histories. Pateman's (1989) critique of contractarianism, particularly, poses an alternative to what she sees as the contractual underpinnings of the 'major institutional bonds of civil society—citizenship, employment and marriage' (p. 180).

Locke's contractarianism, developed in his *Two Treatises of Government*, is a rejection of Robert Filmer's *Patriarcha*, which argues in favour of the divine right of kings and patriarchy. Responding to Locke's critique of Filmer, Pateman argues that social contract theory tells a story of a masculine political birth.

> During this birth the natural paternal body of Filmer's patriarchy is metaphorically put to death by the contract theorists, but the artificial body that replaces it is a construct of the mind, not the creation of a political community by real people. The birth of a human child can produce a new male or female, whereas the creation of civil society produces a social body fashioned after the image of only one of the two bodies of humankind, or, more exactly, after the image of the civil individual who is constituted through the original contract.
>
> (p. 102)

Pateman's reading of social contract theory challenges the view that the social contract establishes liberty and equality for all citizens. The new order, she says, is a fraternal order, in which Locke's civil society emerged the victor over Filmer's patriarchal order. Locke, however, introduces a new patriarchal state, which, in Pateman's words, 'is fraternal in form and the original contract is a fraternal pact' (p. 77). The crux of Pateman's argument is that social contract theories disadvantage women because they are incorporated into civil society as women, not as *individuals*.

Moria Gatens (1996) takes history one crucial step further. She sets out to show how the body acts as a metaphor for 'the political body', or as she prefers to call it, 'the body politic', particularly in the works of seventeenth- and eighteenth-century social contract theorists. She argues that Hobbes's *Leviathan*, the artificial man, reflects a 'masculine image of unity and independence from women and nature' (p. 22). The effect of this is to leave 'natural woman' unprotected, undefended, since she has no 'female leviathan' to represent her (p. 23). She is only included in this artificial body by incorporation, that is, men make the pact, and she just becomes assimilated in the greater body, without having a chance to state her own terms, choose her own representation. Consequently, the 'artificial man' can control and regulate women's bodies 'in a manner which does not undermine his claim to autonomy, since her contributions are neither visible nor acknowledged' (p. 23). Furthermore, since he operates under the (carefully constructed) illusion of unity (propped up by incorporation), he does not need to acknowledge difference. Only one voice will speak for one body. It is only his body 'that is entitled to be represented by this political corporation' (p. 21). Gatens argues that what she calls 'the imaginary body of the body politic' continues to exert force to the present day. Thus, our legal and political arrangements do not take 'female embodiment seriously' (p. 24), although she points out that it is not only females that are excluded.

> At different times, different kinds of beings have been excluded from the pact, often simply in virtue of their corporeal specificity. Slaves, foreigners, women, the conquered, children, the working classes have all been excluded from political participation, at one time or another, by their bodily specificity.
>
> (p. 23)

Carol C. Gould (1988) argues that the problems encountered by the liberal view of democracy can be traced back to the ontological foundations of liberalism itself; the metaphysical assumption of abstract individualism (variously called atomistic individualism, liberal individualism, unitary individualism, rugged individualism, possessive individualism). Gould's description is worth quoting at length.

> It takes individuals or persons as the basic entities that constitute the social world. However, this view abstracts from the particular qualities

that make each individual concretely different from each of the others, and instead characterizes all of them in terms of their universal human properties alone, that is, those properties that they all share in common and that make them the kind of individuals they are. On these grounds, liberal individualism takes all individuals as equal in their basic liberties and rights. Further, these individuals are taken to exist independently of each other and to be related to each other only in external ways. That is, each individual is understood as an independent ego, seeking to satisfy its own interests or to pursue its happiness. The relations among these individuals are external relations in that they do not affect the basic nature of these individuals and leave them essentially unchanged.

(p. 93)

According to this view, the individual is the proprietor of their own capacities and owes nothing to society for them. Further, on the topic of human nature Gould (1988) notes that

this nature is regarded as fixed and at the same time as a universal nature, common to all individuals. Among the basic features of this essential human nature are freedom, rationality and self-interest. Thus these individuals are understood as free agents in the sense of possessing free choice. The motives of each individual's actions are taken to be each one's self-interest, which is pursued by rational choice among alternatives.

(p. 93)

Hobbes, Locke, and John Stuart Mill were among many who appealed to this view of human nature. Liberal feminism accepts the traditional conception of human nature as rational but seeks to do away with the restriction of rationality to men alone. The above discussion of Wollstonecraft's work is an exemplar of this approach.

Alison Jaggar, too, observes that the liberal conception of human nature is connected to an underlying metaphysical assumption that human persons are atomistic individuals which in principle are separable from social groups, that is, individuals exist ontologically prior to society. To use Jaggar's (1983) words:

[H]uman individuals are the basic constituents out of which social groups are composed. Logically if not empirically, human individuals could exist outside a social context; their essential characteristics, their needs and interests, their capacities and desires, are given independently of their social context and are not created or even fundamentally altered by that context.

(pp. 28–29)

The philosophical foundations of liberal political thought are foundational upon a conception of human persons as individuals abstracted from all social conditions, hence, the term abstract individualism.

It should be noted that the acceptance of abstract individualism does not require liberal theorists to deny that the existence of social groups and communities play an important role in the development of human capacities. It does, however, create difficulties, especially for liberal feminists, in defining human nature in terms of being a property of social structures. For this reason and others, many feminist writers from different traditions have challenged the concept of abstract individualism, claiming that it is tied up with a masculinist interpretation of self and reality which has homogenised, repressed, and devalued women's experiences, whilst it has 'absolutised' and 'universalised' the male experience (see Gilligan, 1982; Nash, 1997; Schwartzman, 2006). By rejecting the presuppositions of liberal individualism in favour of an ontology of individuals as *human beings* and their relations as *social relations*, feminist writers can account for some fundamental features of human reality, hitherto unaccounted for. For example, many feminists reject the notion of equality, and hence equality as compared with men. In fact, some strands of feminism embrace sexual 'difference' as a theoretical basis for political action (see Gallop, 1992; Irigaray, 1985; Mitchell, 1974, Stone, 2004). Others, such as Catherine MacKinnon (1989), argue that 'for women to affirm differences is to affirm the qualities and characteristics of powerlessness' (p. 51). Yet other feminists emphasise the experience of familial, social, cultural, and ecological connections and suggest an alternative to the model of the human as relational rather than individual. Among these accounts is *relational autonomy*, which highlights the social context within which all individuals exist and acknowledges the central role of others in social relations that shape identities, needs, and interests as well as autonomy (Mansbridge & Okin, 1993, p. 277).

Moreover, the liberal conception of human nature conceives reason to be the quintessential element that distinguishes humans from other animals. Human beings, the story goes, are essentially rational agents, that is, personhood is defined by the capacity for rationality, and all individuals are thought to have an equal potential for reason. It might be argued that this conception is neither unique, nor is it informative. After all, defining human beings as rational agents has a history in philosophical thought that can be traced back to Socrates in Plato's dialogues, and to Aristotle's *Nicomachean Ethics*, which characterises humans as rational animals. What many consider the distinguishing characteristic of the liberal conception of human nature is that liberal theorists identify rationality by stressing either its moral or prudential aspects. This is to say, reason is defined as the ability either to comprehend the rational principles of morality or to calculate the best means to a desired end. The former idea finds its antecedent in Socrates theories of justice. In the case of the liberal conception of rational principles, the value of individual autonomy is stressed, whereas in the case of the calculation of the best means to a desired end, emphasis is placed on the value of self-fulfilment.

Of course, in Socrates the two are collapsed and reason rules desire and emotion to bring about justice and self-fulfilment. While there are various interpretations of rationality even among liberals, the liberal conception of human nature rests on the assumption that all persons possess a universal and essential capacity for reason. Individuals who fail to develop their capacity for reason are regarded as deficient simply because they have failed to meet their human potential—an idea that is decidedly Platonic. As mentioned, the traditional liberal view assumes an ontology of abstract individualism, which emphasises that the relations among individuals are external relations in that they do not affect the basic nature of these individuals.

Given that democratic theory is dependent upon a particular under-standing of human experience, the human condition or human nature that informs conceptions of citizenship, political philosophers cannot avoid mak-ing assumptions regarding sex and gender. Consequently, there has been a tendency among philosophers of the classical liberal tradition, along with contemporary liberal theorists who emphasise neutrality, to make general-isations about human nature which discount the possibility that social life is governed by gender. For example, when claims about women's nature *are* made explicit, male philosophers have relegated women to the private sphere, and, thus, denied them a central place in the political order. An example of the ways in which women are erased through the application of neutrality in political theory, is John Rawls's 'Veil of Ignorance'. Rawls proposed that ideas of fairness could be tested behind what he called the 'Veil of Ignorance'; a thought experiment, where we are asked to imagine that we do not know who we are. Behind the veil we lack clues to our identity, such as social status, ethnicity, education, career, family, appearance, and other socially relevant information, including sex and gender. Once we are sufficiently abstracted in such a way, we are expected to choose which principles of justice we would select as the basic structures of society. This thought experiment is intended to show how participants can select prin-ciples impartially and rationally. Many critics have drawn attention to the problems involved in the abstraction away from individual and group iden-tity. For example, because Rawls believes his theory of justice to be univer-sally applicable and, thus, able to be applied without modification to women, feminist critics have argued that he fails to address adequately the substantive inequality within the private sphere, especially the family (Walsh, 2012). In terms of hyper-separation, the abstraction away from the earth and earthly relationships also is striking, and a topic to which we will shortly return.

Ecofeminists, such as Plumwood (1993), pick up on the critique of dual-isms of earlier feminists and extend it to the environment.

> Ethical universalisation and abstraction are both closely associated with accounts of the self in terms of rational egoism. Universalisation is explicitly seen in both the Kantian and the Rawlsian framework as needed to hold in check natural self-interest; it is the moral complement to the account of the self as "disembodied and disembedded", as the

autonomous self of liberal theory, the rational egoist of market theory, the falsely differentiated self of object-relations theory.

(p. 170)

Abstract individualism is conceptualised not only as a separation of self from others, but also as a separation of self from earth and all other living things. Such a stark separation between the individual and their environment issues in a dualistic framework through which the world is viewed and understood according to liberal theory.

Plumwood argues that dualisms form a system of oppositional pairs, according to which one side of the equation is superior and defined against the other. For example, reason is thought to be superior to emotion, public superior to private, individual superior to community, theory superior to practice, and so on. To use Plumwood's terminology of hyper-separation, liberalism relies on an atomistic view of the individual, with community understood as merely an aggregate of individuals not relationally connected in any significant way and, thus, liberal-democracy is no more than aggregate individualism. If Plumwood is correct that liberal-democracy has failed both democracy and ecology due to its inability for self-correction, which is inherent in the adversarial nature of abstract individualism and, therefore, in the structure of liberal-democracy itself, then we must reject the liberal conception of the human as well as liberal citizenship.

A radical theory of democratic citizenship

To avoid the problem of democracy being subservient to a normative theory of citizenship, as in the cases of liberal and communitarian citizenship, radical democracy offers a theory of democracy whereby the citizen plays an active role in the ongoing reconstruction of democracy. As such, radical conceptions of democracy are also sensitive to feminist critiques of liberal individualism and liberal theory generally. Radical democracy implies a conception of citizenship which is 'repoliticized by democracy, allowing us to speak of democratic citizenship' (Delanty, 2000, p. 36), rather than confining citizenship to membership of society or the bearer of rights which informs liberal-democratic theory. More specifically, it is a theory of democracy whereby citizenship is seen as participatory citizenship with a democratic aim; that is, of reconstructing the relationship between society and the state. By shifting the emphasis away from a model of citizenship that rests on political foundations, in the sense that a particular model of democracy can be justified only by an appeal to self-evident truth about human nature, natural rights, or other pre-political or normative foundations (such as liberal-democracy's commitment to abstract individualism), toward an emphasis on democratic engagement, citizenship itself becomes the means of reconstructing politics.

What makes theories of radical democracy distinct from liberal and communitarian conceptions is that democracy and citizenship are not treated as separate discourses. *Citizenship is not a theory of the individual but of collective action.* By extending citizenship to democratic participation, rather than confining it to societal membership, citizenship is an active process of social change through political reconstruction. Put another way, the dualisms of the state and society, democracy and citizenship, and the individual and community are dissolved. The state and the community are seen as interdependent, and citizenship the prime mover for democratising both. Dewey's (1916) conception of democracy is exemplary of community tied to democracy; it 'is more than a form of government, it is primarily a mode of associated living, of conjoint, communicated experience' (p. 87). His vision of democracy is a process of community formation founded on deliberative communication. It is a deliberative model of democracy that provides a vision of an ideal democratic society which supports greater participation and deliberation as necessary conditions for democratic life.

Dewey's theory of democracy could be described as a precursor to discursive democracy, as it locates democracy in both the state and society and is concerned with the deliberative process within public communication. Emphasis is not only on participation, but also on the quality of the participation, and, thus, challenges the notion of the liberal autonomous individual subject and the public/private distinction. This shifts the emphasis also onto civic virtues such as tolerance, a willingness to listen and be open to alternatives, and a readiness to reason. It also stresses the relationship between language and a sense of community and locates the justification for democracy as a form of communal deliberation in both the public sphere and the institutional political culture of civil society. This form of deliberative communication implies an intersubjective understanding of self where the 'idea of the public is also recast as a medium of open-ended communication' (Delanty, 2000, p. 42). The epistemology of the community is fallibilism, an ongoing learning process of reconstruction through reflexive scrutiny and self-correction. It is what Jürgen Habermas (1996) calls 'a fallible learning process through which a society gradually overcomes its ability to engage in normative reflection on itself' (p. 444). Citizenship, in this sense, 'is as much about the articulation of problems as it is about their resolution' (Delanty, 2000, p. 46).

Radical democracy recognises that citizenship, like democracy, is a fluid and ongoing process of sociocultural reconstruction; it is never permanent and complete. What we are stressing here is the learning dimension of citizenship as a process of social reconstruction. As a learning process, citizenship takes place in communicative situations arising out of ordinary and extraordinary life experiences and events. Seen in this way, citizenship has a cognitive dimension; it is experienced as a practice that connects individuals to their society, sustained by individual and collective narratives, consisting of memories, common values, and shared experiences. Thus, citizenship has a transformative role to play, not just in enhancing the individual's cognitive competencies, but also in bringing about collective learning. The advantage of framing citizenship as an active learning process is that it shifts the focus of citizenship from membership of a political community onto common experiences, cognitive processes, forms of cultural translation, and discourses of empowerment. Citizenship must be able to give voice to personal identities that come out of communicative relations, rather than as an expression of liberal or neo-liberal values of individualism or shared communitarian values. While coping with diversity is one of the tasks of citizenship, as an active learning process citizenship can become an important means of cognitive transformation of self and other. Put another way, citizenship as a learning process shaped by communicative and deliberative processes and relations is radically democratic. It concerns the task of constructing and enhancing democratic ways of association, such as learning to give new definitions to work, social relations, and ecological relations.

The fact that a genuine deliberative democracy does not yet exist should not be considered a hindrance. If we are ever going to achieve a stronger democracy of the deliberative kind in what Dewey called the 'Great Community', we need to have democratic microcosms in place, such as the classroom. This leads us to the kinds of educational arrangements required to fit deliberative democracy and to facilitate democratic reconstruction.

Cultural citizenship

The liberal characterisation of the citizen as an atomistic individual, the nation as an aggregate of individuals rather than a collective or community, and democracy as the maximisation of private interests with minimal citizen participation, illustrates well the features inherent of liberal-democracy—features that contribute to the emphasis on private interests rather than the common good and, thus, hinder the capacity for adaptation and correction. As such, liberal-democratic nation-states are, as Plumwood (1995) claims, unable 'to articulate and respond to the needs of the least privileged', leading to radical inequality, which, as previously noted, is both a hindrance to, and an indicator of, other hindrances to the democratic correction of social institutions (p. 137).

A neglected dimension in developing the capacity for democratic correctiveness is education. Currently, the predominant liberal discourse on citizenship is indistinguishable from 'disciplinary citizenship' that permeates official policy documents. Delanty (2003) refers to this as the governmentalisation of citizenship:

> In this discourse, citizenship is constructed by codes, categories and modes of classification that reflect a governmental strategy into which the individual as citizen is inserted. Thus, the immigrant [be]comes [sic] a citizen by participating in a discourse that redefines social relations according to fairly fixed categories. What is noticeable in this is that the language of citizenship and learning is taken over by the state and defined according to a set of rigid categories.
>
> (p. 599)

In liberal-democratic nation-states, citizenship is characterised by governmental discourse that has remained within rights discourse and formal membership of the polity with emphasis on equality over difference and advocates the idea of a common public culture regardless of ethnic groupings. Critics claim that such measures dilute non-Western values in favour of Western values and advocate cultural assimilation or exclude worldviews that do not sit well within the framework of non-liberal values (Clarke, Coll, Dagnino & Neveu, 2014; Kapai, 2012).

Consequently, curriculum and syllabus documents on civics and citizenship education tend to emphasise the teaching of shared values and the knowledge and understanding of civic institutions and processes. Typically, the aim of civics is to develop a body of knowledge and understanding of the institutions and processes related to a nation's system of governance, including local, state, national, regional, and global perspectives, such as social and political heritage, democratic processes, public administration, the judicial system, tradition, and national identity. Citizenship, on the other hand, refers to 'the dispositions and skills for participation in the civic life of a nation' (Tudball & Henderson, 2014, p. 5). In other words, civics education provides the knowledge base for civic understanding and citizenship education provides the experiential base for democratic participation. In terms of learning processes, a common distinction is that 'Civics is cognitive whereas Citizenship is dispositional in nature' (Mellor, Meiers & Knight, 2010, p. 5). This is not to say that civics and citizenship are separate. Indeed, they are complementary; the civic realm of the state and the civil realm of the community, for which students must be prepared as future citizens, must be interactive as knowledge and experience inform each other. However, civics and citizenship education programs in liberal-democracies tend to be reduced to formal learning and the assumption is that what needs to be learned is the official values of the polity and the history, traditions, structures, and processes of democracy as interpreted by public officials, policy makers and curriculum designers; all other values and knowledge are subsumed. A further assumption is that *individual* learning processes convert into a *collective* learning outcome, but this view is mistaken. As Delanty (2003) notes, '[c]ollective learning processes operate on quite different levels and the relation between individual and collective learning is complex' (p. 599) and, therefore, cannot be assumed. As citizenship is a process undertaken both individually and collectively, understanding collective learning processes is paramount to understanding citizenship, whereby citizens learn about and shape society.

Delanty contrasts disciplinary citizenship with *cultural citizenship*, which makes a greater connection between learning and citizenship as a collective discursive learning process that occurs on individual, group, and institutional levels. According to Delanty, the learning that takes place at each level is a different kind of learning, as '[t]he way individuals learn is quite different from the way societies learn' (p. 600). Cultural citizenship moves away from 'the fixed, rule learning model implicit in disciplinary citizenship' (p. 600) toward a dynamic view of citizenship 'conceived of in terms of learning processes that have a developmental and *transformative* impact on the learning subject' (p. 605, *italics* added). The cultural citizenship conception of learning, therefore, entails empowerment, as individuals have the capacity to *reconstruct* themselves.

> To be emphasized, then, is the processual nature of learning, which is an open process defined in movement rather than in finality. This view of learning suggests a cultural dimension to it; that is, culture as a making or a doing. Learning involves agency on the part of the learning subject. The cognitive structures operate in learning processes connect different frames and codes. Learning is thus a cultural process of creation and construction.
>
> (pp. 600–601)

Delanty's attention to learning processes emphasises learning as: (1) an individual biography, (2) an intersubjective conduit, occurring as interpersonal cultural narratives that provide interpretations of the world, for social construction, by which individual learning is translated and coordinated into collective learning, and (3) cultural learning that eventually becomes embodied in social institutions. The relationships between the three levels are complex, but he thinks can be summed up as: process, connectivism, development, construction, and transformation (pp. 601–602). Such learning can change normative and epistemic frameworks that provide structures to guide social action and social change. Such changes in learning result from a *constructivist* process of communicative links between 'common experiences, cognitive processes, forms of cultural translation and discourses of empowerment' (p. 602), which can arise out of both ordinary experiences and 'major crises and catastrophes such as the experience of victimhood or injustice. It appears that an essential dimension of the cognitive experience of citizenship is the way in which individual life stories are connected with wider cultural discourses' (p. 602). Cultural citizenship not only enhances the individual's cognitive competencies but has the potential to bring about collective learning.

Unlike disciplinary citizenship, which rigidly views citizenship as a formal body of knowledge or proficiency, cultural citizenship is imbued with mechanisms for democratic correctiveness because citizenship occurs in communicative situations and, therefore, connects individuals to their society through sustained narratives, consisting of memories, shared values, and experiences, which speaks to Plumwood's concerns of separation from 'other' inherent in liberal individualism. Cultural citizenship, conceived of as active learning processes, creates 'discourses for the expression of communicative competencies', which is an 'important means of cognitive transformation of self and other' (Delanty, 2003, p. 604) and one of main factors in facilitating democratic correctiveness. The argument we put forward here is that the individual/community dualism inherent in liberal discourse is problematic.

By connecting the dualism in an experiential way, as a 'cognitive relationship by which learning processes in the domain of citizenship are transferred to the cultural dimension of society' (Delanty, 2003, p. 604), cultural citizenship has the potential to empower people through discursive recognition and collective understanding of citizenship. This is a radical view of democracy, as it relies on a dynamic view of citizenship as ongoing reconstruction of identity through collective self-correction, rather than the fixed identity of liberal individualism implicit in disciplinary citizenship. This view is compatible with Dewey's conception of democracy as a mode of associated living, and education as life itself and not preparation for life, which we will discuss further in Chapter 2.

Conclusion

Plumwood's criticism of liberal-democracy failing both ecology and democracy, due to its inability to bring about the correction of social institutions, cannot be ignored. Nor can the dearth of people's confidence in democracy to represent their interests, be cast aside as mere political apathy. The environmental, social, and political failing we have so far addressed, combined with liberal-democracies lack of correctiveness, leaves citizens feeling powerless to bring about much needed change. These factors, and the ever-increasing presence of social media and media-driven elections, hardly instil confidence in democracy; rather, they only serve to support Plato's contention that democracy would inevitably lead only to tyranny and subjugation. In addition, the accumulating evidence of anthropogenic climate change demands a change in our consumer and citizen habits. The onus is on democracy to mitigate obstacles that hinder the capacity for correction to bring about change, rather than continue in its subordination to the predominant logic of liberal-democratic governmentality and discourses that perpetuate radical inequalities, environmental degradation, and colonisation.

To address these concerns will require democratic correctiveness, that is, it will require re-emphasising the relationship between belief-habits and habitats and, inevitably, the reshaping of democracy. We discuss this at greater length when we outline our framework for a place-based democratic education in Chapter 6. Suffice it to say, such a change requires a move away from abstract individualism toward citizenship as a corrective learning process, that is, civics and citizenship education as a way of reconstructing citizenship as a dialectic process, which enables democratic correction of social institutions. In this sense, citizenship is an educative process that is life itself; a mode of associated living as Dewey called it, rather than a set of rights and duties. As such, citizens have an integral role to play in shaping democracy. In the case of schooling, students would then practice democracy as an ongoing process of collaborative inquiry that aims at self-correction as a fundamental aspect of inquiring communities. The next chapter, therefore, looks at what kinds of teaching methods are suitable for enhancing cultural citizenship as a learning process.

Notes

1 For more on the topic of present instantiations of colonisation, see Moreton-Robinson (2015), Wolfe (2006), Smith (2012), Smith, Tuck & Yang (2019).

2 See Olsson et al. (2014), Chapter 13 of the 2014 IPCC report, 'Livelihoods and poverty', which 'is devoted to exploring poverty in relation to climate change, a novelty in the IPCC' (p. 798). Its addition reflects growing global recognition and concern over the effects of climate change on those already economically and ecologically disadvantaged.

3 For a critical look at the tradition of political philosophy, specifically the works of Plato, Aristotle, Rousseau, and Mill, see Okin (1979). See also Pateman (1988), Shanley & Pateman (1991), Jaggar (1983).

2 Teaching civics and citizenship

Introduction

Across the globe, citizens in many countries vote in periodic large-scale national or regional elections, as well as small-scale local elections, to express their preferences for candidates to hold political office. Many do so because they believe *individuals* can make a difference and that *collectively* they can influence governmental decision-making. Others are not so optimistic, as they feel disenfranchised or that no elected representative or political party has ever helped them—they're all the same! In countries where voting is not compulsory this can lead to low voter turnout. For example, in the 2016 U.S. presidential election between Donald Trump and Hillary Clinton, almost 100 million Americans did not cast a presidential vote, representing 43 per cent of the eligible voting-age population, which was more than the number of votes each candidate received. This might be a shock to citizens who see voting as more than a right, but as an obligation, but to others like Barber voting is not enough to guarantee democracy.

There is a danger in thinking that democracy runs by itself without any effort from citizens, or with minimalist effort of voting, when, indeed, it requires civic work, civic activity. In an interview with Scott London in 1992, Barber had this to say:

> Citizenship is, at its best, a full-time job. It means taking ongoing responsibility for all of the communities in which you live: your family, your neighborhood, your church, your school, your synagogue, the town, the state, the nation, and of course increasingly now we talk about a genuine responsibility to the whole globe environmentally as well […] voting is the *first* step towards citizenship, not the last step.
>
> (Barber, in London, 2021, n.p.)

In other words, a well-functioning democracy requires active and informed citizenship. For Barber, this is so because democracy cannot be premised on foundations, such as appeals to human nature like those of the self-interested liberal individual, as such foundations would be static, unchanging. Rather,

DOI: 10.4324/9781003098089-3

democracy is a process that evolves with each new generation and each new struggle for redefinition of concepts.

> Politically, we may define democracy as a regime/culture/civil society/government in which we make (will) common decisions, choose common conduct, and create or express common values in the practical domain of our lives in an ever-changing context of conflict of interests and competition for power – a setting, moreover, where there is no agreement on prior goods or certain knowledge about justice or right and where we must proceed on the premise of the base equality both of interests and of the interested. Voting involves not a discretionary decision about what is true but a necessary decision about what to do.
>
> (Barber, in London, 2021, n.p.)

For Barber, democracy is paradoxical, insofar as it was created in the spirit of revolution, yet the social and political structures it forms become binding, constricting the very spirit in which they were created. Hence, he stresses that voting is a first step towards citizenship and that gentle revolution is a necessary part of the democratic process. Civic literacy is, therefore, necessary so that 'gentle revolution', which can also be conceived as a type of democratic correctiveness, is informed by active and informed citizen inquiry.

As the long history of democratic protests illustrate, individual and collective action—such as rallies, marches, pickets, civil disobedience, boycotts, press conferences, social media campaigns, and other public expressions of objection, disapproval, or dissent towards a political idea or action—the revolutionary spirit of democracy is equally, if not more, effective in forging change. The rise of school activism and the global school strikes inspired by Greta Thunberg, the #MeToo campaigns, Black Lives Matter protests, the Australian Aboriginal sovereignty political movement, and the global environmental movement Extinction Rebellion (XR) all demonstrate that protest is alive and well as a form of democratic participation. What these protests seek to achieve is what Barber (1984) calls *strong democracy*, in which citizens actively participate to the greatest extent possible in democratic decision-making. However, a strong democracy requires an active and informed citizenry. This brings us back to the question of civics and citizenship education and identity formation. How can we move away from disciplinary citizenship towards a model of cultural citizenship?

To address this question, we will discuss three conceptions of education: teaching as transmission, transaction, and transformation. These different approaches to teaching indicate a tension between present societies and social aspirations, that is, the conservative view that education should reflect and preserve the composite values of the present society and the aspirational view to lead students towards an idealised society. This raises questions of value conflicts and teacher neutrality. We argue that neutrality is an untenable position that tends to privilege the dominant ideology. For education to be effective, all three conceptions need to be integrated. When taken together, education becomes a *corrective process*; an ongoing reconstruction of students' social and intellectual habits, which can enlarge the meaning of their experiences, including social and moral thinking, and, therefore, increases their ability to deal with issues and problems of contemporary social life. To this end, students need to engage in genuine communicative practices, which we argue are best served through student-centred, inquiry-based pedagogy, in which education is seen as a continuous reconstruction of experience that develops students' capacities for active and informed citizenship.

Three conceptions of education

With the onset of the global information age, came an increase in connections with others through social media and communication platforms for instant messaging, document sharing, screen sharing, and video or audio calls. At the same time, emphasis on individualisation, rather than autonomy, increasingly became an integral part of selfhood in neoliberal discourse that has permeated liberal-democratic politics and consequently identity, to a lesser extent, is 'being determined by group affiliation', with 'dominant norms plac[ing] the individual, not the group, in first place' (Bjereld, Ekengren & Schierenbeck, 2009, p. 267). This has manifested internationally as stronger claims for individual rights but at the expense of state sovereignty, whereas nationally it has meant, for example, 'an increased importance of the specific competencies of the individual in the labour market and a decreasing interest in collective political activities' (Bjereld et al., 2009, p. 263). Under the current conditions of individualisation and connections with others due to global communications, 'identity is such a central and deep aspect of life that education cannot afford to neglect it' (Flum & Kaplan, 2012, p. 244). Such a response is hardly surprising as education is prescribed as a 'cure all'. It is viewed variously as a pre-requisite for transmitting skills and knowledge considered necessary for the reproduction of existing societies, 'as an antidote for a range of apparent ills', and as the foundation of 'a stable society, social change, a new economy, economic stability, female empowerment, male rights, traditional values, progressive values, and so on' (Thornton, 2022, p. 1). The multiple and often somewhat contradictory aims and theories of education leads to the question: What counts as education, and how can education promote the development of students' identities in a democracy?

There exists an ever-burgeoning body of scholarly literature devoted to the philosophy of education, in which many authors have attempted to carry out arguments concerning the purposes of education by appealing to the historical use of the word 'education'. In its broadest sense, education refers to, as Dewey pronounced, the social continuity of life. In a much narrower sense, it can be applied to the deliberate transmission and fostering of culture. Whilst Dewey's definition could be said to exclude from education very little that is not potentially a learning activity, the latter definition generates a host of difficulties for anyone who has seriously considered democracy.

Looking for the 'true' meaning of words by delving into their etymologies, brings us no closer to the truth. Scholars are unsure whether the word educate derived from the Latin word *educere* meaning to 'lead out', or *educare* meaning to train. Plato, for example, believed education to be a process of 'leading out' or 'bringing out' what he saw as already innate in the child.[1] Some writers have argued that both words were used interchangeably, or that each incorporated the other. To add to the controversy, some writers have postulated that to educate is more closely related to the word *educe*, which is supposed to give evidence in favour of their view of education (see Postman & Weingartner, 1969). We will not attempt to carry on the arguments any further here; suffice to say that, even if it were an established fact that the word education derived its meaning from a particular Latin word, such evidence does not settle the question of how we should approach education in the twenty-first century.[2] What is evident is that the word education can incorporate either or both meanings without straying too far from the word's etymological roots or its original usage.

So, what kind of education is required for facilitating identity formation in a democracy? Debates continue on the merits of (1) teacher-centred education or traditional pedagogy, often aligned with the *transmission* of information, an educational process that creates a learning environment in which students can understand and apply knowledge, values, and skills, (2) knowledge as construction through *transactions* between teacher and students, and (3) learner-centred or student-centred education, usually aligned with the *transformation* of knowledge, which often is linked to inquiry-based conceptions of education, including philosophical learning communities. This debate has direct bearing on our proposal for democratic education, for which our starting point is the question we raised above on reconstructing civics and citizenship education underpinned by cultural citizenship as a learning process.

Teaching as transmission: The banking model

The transmission model of education refers to the view that the primary role of education is to transmit or inculcate certain knowledge, values, and skills, thereby contributing to the stabilisation of social and cultural norms. Its underlying principle is atomism: 'Reality is seen in terms of separate, isolated building blocks. Information or ideas can be broken down into small, manageable units that make it easier for students to learn' (Miller, 2010, p. 16). The learning environment is, therefore, usually very structured; the teacher designs lessons with predetermined goals and presents them in a predetermined order, often using a sequential approach to learning, so that students passively acquire teacher-specified knowledge and skills in order to inculcate cultural values and mores (Arends, 2012; Slavin, 2012). Academic achievement is measured by students' ability to demonstrate the designated knowledge and skills to the teacher or other evaluation agency, such as state government administered testing. Emphasis is, therefore, on the mastery of traditional school subjects (included in the subject-oriented curriculum) through traditional teaching and learning strategies or methods. These include rote learning techniques (i.e., memorisation and recall based on repetition); mastery learning, an instructional strategy that requires students to attain a level of prerequisite knowledge before moving onto the next stage of learning (Bloom, 1968); phonics, the process of decoding words, sounding-out words, or using print-to-sound relationships; and cultural literacy, the ability to understand and participate fluently in any given culture. Evaluation methods include fill-in-the-blank tests, multiple choice tests, and standardised tests which are considered apt measures of students' learning.

Once the dominant mode of education, the transmission instructional model has a very long history and continues to be prevalent in classrooms, albeit to a lesser extent, and has advocates who see it as the most efficient way of teaching basic cultural values. However, as the learning experience is assimilative, it is often a vehicle for cultural assimilation. Students are likely to be assimilated into the existing social and political structures, which, in Western-style democracies, includes the perpetuation of the predominant conception of liberal individualism, citizenship, and national identity. This model is, therefore, unacceptable as a critical approach to civics and citizenship education. Paulo Freire (1970), a leading advocate of critical pedagogy, has this to say:

> A careful analysis of the teacher-student relationship at any level, inside or outside the school, reveals its fundamentally narrative character [...] The contents, whether values or empirical dimensions of reality, tend in the process of being narrated to become lifeless and petrified [...] Worse still, it turns [students] into 'containers', into receptacles, to be filled by the teacher [...] Education thus becomes an act of depositing, in which the students are the depositories and the teacher is the depositor [...] This is the 'banking' concept of education, in which the scope of action allowed to the students extends only as far as receiving, filing, and storing the deposits. They do, it is true, have the opportunity to become collectors or cataloguers of the things they store. But in the last analysis, it is [people] themselves who are filed away through the lack of creativity, transformation, and knowledge in this (at best) misguided system.
>
> (pp. 45–46)

Freire's metaphor of the transmission process as the 'banking concept of education' provides a powerful image of a 'misguided system' in which students are 'containers' that simply store the information relayed to them by the teacher. It is a teacher-centred approach in which the teacher is the instructor; 'the dispenser of knowledge, the arbitrator of truth, and the final evaluator of learning' (Johnson, 2010, p. 1). As knowledge, skills, and values are transmitted from the teacher's head to the students' heads without critical examination, students are more likely to be susceptible to the hidden curriculum, and, therefore, for Freire, the banking model of education aligns with oppression.

The crux of Freire's critique of teacher-centric learning is that it precludes the need for students to recognise their own oppression. Because the uni-directional transfer of knowledge does not engage students in dialogue or allow them to think critically and creatively and, instead, requires them to passively adapt, it dehumanises students. Not only are students socialised to believe that the teacher knows all and that as not-yet-adults they are inferiors that must accept what they are taught and not question the world or their teachers, consequently, they will not have the intellectual and social capacities and dispositions to question the world if they need to. To quote Freire (1970): 'The more students work at storing the deposits entrusted to them, the less they develop the critical consciousness which would result from their intervention in the world as transformers of that world' (p. 73). As a result, they are unlikely to recognise their own oppression let alone that education is their oppressor.

Freire's apprehension of transmission education as an effective model for civics and citizenship education is more than understandable. Even more so is this concern understandable today given our global interconnectedness and the complex new social, political, and cultural realities interconnected-ness brings for nations and regions in developing more inclusive societies and strengthening democracy. Over 50 years after the English translation of *Pedagogy of the Oppressed* was published (in 1970), Freire's thoughts on the banking concept of education are still pertinent today, as the knowledge, skills, and values, as well as dispositions, required to be active and informed citizens in a highly stratified and unequal global socio-political context, places new and increased demands on educational institutions. Empowering students to be actively engaged in their world, and more informed, respon-sible, and caring citizens is, therefore, of increasing priority. We will address these issues in more detail in later chapters but for the moment, suffice it to say that learning by transmission has a limited role to play, insofar as it can be useful to divide learning into sequentially manageable tasks or deliver a 'chalk and talk' lecture to disseminate information or learn new skills through imitation and repetition such as learning a new sport, a musical instrument or how to drive. However, it serves best in conjunction with transactional and transformative teaching, in order to facilitate connections with all areas of students' development and learning—social–emotional, physical, and cognitive—to develop the *whole child*.

Teaching as transaction: Constructing knowledge

According to the transactional model of developmental psychology, 'develop-ment of any process in the individual is influenced by interplay with processes in the individual's context over time' (Sameroff, 2009, p. 3). This model is homologous with the constructivist perspective of cognitive development expressed in the theories of psychologists Jean Piaget and Lev Vygotsky. Piaget, who focused on both understanding how children acquire knowledge and the nature of intelligence, was a forerunner of the constructivist theory of knowing, for which the origins can be traced back to his theory of cognitive development, based on biological maturation and stages. According to Piaget (1936), children move through four stages of development: (1) sensorimotor stage, (2) preoperational stage, (3) concrete operational stage, and (4) formal operational stage, and should not be taught certain concepts until they reached the appropriate stage of cognitive development. However, he believed that children take an active role in the learning process, partaking in experiments, observations, and learning about the world around them, continually adding new knowledge, building on existing knowledge, and adapting existing beliefs to accommodate new information.

Unlike Piaget, Vygotsky's social constructivist view of learning places emphasis on the social and cultural nature of development rather than developmental stages. According to Vygotsky (1978), human social and intellectual development is a process wherein the interpersonal communicative functions of language are internalised. The process is from an interpersonal communicative function to an individual psychological one, which is necessary for the development of the higher-order cognitive functions. Note the emphasis on the role of collaborative situations for achieving greater intellectual development. In other words, development cannot be separated from its social and cultural context.

> Every feature in the child's cultural development appears twice: first on the social level, and later, on the individual level; first between people (interpsychological), and then inside the child (intrapsychological). This applies equally to voluntary attention, to logical memory, and to the formation of concepts. All the higher psychological functions originate as actual relations between human individuals.
>
> (p. 57)

The internalisation process is vital to the acquisition of the culture to which the child belongs. However, children cannot discover their meaning without the assistance of adults. Thus, Vygotsky underscored the significance of collaborative situations, such as teacher–student and student–peer interaction, in the learning process.

Engaging students in cooperative dialogue with their peers under the facilitative guidance of a teacher enables them to experience the interactive processes happening externally which in turn become internalised through shared or intersubjective understanding. To promote development, students require guided participation in genuine collaborative learning experiences which are assessed not only on the current level of an individual's achievements but also on potential development. As Vygotsky (1962) put it, 'what a child can do in cooperation today, he can do alone tomorrow' (p. 104). The distance between what an individual can do with and without assistance he referred to as the 'zone of proximal development'. The process of internalisation is made possible in the zone of proximal development as collaborative performance leads to independent performance, and at the same time individuals acquire a culture of social interaction, collaborative dialogue, problem-solving, and deliberative decision-making. Individuals not only internalise the methods of collaborative performance, but they also internalise the characteristic behaviours that come from such engagement. Significant among these are openness to alternative views and a commitment to self-correction. These characteristics could be thought of as necessary for civic engagement and the democratic correction of social and political institutions.

Comparisons have been made between Piaget's and Vygotsky's constructivist theories (see Lourenço, 2012; Slavin, 2012; Thomas, 2000). Both focus on cognitive development, and both claim that cognitive conflict can initiate and further such development, that biology and language have roles in cognitive development, that egocentric language is vital to that process, and that children are active participants in their own learning. However, Piaget believed that development precedes learning (i.e., development occurs in distinct stages and that each stage needs to be reached for learning to occur), whereas Vygotsky rejected stage development and believed that social learning precedes development. Piaget believed that cognitive development starts in the individual and continues to the social world, that egocentric speech is evidence that children are self-centred and, thus, see only from their own point of view, that language stems from thought, and that children learn independently. Vygotsky believed the contrary, that development begins in the social world and gradually is internalised in the individual, that egocentric speech occurs when children progress from using language to communicate socially to using language as private speech and eventually as thought (or inner speech), and, thus, that thought stems from language, and that children depend on social interaction to learn.

Piaget's stage theory and Vygotsky's sociocultural theory of cognitive development are often linked to transactional teaching, as 'there is a strong cognitive focus to the transaction orientation', but it is also based on the scientific method which has links to Dewey (Miller, 2010, p. 21). Dewey (1938) argued that the scientific method is 'the only authentic means at our command for getting at the significance of our everyday experiences of the world in which we live' (p. 88). His conception of the scientific method as inquiry, which he applied to his method for problem-solving in groups called reflective thinking, is considered a general teaching method in education; the active, persistent, and careful consideration of generally accepted knowledge, the grounds that support it, and the conclusions to which it leads. The method comprises five steps: (1) confronting a problematic situation that needs to be resolved, (2) defining the problem, (3) analysing the underlying factors that contribute to it, (4) developing hypotheses that offer possible solutions and evaluating and testing them, and (5) deciding on a mutually acceptable solution, implementing it, and thereafter evaluating the solution.

The influences of Piaget, Vygotsky, and Dewey on transactional teaching can be seen in its emphasis on student-centred pedagogies, such as inquiry-based learning, problem-based learning, and critical thinking pedagogy, which is a move away from instructional teaching and knowledge transmission as its aim is to generate alternative possibilities and interpretations. Learning occurs when participants are actively involved in a process of meaning-making and knowledge construction, rather than passively receiving information, as described by Freire's banking concept of education. The task of the teacher is to create educational environments in which students are given opportunities to interact with the classroom materials so that their understanding of the world (i.e., past knowledge and experiences) can *transact* with their interpretation, understanding, and meaning to construct new meaningful knowledge (Johnson 2010; Santrock 2004). In other words, teaching as transaction connects knowledge to something students already know, information that has been transmitted through formal education, or informal education, such as the family, church, local community, and social media.

For the transactional model, the aim of education is to foster students' ability to inquire and think critically in order to solve real-world problems. Teaching and learning strategies include problem-based learning, the case study method or moral dilemmas approach, and disciplined-based inquiry. Evaluation methods include observation, interviews, and rubrics. Unlike the teaching and learning strategies and evaluation methods of the transmission model, the transactional model is more interactive as dialogue is central to teaching and learning, and, therefore, has a vital role in whole child education (rather than being limited to atomism), insofar as it can facilitate students' ability to think clearly and to problem-solve—skills required for civic engagement.

A major criticism of the transactional teaching model is that 'analysis is stressed more than synthesis and thinking is emphasized over feeling', and, therefore, it is 'primarily limited to the cognitive domain' (Miller, 2010, pp. 11, 29). Arguably, this could be said of Piaget's stage theory of cognitive development, but not so for Dewey's and Vygotsky's constructivist theories. Dewey rejected the supposition that emotions are states or processes located within an individual's brain. Emotions are composite parts of a concrete whole, 'both internal (neural and physiological activity, phenomenal properties, cognitive judgments) and external processes (expressive behavior, ongoing "transactions" with the surrounding environment)' that are an 'interrelated, distributed process spanning brain, expressive body, and world', which 'not only receives support from current research in cognitive and neuroscience', but also 'highlights the central role that agency and the social world play in the development and experiential character of our emotional life' (Krueger, 2014, p. 140). As Dewey emphasised experiential education, in which learners engage directly with their environment, the self in dialogue is an expression of brain, body, and the environment and, therefore, emphasises both thinking and feeling, as well as analysis and synthesis. Vygotsky, too, did not neglect emotions. Instead, he acknowledged a relationship between cognition and other types of emotion, arguing that 'intellectual feelings (such as interest, curiosity, awe) are a result of the way thinking conducts emotions' (Mesquita, 2012, p. 813).

In addition, both Vygotsky and Dewey stressed the 'roles of social history, experience/ culture, and human inquiry in the education process' (Glassman, 2001, p. 3). Vygotsky 'emphasized the role of cultural forms and meanings in perpetuating higher forms of human thought' (Mayer, 2008, p. 6) and Dewey's notion of experiential education 'provides a flashpoint for connecting Vygotskian-inspired constructivism and learning through cultural mediation' (Razfar, 2013, p. 129). Dewey's interactional, organic model of inquiry, which appeals to psychological informed theories of learning and knowledge, is an *integration of mind-body in action* that rejects dualistic divisions between emotion and reason (Hildebrand, 2018, n.p.). Education is, as Dewey (1916) put it, 'the process of forming fundamental dispositions, intellectual and emotional, toward nature and fellow-men' (p. 328). We will revisit Dewey's constructivist accounts of inquiry, as part of a larger discussion on education as reconstruction later in this chapter. But first, we look at the last of the three conceptions of education: teaching as transformation.

Teaching as transformation: Developing meaningful lives

The development of various learning principles and strategies, particularly student-centred learning, active learning, collaborative learning, experiential education, and problem-based learning, have had significant influence on contemporary approaches to education. Each share underlying characteristics that are complementary components of the transformation conception of teaching, which emphasises 'creating dynamic relationships between teachers, students, and a shared body of knowledge to promote student learning and personal growth' (Slavich & Zimbardo, 2012, p. 576). Unlike transmission teaching, which has atomism as its underlying principle, transformative teaching is underpinned by the view that everything is connected (Miller, 2010, p. 29). It involves creating conditions with potential to transform students 'on many different levels (cognitive, emotional, social, intuitive, creative, spiritual and other)', in which learning occurs 'when these experiences elicit a transformation of consciousness that leads to a greater understanding of and care for self, others, and the environment' (Johnson, 2010, pp. 1–2). Put another way, transformative learning is that which occurs when 'a deep, structural shift in the basic premises of thought, feelings, and actions' is experienced; a 'shift of consciousness that dramatically and irreversibly alters our way of being in the world' (Morrell & O'Connor, 2002, p. xvii).

As a teaching method, transformative education incorporates elements of constructivism: participants are actively involved in a process of meaning making and knowledge construction, with an emphasis on inquiry-based learning, problem-solving, and thinking skills to foster students' ability to inquire and think critically in order to solve real-world problems.

However, academic achievement is closely connected to self-actualisation (Johnson, 2010, p. 2) and, thus, transformative teaching has the additional purpose of 'shift[ing] perspectives and to transform student's conceptions of self' (Thornton, 2019, p. 612). In other words, it is *purposeful engagement in identity formation.* To this end, it aims to develop independence in decision-making by encouraging students to examine alternative options and values of life. It also looks to develop reflective thinking about ideas and opinions of others. For that to happen, schools need to provide a learning environment that is, among other things, diverse, supportive, and stimulating. Under these conditions, students can become the creators of their community while also making a difference to the society of which they are a part.

The use of various approaches to learning that complement transformative learning theory provides pedagogical synergy, that is, the process whereby the level of comprehending teaching material is increased, the practical focus strengthened, and the coherence of an educational environment enhanced (Mascall & Rolheiser, 2006), which has the potential for maximising students' intellectual and personal growth. Such growth has been variously described as 'enhancing students' learning-related attitudes, values, beliefs, and skills' (Slavich & Zimbardo, 2012, p. 576) or fostering 'wisdom, compassion, and sense of purpose in one's life' (Miller, 2010, p. 30). According to transformative learning theory (Mezirow, 1997), to achieve this, certain conditions and processes must be in place, in which students are:

1. exposed to the limitations of their current knowledge,
2. provided with opportunities to identify and articulate the underlying assumptions of their current knowledge,
3. engaged in critical self-reflection to consider the origins of these assumptions and how they influenced or limited understanding,
4. engaged in critical discourse with other students and the teacher as a learning community to examine alternative ideas, and
5. provided with opportunities to test and apply new perspectives.

Only when these conditions and processes occur, are students likely to revise their assumptions, and adopt and apply new paradigms (Cranton, 2002); hence the learning experience is transformative rather than assimilative. It should, however, be noted that transformative learning theory acknowledges that challenging and changing perspectives is not merely a rational process, but also an emotional experience; student learning and personal development occurs through reflective group-based activities that foster intellectual openness in order to empower students to apply new knowledge, and, thus, move from thought to action.

By adhering to the values or principles of active learning and student-centred learning, and the teaching methods of collaborative learning, experiential education, and problem-based learning, transformative teaching immerses students in the processes of social interaction and mutual learning in search of understanding and meaning through the experience of reflecting on open-ended problems and adapting and applying new knowledge in context. To this end, classroom strategies include autobiography or journals, role-playing, observation and experimentation, and service learning (both engaged service and community-based work). Accompanying evaluation methods often used are self- and peer-assessment, self-report questionnaires, portfolios, and performance tasks.

Many criticisms have been levelled at transformative learning theory. One concern is that too much emphasis is placed on critical self-reflection and that any link to emotions is at best tenuous. However, neurobiological research provides some insight into the interplay between emotion and rationality in the transformative learning process (see Taylor, 1998, 2001). Another criticism is that the process of transformation cannot be clearly articulated and, hence, there is no clear understanding among theorists. Transformative learning overlaps with concepts like 'meaning making' and 'critical thinking' as found in constructivist approaches to education and, therefore, research into transformative learning as a reflective meaning-making process, arguably, is in fact research into transactional learning (Cragg et al., 2001). Dewey and Vygotsky, especially, could easily fit into both categories.

In addition to transformative teaching incorporating elements of constructivism, it focuses on the whole child with attention to students' social, emotional, mental, physical, and cognitive development. To do so, it must operate on the assumption that transmission is necessary for transformation to occur. That is, values and social mores are necessary for the continuance of social groups, culture, and societies, However, while transmission may be necessary, it is not sufficient for teaching. As Dewey (1916) notes, '[s]chools are, indeed, one important method of the transmission which forms the dispositions of the immature [the young child]; but it is only one means, and, compared with other agencies, a relatively superficial means' (p. 4). Nevertheless, for the transformative model the purpose of schooling is to develop future citizens and, thus, teaching is seen as a process for providing a basis for children to fulfil their potential. Conversely, Dewey's vision of teaching is that education is life itself and not preparation for life. We will speak more on this later, but for the moment, it will suffice to say that for Dewey meaning emerges from student and teacher experiences; a process of reconstruction that results in an enlargement of the meaning of our experience and, consequently, enlarges the capacity for further education. We will argue that Dewey's notion of reconstruction not only better articulates the education of the whole child than the concept of transformation, but that it also provides an explanation as to how components of the three conceptions of teaching are necessary to the development of the whole child. It also serves Delanty's conception of cultural citizenship as a learning process, and is, therefore, attune with the kind of civics and citizenship education aimed at developing the capacity for correctiveness and required for civic engagement in democratic societies.

Teaching values in a changing society: Can teachers be neutral?

The three conceptions of education indicate that there is a constant tension between present societies and social aspirations. On the one hand, those who favour transmission stress that the education system should reflect the composite values of the present society; the preservation of culture from one generation to the next. On the other hand, those who argue in favour of transformation base their views on the notion that education must aspire to lead students towards an idealised society. This raises questions of value conflicts, the acceptance of common values, and the transmission of such values in the education provided by schools. More broadly, it raises questions about the inseparable relationship between culture and education, and the pedagogical implications of facilitating cultural development in a changing society. This brings us back to the teacher's role in identity formation, including the process of national identity-building reflected in education policies and national curriculum, and in the hidden curriculum.

While education plays a major role in the transmission of culture, insofar as it cannot be avoided, culture also cannot avoid having an impact on education; a process in which we all have a stake. Formal educational systems must, therefore, not only transmit cultural heritage, but also enable children and adolescents to adapt to and create cultural change over time; as existing members of a society grow older and die and new-born babies grow to maturity, so too do accumulated knowledge, values, and skills adapt and change in response to social and ecological changes. It seems reasonable to assume that education should be geared towards diversity so that values do not go unchallenged, but, instead, stimulate discussion on cultural norms, including values, beliefs, knowledge, and experiences. However, confronted by the assertions of some contemporary philosophers who herald the end of philosophy's role as a privileged, truth-telling discourse, some teachers might be uncomfortable with taking such a position, mistakenly viewing the recognition of a diversity of values with promoting moral relativism and, thus, anything goes, whereas others might be reluctant to challenge students' values as they view doing so as disrespectful to students. In the classroom, this can lead to 'teacher neutrality', the practice of taking no position on issues as a pedagogical strategy.

Neutrality has a long history outside debates on ethics and classroom practice. For example, the ancient Skeptics suspended judgement about beliefs as they thought there to be no truth or certainty. Neutrality as an educational ideal can fall into two broad categories: procedural neutrality and content neutrality. *Procedural neutrality*, also referred to as instrumental neutrality or pedagogical neutrality, is the view that teachers facilitate classroom discussions impartially and refrain from expressing their own views or 'taking sides' on the topics under discussion. The idea of a 'neutral chair' was first promoted in the 1970s by Lawrence Stenhouse (see Stenhouse, 1971; Elliot, 1971) but continues to attract support as an approach to teaching values in schools.

> The teacher, as a neutral chair, was positioned to impartially manage the discussion of values ensuring that everyone had a chance to express his or her viewpoint and rationally consider alternatives. The teacher, however, did not express a viewpoint or indicate a preference for any of the alternatives. Rather the teacher was expected to explain that his or her deliberately neutral stance would enable students to freely consider the arguments without feeling the weight of the teacher's viewpoint.
>
> (Renshaw & Tooth, 2018b, p. 22)

Content neutrality, which can be curriculum neutrality or more broadly structural neutrality, is the view that curriculum or education policy can be free of ideology or cultural bias toward diversity of cultural positions. Claims of procedural and content neutrality commonly refer to taking a neutral stance or refraining from making judgements on values, but neutrality can apply also to beliefs, knowledge, skills, attitudes, and norms. Neutrality also implies tolerance, not being judgemental, and acting without bias.

The notion of neutrality conflicts with claims about knowledge by both absolutists and relativists. As absolutism assumes there to be a fixed, objective reality and that truths are thoughts, ideas, judgements, statements, assertions, utterances, propositions, or beliefs that accurately represent or correspond to this reality, it assumes that a meta-justification for our evaluative or normative systems can be found. However, this requires us to start and end somewhere, namely, with knowledge-seeking humans who are fallible epistemic agents not disembodied, impartial, and objective observers. On the other hand, relativists claim that truth is constructed and relative to a particular culture, time, place, or individual, and, thus, that justifications are perspectival and interest relative. To the relativist,

> we are never able to transcend or suppress our own situatedness and interests. Thus, even if there is some ultimate, fixed reality we would not be able to know it as it 'really' is. Rather, all experience and inquiry is conducted through our personal interests, values, and concrete situatedness. Consequently, truth claims reflect the individuals who construct them.
>
> (Bleazby, 2011, p. 455)

The practice of student-centred learning—such as the use of philosophical inquiry in the classroom and other transactional and transformative learning methods—is often thought to require teachers not to express their particular ethical point of view as being the correct one. A common concern is that this approach invites relativism, or that it succumbs to, and embraces the so-called postmodern ideology. But this is a mistaken view of the teacher's role as a value-free, neutral facilitator of learning. It also buys into the absolutist/relativist dualism; that by suspending judgement, the teacher supports the view that all positions are equally valid.

The problem that arises with relativism is the inability to judge other people's opinions, beliefs, and actions. However, the ability to pass such judgements forms the basis of many of the institutions in Western-style democracies, most notably the legal system, whereby passing judgement precedes punitive measures. In education, judgement forms the basis of formative assessment; tests are used to judge where students sit in a hierarchal order with their peers. Judgement also plays largely in selecting appropriate curriculum materials and classroom strategies for teaching, as well as what seeps into the hidden curriculum. There are complex frameworks of belief operational behind all such judgements. This indicates that neutrality, the practice of taking no position, of passing no judgement on an issue, is untenable. In response, those who advocate procedural neutrality, view neutrality—withholding judgement or taking a disinterested position—as an effective classroom strategy for opening 'opportunities for discussion between the posing of a problem and the decision on a solution', a means to an end to develop 'certain critical thinking skills' (Furlong & Carroll, 1990, p. 159). And yet this is also problematic.

A supporting example can be found in David E. Denton's (1963) analysis of the shift in education from a religious to a secular, naturalistic base. This included a shift away from religious-based moral education, brought about by the separation of church and state (facilitated by the Establishment Clause in the First Amendment of the U.S. Constitution) which was extended to the separation of church and public education (through the 1947 *Everson v. Board of Education* and 1962 *Engel v. Vitale* rulings of the U.S. Supreme Court). This shift was characterised at the classroom level by the transition, 'from an emphasis on values to an emphasis on techniques of teaching Skills' (p. 1), as it was thought that skills were value neutral. To the contrary, Denton argues that the push to create a value neutral, skills-based educational system is lost the moment judgements regarding content and methodology of what and how we teach are made, as 'norms constitute the nature of those decisions' (p. 2). Viewed in this way, skills training did not replace the transmission of values; it made it implicit, unexamined, and unintended; or put another way, the transmission of norms, values, and beliefs in the classroom seep in from the social and political environment through classroom teachers and curricula. The general result is that values are taught, but not well. As it stands, young people are, as Denton says,

> inducted into a system of ethical decisions which, in the main, have already been made for them. In addition, the teacher is almost invariably concerned, not only with facts, but with goods and preferences and desires and "shoulds" which eventually reveal the kind of Universe the teacher feels ought to be.
>
> (p. 4)

The process of instilling values becomes the realm of individual teachers, whereby their values can be transmitted uncritically and often unwittingly to their students in their attempts to maintain neutrality.

Freire further problematises the idea of a neutral educational process as it is, he says, part of the dominant ideology, which tries to convince teachers that they must be neutral to respect students. But it is a false sense of respect, for the more teachers 'say nothing about agreeing or not agreeing out of respect for the others', the more they are 'leaving the dominant ideology in peace!' (in Shor & Freire, 1987, p. 174). In other words, by refraining from comment, teachers leave the dominant ideology unchallenged and not open to correction. As Richard Shaull (1970) points out in the Foreword to *Pedagogy of the Oppressed*, for Freire, a neutral educational process is not possible:

> Education either functions as an instrument which is used to facilitate the integration of the younger generation into the logic of the present system and bring about conformity to it, or it becomes "practice of freedom", the means by which men and women deal critically and creatively with reality and discover how to participate in the transformation of their world.
>
> (p. 34)

If we accept Freire's critique of neutrality, then education requires rethinking neutrality which necessitates rethinking pedagogy and curriculum. So, while remaining cautious of their position of authority, teachers can and *should* express their views, but only insofar as these views, alongside the views of the students, are regarded as contributing to the views of the classroom community and not as knowledge that cannot be contested. In the hands of an experienced teacher as facilitator of inquiry, students can gain an awareness of what values dominate their world, while at the same time questioning those values, as well as formulating and incorporating their own. This approach fits with Freire's view of education as a practice of freedom rather than an instrument of conformity. Pedagogical emphasis is on transactional and transformative learning, and less so on transmission, although the non-authoritarian transmission of information is still necessary for students to transact with new information in order to transform knowledge.

The transmission/transformation dualism represents the ongoing political and cultural struggle experienced, generally, by modern societies, expressed in the adversarial two-party systems in liberal-democracies and in the debates on conservative versus progressive education. In education, this struggle is also reflected in government policy and the curriculum, and in teachers' attitudes and practices. Teachers are themselves part of the political and cultural struggle and, therefore, cannot remain value-neutral (if, indeed, such a position is at all possible), lest they 'leave the dominant ideology in peace'. Interaction between the teacher and students is such that teachers express their values in the selection of material and their reaction to their students, so they must make it explicit that their role is not only to transfer current knowledge and values, but to also develop in their students the skills necessary for the development of values. Hence, the transmission/transformation dualism is over-simplified as education requires a balance between transmission, transaction, and transformation.

We will pursue the issue of neutrality in various teacher–student contexts in chapters to come, but next we look at Dewey's view of education as the reconstruction of experience, which provides a conceptual framework for explaining the integration of the three conceptions of teaching and learning, and why reconstruction is necessary for civics and citizenship aimed at developing the capacity for democratic correctiveness.

Education as reconstruction

The importance of Dewey's thoughts on the connections between democracy and education cannot be exaggerated. Although writing in the early 1900s, his influence still resonates today, and there is much we can still learn from him. As Philip Cam (2000) aptly asserts:

> Not only does the quest for democracy animate the whole vast canvas of his work, but Dewey also has an abiding concern with both education and the social value of philosophy, which makes the intersection between philosophy, democracy and education Dewey's home ground. Nor is Dewey's work lacking in contemporary social relevance. His vision of the democratic society as one that is democratic throughout the whole of its social fabric, and which thereby supplies everyday life with greater opportunities for human fulfilment, remains vital today, when democratic societies are still popularly conceived of merely as those that enjoy a certain form of government.
>
> (p. 158)

We will talk about Dewey's concern with the social value of philosophy in Chapter 4. Our task, here, will be to explore Dewey's views on democratic society and education premised on his notion of reconstruction.

Undeniably, for all peoples—small groups, larger societies, and nation-states—continuing survival relies on educational processes, whether formal or informal. As Dewey (1916) says, 'in its broadest sense' education is the means of the 'social continuity of life' (p. 3). It is noteworthy that he does not see education as equipping individuals for future life. Rather, the purpose of education *is* the social continuity of life, and herein lies its value: 'Since education is not a means to living, but is identical with the operation of living a life which is fruitful and inherently significant, the only ultimate value which can be set up is just the process of living itself' (p. 239). Education, therefore, is a social process; 'a process of living and not a preparation for future living' (Dewey, 1897, p. 78). In this sense, education is a form of cultural renewal, a learning process responsible for the continuity of what it means to be part of culture. But, for Dewey (1916), education is also growth. In contrast to education as the 'unfolding of latent powers from within' (the Platonic view of education as 'leading out') and 'the formation from without' (the reproduction of knowledge of the past), education *is* the constant 'reconstruction or reorganization of experience which adds to the meaning of experience, and which increases ability to direct the course of subsequent experience' (p. 76). Growth is, therefore, 'a continuous leading into the future', but this should not be mistaken for

> attaching importance to preparation for future need, but in making it the mainspring of present effort. Because the need of preparation for a continually developing life is great, it is imperative that every energy should be bent to making the present experience as rich and significant as possible. Then as the present merges insensibly into the future, the future is taken care of.
>
> (p. 56)

This growth as continuous reconstruction of experience increases auton-omy—the ability to direct and control our lives. Hence, the future is taken care of in the present; what children and adolescents experience today will merge with their experiences tomorrow as active and informed adult citizens.

The process of education Dewey describes is both conservative and pro-gressive. It is conservative in the sense that social continuity of life relies on transmission, which forms the dispositions of children and adolescents. However, this is only a 'superficial means' but a necessary one, as they need to 'have grasped the necessity of more fundamental and persistent modes of tuition' which ensures 'participation in a common understanding' (p. 4). This transmission takes place 'by means of communication of habits of doing, thinking, and feeling', for without such communication from gen-eration to generation 'social life could not survive' (p. 3). This process is progressive because learning is more than mere transmission of information, but a transformation of the quality of experience. By communication, Dewey means more than verbal ties, but those things we come to possess in com-mon in the formation of community or society, such as shared aims, beliefs, aspirations, and knowledge. As such, '[n]ot only is social life identical with communication, but all communication (and hence all genuine social life) is educative', for being the recipients of communication 'is to have an enlarged and changed experience' (p. 5). Past knowledge and experiences are not merely passively received, but can transact with new information, which, in turn, affects learning to create new knowledge and experiences. Put another way, through communication with each other, knowledge reproduced through transmissive communication interacts with our interpretation, understanding, and meaning of our experiences of social life to transform our experiences, both individually and collectively. Dewey's education as reconstruction is, therefore, a process of ongoing transmission, transaction, and transformation. To facilitate this educative process, neutrality is not pos-sible, as the transmission of certain prior knowledge and skills necessary for communication requires partiality; in other cultures, the requisite knowledge and skills may be different.

Dewey's definition of education, not as 'recapitulation of the past' or 'preparation for a remote future', but as life itself means that the process of living together is educative. Herein lies his connection to democracy and to his democratic conception of education. Dewey's main concern was not with the institution of government (i.e., the political dimension of democracy), but with a specific kind of community he thought homologous with democratic society (i.e., the social dimension of democracy). He regarded democracy not as an alternative to other principles of associated living, but as communal life itself; 'a mode of associated living' or 'conjoint communicated experience' sustained by deliberative agreement and undertaken for the 'good of all its members', wherein 'each has to refer his own action to that of others, and to consider the action of others to give point and direction to his own' (p. 87). The democratic ideal for Dewey, then, is twofold: 'shared common interest, but greater reliance upon the recognition of mutual interests' and 'continuous readjustment through meeting the new situations produced by varied intercourse' (pp. 86–87). Emphasis is on open inquiry, defined as dialogue and communication, cooperation, and active social participation with others in the greater community which intersects a diverse and wide range of associated groups. Putting together Dewey's claims that education is growth, a process of reconstruction of experience which increases ability to direct the course of subsequent experience, with democracy as a mode of associated living, his democratic conception of education is that of community as the provision for growth. We can say that his is a vision of cultural citizenship as communication and continual learning processes, and a rejection of the idea of disciplinary citizenship as a fixed set of cultural ideals, norms, or values, and, thus, a rejection of 'citizenship training'.

The relations between democracy and education as one of community and growth means a reciprocal relationship between the habits of each citizen and their habitat, namely, the democratic community and the local environment in which they are situated. There is no duality of individual/community or human/environment as they are inseparable and influence each other, hence, life and education, too, are inseparable. Consequently, '[t]he variety of peoples and environment, their contrast with familiar scenes, furnishes infinite stimulation' (p. 212). However, when an organism is no longer able to affect its habitat, but must only adapt to it, the habitat has become dominant. Such a dominant habitat can render existing habits obsolete, and subsequently individuals, groups, and even cultures can become alienated as their habits are no longer suited to the environment. In 1934, Dewey gave an example: in the ever-increasing industrialisation of the world '[i]ndividual groups, tribes and races, once living completely untouched by the economic regime of modern capitalistic industry, now find almost every phase of their lives affected by its expansion' including an 'unprecedented wave of nationalistic sentiment, of racial and national prejudice, of readiness to resort to force of arms' (Dewey, 2010, pp. 244–245). In the context of our discussion on liberal-democracy, liberal discourses and structures create the habitat, which backgrounds and nullifies the habits of some groups or cultures and natural processes—the colonisation of Indigenous lands and dispossession of Indigenous peoples and subsequent displacement of their law, culture, and languages are notable historical examples. The dominant habitat has the potential to not only restrict habits but create obstacles to further changes and reconstruction of the habitat on which humans depend; in this case, the liberal-democratic habitat constructs obstacles to the democratic correction of social and political institutions, which fails to be the kind of democracy that Dewey described as a 'mode of associated living, of conjoint, communicated experience'.

Education, as a foundational building block for Western-style democracies, tends to be cast in terms of the individual, in the liberal sense as abstract individualism discussed earlier. It focuses on equipping students with the skills and knowledge to define and pursue their own goals and to contribute as

> discrete individuals whose interests are aggregated with those of others in pursuit of shifting conceptions of self-interest. Only individuals are conceived of as holding rights and bearing claims; groups are merely aggregates of individuals whose status in law and politics arises not from their collective identity, but from the rights and interests of the individuals of which they are composed.
>
> (Svensson, 1979, p. 421)

However, in pluralistic societies not all groups see themselves as liberal individuals. Feminists and communitarians, as we have seen, have questioned the liberal view of the individual. So too have Indigenous peoples. Calls for Indigenous rights is an appeal to collective self-determination and sense of belonging, home, and place connected to land—this will be further discussed in Chapter 6 in relation to place-based education.

What these criticisms have in common is that the notion of an abstract individual, the hallmark of liberal-democracies, is seen to weaken or challenge a group's communal relations and ways of knowing, being, and doing. In terms of cultural continuity, survival is threatened, and formal or state-provided liberal education is often active in blocking attempts for renewal. Dewey's pragmatist view of the world, which is a naturalistic approach to knowledge as the result of an active adaptation of the human organism to its environment, can help to educationally challenge rigid thinking. To Dewey, endings are adaptations that signify new beginnings, as he recognised that an end is also a means to yet another end, in a continual process of change, a continual reconstruction, and, hence, growth. Reconstruction is not progress towards any definitive or known end or final goal, but rather the adaptive ability of the organism and environment. Reconstruction, therefore, is always incomplete, and further problematic situations alter the relationship between the organism and the environment. For humans, it is the relationship between belief-habits and habitat that needs to be a dialectic relationship for cultural citizenship to be effective. Dewey's emphasis on habit and habitat is at the heart of his epistemology. His shift toward a biological concept of experience, and by extension education, recognises the plasticity of humankind as part of the greater plasticity of nature.

Dewey, as well as Vygotsky, can shed light on the importance of genuine collaborative dialogue, wherein individuals internalise values and intersubjectively work towards autonomy, in the development of behaviour characteristics or dispositions of active citizenship. Dewey was convinced that *learning through doing*, namely, that we learn from reflecting on our experiences, is the best approach to education—both formal and informal. Vygotsky shared similar ideas in this regard, especially the view that human development cannot be understood independently of sociocultural context. Humans are active agents in their own social and intellectual development which occurs through communication with others or social dialogue.

The lessons we gleam from experiences both inside and outside the classroom, shape how we see and interact with others and the world, that is, with our habit and habitat. Moreover, emphasis on learning through doing links student's experiences outside of the classroom, their home, neighbourhood, and local community, which is part of the greater community, to that which happens in the classroom. As learning is unavoidable, from the earliest beginnings of a child's life through family, friends, and community, until they start school and are influenced further by friendships, teachers, and both the set and hidden curriculum, attention to the relationship between schooling and life, both inside and outside the classroom, is vital to educating citizens. While being consumers in the greater society is today a part of life for most people, attention also needs to be on dissolving the dualism between consumer and citizen. This is especially vital in relation to civics and citizenship education if we are to address Plumwood's contention that liberal-democracy has, through its failure to be corrective, failed democracy.

Conclusion

Transmission, transactional, and transformative approaches to learning fail to provide an informative explanation of the process of identity formation, which we have argued is better captured in Dewey's democratic conception of education as a relation between growth and community—the process of ongoing reconstruction of experience through open inquiry. This is because democracy is a mode of associated living that relies on communicative practices to navigate diversity. To this end, we believe education in a democracy needs to go beyond transmission teaching and learning, critical thinking, or the acquisition of skills and, instead, be aimed at adaptive construction of identity though collaborative practices to promote 'students' confidence, agency, and skills in questioning and revising current self-aspects and identifications' (Kaplan & Flum, 2012, p. 172). This is so because the primary strength of democracy is its capacity for adaptation and correctiveness, and the strength of Dewey's democratic conception of education is its emphasis on reconstruction of experience, which is itself a process of adaptation through self-correction at both the individual and community levels. Therefore, in the next chapter, we examine the role of education in a democracy.

Notes

1 Plato's contention is illustrated in his dialogue in the *Meno*.
2 Such appeals are often referred to as 'etymological fallacies', namely, that the present-day meaning should necessarily be similar to its historical meaning.

3 Democracy, curriculum, and pedagogy

Introduction

Dewey's conception of democracy as a mode of associated living rather than as a form of government is at odds with how democracy is perceived today. Defining democracy in this way, primarily as a process, as a form of social democracy, also has implications for how preparation for citizenship is conceptualised as the basis for teaching democracy, and more broadly, the role of education in a democracy. Whereas Dewey thought government institutions and processes subsidiary to the broader issues of communication within a community, today, even with public trust in governments at an all-time low, there is a tendency to see reforms to the political system as the solution for revitalising political life, such as anti-corruption measures, political fund regulation, constitutional amendments, and changes to electoral systems. Indeed, few political debates pay particular attention to ideas on how to improve and sustain communal life in forming political opinion, and, therefore, what constitutes democracy. Much more has been said by politicians and political analysts on whether liberal-democratic institutions meet the expectations of citizens or whether they are becoming illiberal autocracies. For example, it is not uncommon to hear Western-style democracies described as bureaucratic political systems with oligarchical tendencies—rule by conservative elites who try to restrict majority rule or even access to the ballot box, fearing mass democracy poses a threat to the status quo with its entrenched hierarchies of power and wealth. These debates take aim at institutional practices such as gerrymandering, the role of money in politics, and powerful lobby groups in shaping government policies, to the detriment of mass-based interest groups that represent the interests of less well-off citizens who have far less influence.

Today, the number of people who think democracy is in crisis steadily grows and, indeed, relatively few now think there is nothing amiss about representative democracy. Discontent with the economy, the justice system, political corruption, out-of-touch elites, the electoral system, and partisan politics, people's opinion about the performance of democratic systems in their own country is generally negative to say the least. But are disgruntled citizens warranted in believing that democracy is not working? Politicians,

DOI: 10.4324/9781003098089-4

political parties, and governments have failed to be responsive to many issues of concern to their constituents and, therefore, have failed in their principal objective of being representative, not only leaving broad cross-sections of citizens dissatisfied, but creating socio-economic inequalities that lead to a weakening of democracy and, hence, to a reduced capacity for democratic correction of social and political institutions. Plumwood's claim that liberal-democracy has failed democracy cannot be ignored, as it does appear that Western-style democracies around the world are unable to deal with citizens' concerns, including major ecological concerns and radical inequality. Short of revolution or radical political reform, the weight is put on the shoulders of formal education to prepare future citizens. However, because the dearth of democracy has been blamed on factors such as voter turnout, party membership, distrust in politicians, and disinterest in politics, the persistent claim is for a greater understanding of civics and citizenship to increase participation and interest in politics. But a question still remains: Should our efforts as educators be aimed towards democracy as a form of government or, as Dewey did, towards democracy as a mode of associated living?

This brings us back to the role of civics and citizenship education in a democracy. Societies have vested interests in preparing children and adolescents for citizenship and how they learn to participate in civic life—this interest is also extended to adults through adult migration education schemes. The governmentalisation of citizenship means that the socio-legal values that permeate official policy documents are inserted into educational standards and inform curriculum and teaching practices. In the case of civics and citizenship education, these values extend beyond individual and collective identity formation to national identity building. As Wiel Veugelers (1995) points out, the 'task stems from the role played by education in the transfer of culture, in socializing the youth in order to help them function in society' (p. 2). Many governments do this through values education, which is the process of initiating children and adolescents into values; developing their understanding of the social norms, moral standards, cultural practices, and of the underlying principles, as well as the dispositions to intelligently apply them, in order to relate to other people (Aspin, 2000).

It should be noted that the term 'values' is not only vague, but it is also fraught with ambiguity. When we say that we *value* something, we are making a claim that something is of worth or that it is important to us. Value in this sense is what matters. For example, we can value friendship, freedom, security, health, education, beauty, art, wealth, or any number of things within the realm of human experience. When we use the word in its plural form, it indicates someone's opinions as to what is important or worthwhile. Of course, valuing something or having certain values does not guarantee that we will act in accordance with what we cherish as worthwhile. It could be said then that not everything we value has genuine worth. Valuing, therefore, requires value judgements. There is always room for improvement of judgement and reappraisal of the things we value. What we value initially may reflect our impulses or unreflective preferences, whereas enduring value is derived from thorough reflection and sustained inquiry. We can never be certain what values will be worthwhile nor can we be certain they will endure, but this should not be considered as grounds for disengaging with value inquiry. However, '[b]y examining the grounds and consequences of particular values, value inquiry moves away from subjectivity toward objectivity in assessing what is important or worthwhile, whether the values in question be aesthetic, political, environmental, ethical, social, or any other of the countless categories in which values fall' (Lipman, 1988, p. 56). While these words may ring true for many of us, values education is not without contention.

In formal education, values education is associated with pedagogies, methods, or programs that teachers use to create student learning experiences regarding value questions (Cox, 1988; Halstead, 1996). Some educational approaches explicitly teach values through purposefully written curricula. However, as we mentioned earlier, values are inevitably taught through the hidden curriculum, wherein the inculcation of values need not be intentional or deliberate. The question of inculcating values is magnified even further when understood as moral development.

> Whether teachers like it or not, even accept it or not, they are inevitably influential in the moral development of the child. Much of this influence is incidental (which is not to say it is beyond the control of the teacher). It occurs through the model of moral concern and action that the teacher presents, through the expectations the teacher has of children in the class, through the rules of the classroom, through the habits of behaviour that the teacher inculcates. Nor does the teacher exist in a vacuum. The school as an institution has its own impact on the moral development of the children through many avenues, as diverse as the school rules; the model it presents through its discipline policies; the informal interactions that the school encourages, accepts, ignores and discourages; the formal messages conveyed at assemblies and other occasions of public messages; and the interactions it has with the wider community.
>
> (Sprod, 2001, pp. 3–4)

While many of the practices Sprod mentions are inevitable, they are not necessarily undesirable. Rather, 'each can be implemented well or badly—that is, to assist or hinder the development of ethical persons' (p.4), which can have implications for the role of schooling in identity formation.

The connection between identity formation, curriculum and teaching practices, and the transmission of values is exacerbated if we consider that the experiences of students during childhood and adolescence bear crucially important meaning in their lives, particularly with the onset of adolescence, 'increasingly occurring in earlier ages' (Kaplan & Flum, 2012, p. 172), when students' emerging cognitive capacity 'elevates their self-reflection ability and develops in tandem with identity' (Flum & Kaplan,

2012, p. 241; see also Cole & Cole, 1989; Erikson, 1968). Bearing all these factors in mind, and that formal education is the most deliberate form of human instruction (Gutmann, 1987, p. 15), it is imperative that we confront the following question: For what kind of society should students be educated, and, to this end, what values are required? This links back to our question above on whether civics and citizenship education should focus on formal knowledge of how government works, including responsible citizenship, in preparation for future citizenship or on a Deweyan democratic conception of education as a relation between growth and community through open inquiry.

Western-style democracies are confronted with the challenge of providing education that is responsive to an increasingly complex world, and responsible to the differing needs of students, especially in providing multidisciplinary and cross-cultural learning experiences. This challenge is compounded by the fact that in any society that claims to have democratic aspirations, there are bound to be different views on how democracy should be practiced. An illustration of this is that civics and citizenship education programs have been criticised for their narrow focus on institutions of government and therefore, for producing a limited notion of citizenship, or to use Delanty's term, disciplinary citizenship, which downplays or ignores both the social dimensions of democracy and the development of students' capacities for communal inquiry, both necessary components for the development of democracy as a corrective process. However, this challenge should be viewed as a positive one; not to seek to instil the values of a certain model or conception of democracy, but to foster autonomy and responsible citizenship, including the ability to imagine different ways of organising society for enhancing democracy as a mode of associated living. When we look at what is involved in meeting this challenge, it is inevitable that consideration needs to be given to the kinds of educational provisions and teaching practices that will facilitate these goals.

We argue that education can foster democratic practice itself as a process of deliberative communication, in contrast to education merely preparing students to function effectively as future democratic citizens. Acceptance of such a view raises further questions about the purpose and aims of education consistent with this conception of democracy, which, we argue, requires an educational approach that is committed to aligning curriculum, pedagogy, and assessment to produce a transformational environment that will inform our social, cultural, and political structures—a commitment to democratic education and not merely education for democracy (a distinction we will examine at length a little further on). We contend that more emphasis needs to be placed on Dewey's notion of reconstruction, including accounting for the primacy of democracy as social inquiry, which requires the development of deliberative and communicative relationships, and placing emphasises on a cultural conception of citizenship as a learning process, wherein citizenship is experienced as a practice that connects individuals to their society, sustained through social reconstruction.

Education and democracy

Civic participation is integral to democracy. It is a process in which people take action to arrive at better collective decisions in order to address issues of public concern, facilitate increased well-being of the population, and promote the quality of the community (Australian Bureau of Statistics, 2006; Checkoway & Aldana, 2013). This process could be seen in two ways: (1) as collective and individual activities reflecting interest and engagement with governance and democracy, and (2) as the *quality* of the engagement regarding deliberative processes and collective decision-making. The latter, especially, has educational implications. Developing students' skills in social inquiry and communication as an integral component of schooling is crucial if education is to contribute to social democracy and the cultivation of democratic competencies and values to enable effective civic participation. However, the realisation of democratic ideals in schools is significantly constrained 'by the dominant rationality which informs much of the theory and practice of educational administration' (Rizvi, 1989, p. 54). So, our task now is to explore the theoretical and practical implications of introducing democratic reform in schools.

To begin, we distinguish between education for democracy and democratic education to delineate the relationships between theories of democracy and education (see Burgh, 2003a, 2003b, 2009, 2014). This classification provides a framework for comparing different approaches to education in terms of their effectiveness on civics and citizenship according to the above measures. It differs from an earlier attempt by R.S. Peters (1966) to classify the relationship between democracy and education that offers three ways in which education could be democratic: (1) the democratisation of education, (2) the school as a democratic institution, and (3) education for democracy. It also differs from Gutmann's (1987) ground-breaking critical examination of the education of citizens in a democracy through three normative theories of the educational purposes of society: (1) the family state, (2) the state of families, and (3) the state of individuals, which leads her to propose a fourth theory: a democratic state of education. Instead, we focus on the relationships between democracy and education in pedagogical terms, in order to categorise and examine the various approaches to education pertaining to democracy, such as values education and civics and citizenship education, to illustrate how they are positioned in Western-style democracies. The framework also can be used to explore new pedagogies for education reform. The distinction between education for democracy and democratic education is further broken down in the following ways: under education for democracy, we include (i) teaching values, (ii) political education, and (iii) critical citizenship as a competency, and included under democratic education are (i) freedom-based education, and (ii) communication and deliberation.

Whereas *education for democracy* focuses on the acquisition of knowledge and skills to improve the capacity of future citizens to participate effectively in civic life and contribute to the social, political, and economic future of their communities and the political system, *democratic education* recognises the social role of schooling as that of reconstruction and that children and adolescents have an integral role to play in shaping democracy. Our contention is that education for democracy serves political leaders, as they have vested interests in the promotion of disciplinary citizenship, which plays out in official education policy documents and teachers' thinking. The focus is on the substantive aspect of citizenship, with the purpose of fostering the capacities required for formal membership of a political community. Conversely, democratic education is more attuned to the procedural aspects of democratic societies, namely, democracy as a process of communication, deliberation, and social decision-making.

Education for democracy

The primary goal of education for democracy is the development of an educated citizenry competent to participate in democratic societies, which is achieved through 'the proper preparation of young citizens for the roles and responsibilities they must be ready to take on when they reach maturity' (Kelly, 1995, p. 101). Accordingly, the role of civics and citizenship education is to prepare children and adolescents to function effectively as future citizens. Typically, civics and citizenship are taught as either a subject or as part of a multi-subject learning area, commonly the humanities and social sciences, alongside history, geography, and other related subjects. Civics and citizenship can also make connections to cross-curriculum priorities (i.e., considered and focused content that aligns with the content descriptions of subjects) and general capabilities (i.e., knowledge, skills, behaviours, and dispositions) to make for richer learning experiences for students, in order to apply knowledge and skills confidently, effectively, and appropriately in complex and changing circumstances, both at school and outside of school. What priority civics and citizenship education receives in the curriculum varies from country to country. Implied is that formal civics and citizenship education can serve as an integrative mechanism to reinforce the competencies for democratic culture as a way of sustaining democratic societies, which requires the reproduction and preservation of democratic values and political institutions of liberal-democracy, and, therefore, to embrace the principles of liberty, equality, and justice upon which liberal-democratic nation-states were founded.

However, as political ideologies influence perceptions of democracy, disagreement over what values are culturally appropriate, whether conceptions of the collective good should take precedence over individual rights, and what framework for socioeconomic and political organisation best advances the principles of pluralistic societies, raises questions about the design of civics and citizenship education curricula. Moreover, established liberal-democracies such as Australia, New Zealand, Canada, and the U.S. were founded on historical injustices resulting from colonialism, further highlighting the highly contested and contentious nature of the values identified in curriculum documents related to civics and citizenship education. We will revisit these issues in Chapter 4. For now it is enough to stress that crucial to education for democracy as an approach to civics and citizenship education is the development of a sufficient degree of social understanding and judgement in students, and the population generally, so that they have the capacity to think intelligently about public issues.

Education for democracy does not prescribe any particular teaching method, but rather it is an approach to teaching that has been interpreted in various ways. We outline three different interpretations: teaching values, political education, and critical thinking as a citizenship competency. It should be noted, however, that there are overlaps between each and that while civics and citizenship education programs may focus primarily on one, it is likely that, in practice, teachers will combine all three to varying degrees. Nevertheless, categorising them as such allows for making comparisons between different forms of civics and citizenship education that focus on preparing students as future citizens for civic participation.

Teaching values

One curricular approach to civics and citizenship education is to foster an understanding of society and citizenship by focusing on the promotion of a common set of shared values linked to national identity, which prepares children and adolescents to live together as adult citizens in a pluralist society. Many countries do this through values education programs in their national curriculum, although not all recognise or call it by name. For example, in the U.K., values are taught in the guise of spiritual, moral, social, and cultural development (Starkey, 2018). In Japan, civics education is part of social studies in elementary and middle schools and a separate subject alongside history and geography in high school. Emphasis is on social and moral responsibility and school community involvement so as to respect responsible engagement, rather than emphasis on political literacy (Davies, Mizuyama & Thompson, 2010).

Singapore has implemented various civics and moral education programs, but currently there are two subjects associated with civic education: character and citizenship education, and social studies. The underlying theme of both is citizenship training as a facet of formal values education, which aligns with the education agenda, underpinned by a revitalised conception of national identity and citizen loyalty, in response to globalisation. For Singaporean society, this conception 'is rooted in the "survival" ideology, emphasizing social cohesion and economic growth' (Neoh, 2017, p. 31). The Ministry of Education (MOE) maintains control over the national syllabi, textbooks, and assessment.

In Australia, the *National Framework for Values Education in Australian Schools* identifies nine values for Australian schooling that are said to reflect a 'commitment to a multicultural and environmentally sustainable society where all are entitled to justice' (DEEWR, 2005, p. 5).[1] Since values and civics and citizenship education are intricately related, these values have been controversial, as any attempt to define common, shared, or universal values in a pluralistic society are likely to be divisive, which 'can explain why Australia has had a history of shying away from teaching values, and has clung to the myth of value neutrality' (Macintyre, 1995, p. 15). Focus is on the development of knowledge, skills, dispositions, and attitudes, and the 'values that are important to Australian democracy and social cohesion' (DEEWR, 2010, p. 7), which are based on Australian society and the Westminster model of liberal-democracy (ACARA, 2020). In all cases, precautions need to be taken as to how the values are taught, lest they seep into the hidden curriculum.

Given the contentious nature of values, unsurprisingly, the question of how best to approach teaching them is not without contention. Some approaches place no emphasis at all on discussion, assuming morality to be a matter of transmitting values to students through unreflective moral shaping or moral instruction. Unreflective moral shaping includes 'those practices which require students to act in certain ways, or model such actions to students, with little or no explicit reference to the moral import of the actions involved' (Sprod, 2001, p. 4). The transmission of values in schools is often the result of unreflected moral shaping as part of the hidden curriculum. Moral instruction, on the other hand, does make explicit moral transmission, and includes 'sermons or lectures; moral influence purely through one-way talk' (Sprod, 2001, p. 4). Other proposals, such as the moral dilemma-based programs that grew out of Lawrence Kohlberg's work, acknowledge the role of classroom discussion in moral development. A number of authors have made comparative assessments of these and other approaches to education in a democracy (e.g., Gutmann, 1987; Jarrett, 1991; Weinstein, 1991). We will not elaborate on all of the possible approaches here, rather we draw attention to three widely used and broad characterisations: character education, values clarification, and developmentalist theories.

Character education is a term used to capture a broad range of values education programs or teaching methods aimed at developing moral character or virtues through modelling exemplary character traits. Also known as the 'exemplary model', this approach focuses on 'appropriate behaviors which are modeled by presenting instances of appropriate moral and political behavior to students' (Weinstein, 1991, p. 17). Most importantly, teachers must 'live the difference (between right and wrong) in front of pupils' (Bennett, 1985, n.p.). Competing exemplary models may articulate the principles or core values (e.g., honesty, kindness, empathy, integrity) that underlie appropriate behaviours and exemplifications of 'good character' or what it means to be a 'good' person; typically, someone who exhibits personal qualities that a society might consider desirable for its citizens. A common method is to provide a list of principles, values, or virtues around which teachers plan classroom activities, although no agreement exists on what values must be included, nor are there set standard means for assessing, implementing, or evaluating programs. Moreover, there is a diversity of opinion on what constitutes a 'good citizen'—that is, what it means for individuals to fulfil their role as a citizen—and, therefore, what core values are necessary to promote good citizenship.

Despite this lack of agreement, character education is based on several common assumptions: that character is deficient in some or all children and adolescents (Fabes et al., 1989); that it is possible to identify a set of universally shared values, that values can be prescriptively taught, and 'that students will accept and enact them as "guides to behaviour"' (Gilbert, 2004, p. 9); and lastly, that role modelling is considered to be 'the most important moral lesson in the character curriculum' (Lickona, 2004, p. 118). However, there is no clear evidence that values can be effectively taught through role modelling, as it is not commonly used as an explicit teaching method because 'many teachers consider "respect" to be the most important virtue', and in the studies conducted a 'very small percentages of students mention teachers as role models' (Sanderse, 2013, p. 39). Indeed, the majority of studies on character education indicate that there are no improvements in student behaviour or academic performance (Davis, 2003; Social and Character Development Research Consortium, 2010). There is also disagreement over what counts as effectiveness (Was, Woltz & Drew, 2006). Further, critics have noted the problem of confusing morality with social conformity (Dune, 1997) and that many programs lean toward ideological and religious ends (Yu, 2004). Agreement on which character traits are desirable is a further obstacle and the idea of universally shared values has received sustained criticism.

Character education can also be criticised on theoretical grounds. Mark Weinstein (1991) contends that 'exemplifications taken alone, do not include the criteria upon which the justification of the exemplary act relies. Imitation of good behaviours can hardly be relied on to foster the ability to generalize to new and, perhaps, apparently dissimilar circumstances' (pp. 17–18). Indeed, even if justification could be grounded in principles, these 'frequently underdetermine their application to cases', as they 'need to be informed by consideration of the context of their application' (p. 18). This not only requires practice in applying principles in context, but the development of intellectual and social capacities and dispositions to deliberate over what principles are to be correctly applied (Gutmann, 1987, p. 57). A related, and more fundamental, problem for exemplary models, then, is the requirement of self-correction. As Weinstein (1991) puts it: '[t]he authority of past practice is not the court of last resort in a democracy. Rather, democracy requires ongoing renegotiation of basic commitments, and a reassessment of particular values' (p. 18). Civics and citizenship education that is restricted to exemplification is, therefore, inadequate, as it does not develop students' abilities to 'deliberate critically among the range of good lives and good societies' (Gutmann, 1987, p. 44). Recall Plumwood's claim that the strength of democracy lies in its capacity for correctiveness. Students' capacity for self-correction is, therefore, vital for the correction of the values underpinning social and political institutions, otherwise education fails democracy.

Unlike character education, which promotes the process of teaching core values and virtues to foster exemplary traits for good citizenship, *values clarification* aims at developing students' internal cognitive and affective processes, thereby allowing them, rather than external factors such as core values or exemplification, to be the primary determinants in the valuing process. First explicated by Louis Raths, Merrill Harmin and Sidney Simon (1966), values clarification is used in cognitive-behavioural therapy and various helping professions, but it is also used as an educational intervention designed to actively involve students in the presentation and analysis of values in order to guide their behaviour in diverse interpersonal and social contexts. The valuing process central to values clarification is intended to help students to 'understand and develop their own values' and to 'teach them respect for the values of others', rather than transmit values, as 'none of us has the "right" set of values to pass on to other people's children' (Simon, 1976, p. 132). In doing so, students can gain a better understanding of themselves in relation to social norms, and, thus, of their choices as future citizens in responsible decision-making.

Communicating and clarifying values involves students defining, listing, ranking, and rating that which they value, as well as listening to and learning from one another. Pedagogically, the teacher's responsibility is to help students clarify their values, refraining as much as possible from the inculcation of values; while teachers do not correct, evaluate, or validate students' responses, nor do they lead students toward a predetermined response, their role is to facilitate classroom discussion so that students can consider the consequences of their choices (Simon, Howe & Kirschenbaum, 1972). This claim is not without contention, as not correcting, evaluating, or validating student's responses assumes value neutrality regarding the content of the methodology, which, as discussed in Chapter 2, is an appeal to *procedural neutrality*, an untenable position which holds that teachers can be impartial while facilitating critical discussion about values. This approach does not account for values built into the methodology, that is, into educational questions, techniques, and strategies. Bearing this criticism in mind, it is not clear that value clarification activities and exercises can provide students with a critical awareness of their own attitudes and that of others.

Arguably, the relationship between values clarification and democracy is that the process of clarifying values reflects citizen engagement in the articulation of their values and the consideration of others' values, which, 'presumably, prompts an awareness of the range of considerations that underlie political decisions reflected in democracy' (Weinstein, 1991, p. 19). However, a major criticism frequently levelled at values clarification is its advocacy of moral relativism (Craig, 1981; Kohlberg, 1981; Stewart, 1975), although it has been dismissed by advocates who remain committed to Raths' theory which values clarification has inherited. Some attempts have been made to reformulate the theory. Howard Kirschenbaum (1976), for example, argues that 'values clarification is best achieved when combined with other thoughtful approaches to human growth and development' (p. 99).

John S. Stewart (1975) maintains that values clarification theory 'is philosophically indefensible and psychologically inadequate' (p. 686), arguing that 'it will have to make some major reformulations and extend itself far beyond its present theoretical and empirical base' (p. 688). His criticisms are twofold. First, the research in support of 'the validity and efficacy of Values Clarification is weak and seriously flawed' (p. 687). Second, values clarification theory's reliance on Dewey's theory of valuation 'possibly reflects a misunderstanding of Dewey's thought'; not only is Dewey's understanding of democracy 'quite different from theirs [Raths, Harmin & Simon]', they fail to recognise that he was a contextualist, 'not an absolute relativist' as claimed (p. 687). Values clarification could, therefore, be said to suffer from theoretical confusion, that is, writers have 'failed to conceptualize values, valuing, and other fundamental concepts adequately in their framework' (p. 687). Consequently, it fails to 'furnish the necessary conceptual apparatus to support rational deliberation in respect of the values appealed to, and in light of competing points of view' (Weinstein, 1991, p. 19). Like character education, values clarification fails to provide criteria for judgement necessary for self-correction, and, therefore, makes it inadequate as a basis for democratic correctiveness.

Developmentalist theories of moral reasoning concentrate primarily on moral values, such as fairness, justice, equity, and human dignity, which have direct bearing on civics and citizenship education. The method most favoured is to present students with a hypothetical or factual value dilemma scenario—a decision-making problem between two possible moral imperatives—followed by group discussion of the various viewpoints raised in response to finding possible solutions. This approach, as discussed in Chapter 2, assumes that children progress through stages of moral development; a view which grew out of Piaget's research and was developed further by Kohlberg. Rather than merely gaining more knowledge or instilling values, moral development is argued to be the result of developing to the next stage of moral reasoning, creating a sequence of qualitative changes in the students' thinking. As the child or adolescent interacts with their environment, at some point they will encounter information that does not align with their beliefs and so they will need to accommodate this information and rethink their beliefs accordingly. It is through this process of equilibration that moral development occurs.

The purpose of moral dilemmas in the classroom is to seek to encourage students to reflect on the contradictions inherent to their present stage of moral development. An appropriate dilemma consists of a story in which the central character is presented with a problem of genuine conflict, which must be able to 'generate differences of opinion among students about the appropriate response to the situation' and requires a classroom environment that encourages students to express their views freely and the teacher to facilitate discussion focused on moral reasoning (Galbraith & Jones, 1975, p. 18). However, moral dilemmas can be problematic because they 'are constructed by arbitrarily ruling out meaningful options and by limiting those that remain to those that contradict either one another or themselves' (Lipman, 1988, p. 69).

Not only does such a technique focus on contradictions, but it creates an abstraction, an artificial setting divorced from context, containing only what is deemed to be morally significant factors. Viewed in this way, moral dilemmas fail to capture the richness of real-life situations that citizens face, which require more than an appeal to the cognitive and rational aspects of ethical decision-making, such as personal relationships between the characters and extended social, political, economic, and environmental settings in which they are situated. The articulation and application of values and principles to cases becomes a matter of accepting the abstraction of how the hypothetical dilemma was presented and dealing with it as a logical problem, whereas were students more informed of the context and circumstances surrounding the central character's dilemma they might decide differently. In other words, rather than interpret a moral choice in terms of abstracting that choice from its particularities and analysing it as if it represented some sort of universal standard from which to evaluate moral choice, moral choice can be interpreted within the context of the personal, social, and historical circumstances that have produced it.

A broader objection against developmentalist theories in favour of the use of moral dilemmas, is that of the use of moral hierarchy, such as Kohlberg's normative assumptions about the central role of universal norms in moral reasoning. The priority of principles over context and circumstance in moral reasoning has been challenged by philosophers and psychologists alike (e.g., Gilligan, 1982; MacIntyre, 1988). According to American feminist, ethicist and psychologist Carol Gilligan (1982, 1987), abstract categories of moral reasoning are inadequate as a general account of moral discourse, as they paint an incomplete picture. Gilligan criticised Kohlberg's claim that women are deficient in moral reasoning compared to men, because it was based on his research using all male subjects. Her studies on moral development, with both male and female subjects, revealed two moral orientations: justice and care. The dominant justice orientation regards moral reasoning as dictated entirely by the principles of equality, impartiality, and universality, and humans as abstractly conceived rights-bearers, understood as the liberal paradigm of citizenship that Kohlberg prioritises. The under-valued care orientation emphasises interconnectedness and responsiveness that arises from interpersonal human relationships, situatedness, and partiality, and acknowledges real inequalities as a salient feature that distinguishes us for the purposes of moral reasoning. The use of moral dilemmas must, therefore, take both orientations into account.

Many commentators have found fault in Gilligan's methodology, arguing that not only should she have been attentive to differences other than gender, but that she left many questions unasked. For example, one of the studies sought women's views on abortion while neglecting to discover men's attitudes. While such criticisms may have repercussions for the results of Gilligan's empirical studies, they do not detract from subsequent philosophical developments which reinforce the view that an ethic of care serves as a legitimate alternative to the justice perspective prioritised in Kohlberg's and other similar studies in stage development and moral dilemmas. It is noteworthy that the different voices Gilligan describes are characterised not by gender but by theme. She is *not* making an essentialist claim about women's ethical or moral orientations. The association of a care perspective with women is an empirical observation, and it is primarily through listening to what women have to say about ethical reasoning that she traces its development. This association is, as Gilligan (1982) puts it, 'not absolute, and the contrasts between male and female voices are presented here to highlight a distinction between two modes of thought and to focus a problem of interpretation rather than to represent a generalisation about either sex' (p. 2). Other critics have interrogated Gilligan's motives regarding what they see as a claim on the superiority of the care perspective. However, Gilligan insists that we must vacillate between the two orientations, and that they are, indeed, compatible. What Gilligan is suggesting is that 'development may proceed along more than one line. One line of moral thought focuses on logic, justice, and social organization, the other on interpersonal relationships' (Crain, 2010, p. 179). The focus is, therefore, shifted away from formal adherence to developmental stages to also considering context and issues, as a way of developing and improving moral reasoning.

Critics have also criticised Kohlberg's developmental stages for being culturally biased, particularly the final stages which prioritise Western ideals of liberal justice and individualism, and that he has applied his theory to non-Western cultures with no consideration of cultural difference (Simpson, 1974). As William Crain (2010) observes: 'One wonders how well Kohlberg's stages apply to the great Eastern philosophies' or 'if his stages do justice to moral development in many traditional village cultures. Researchers find that villagers stop at stage 3, but perhaps they continue to develop moralities in directions that Kohlberg's stages fail to capture' (p. 179). Consequently, Kohlberg's cultural bias extends to cultures that focus on relations and community, which in many Indigenous cultures are intertwined with land and notions of care for country. These issues will be taken up again in Chapter 6 when we discuss place-based education.

To sum up, neither of the approaches for teaching values identified here are in themselves adequate. An effective approach must recognise the epistemological relations between the development of dispositions and the development of reasonableness. This relation is a complex one that demands more than prescriptive role-modelling and value clarification activities, both of which tend toward superficiality, or moral dilemmas, which fail to capture the particulars of a given situation and tend toward abstraction and universalisation. Formal values education programs fall into the trap of presupposing a common identity—one in which values, beliefs, and knowledge are congruent with those that are dominant within the society at the time, notably those identified with liberal-democracy. The assumption of a common identity is displayed in the calls for teaching values designed to promote national identity, global identity, or multicultural identity. The key point is that the values education approach to civics and citizenship education does not improve students' competence to make deliberative judgements essential for the preparation of citizens in a democracy. To effectively teach values requires genuine inquiry and engagement in ethical discourse.

Political education

Another approach to preparing children and adolescents for future citizenship is political education, sometimes referred to as the classical approach to civic education. According to this approach citizens are conceived in the narrow sense as citizens of the state and starts with the presumption that democracy needs a politically educated population. At the very least, citizens need an understanding of how democratic institutions function, knowledge of how to vote, and the ability to discern between the policies of political candidates, in order to participate in the process of electoral democracy. The purpose of civics and citizenship education, therefore, is to develop students' capacities for informed citizenship. This requires a focus on content to develop institutional and procedural knowledge, namely, civic knowledge and understanding of the institutions and processes related to a nation's system of governance, as well as an understanding of citizenship as the legal relationship between an individual and the democratic state relating to rights and responsibilities, duties, and privileges. To this end, schooling must prepare students to fully grasp the relations between civics and citizenship, which necessitates knowledge and understanding of the social and political institutions and practices in which students as future citizens will partake, so as to be adaptable and socially responsible contributors to the democratic society in which they live. In other words, to develop citizenship competencies, students require civic knowledge, including that of the institutions of liberal-democracy and its practices, as well as an understanding of civil society and how it contributes to a functioning nation, that is, the role of citizens in contributing to social and political decision-making.

Focus on the political aspects (i.e., the civic and civil) of democracy as a way of teaching civics and citizenship need not be purely descriptive. Emphasis on political institutions and practices also can provide opportunities to expose students to concepts and values related to democracy, such as social justice, rights, equality, freedom, choice, culture, identity, ecological and economic sustainability, and so forth. So, too, can modelling procedures to develop political competence, such as classroom elections or mock parliaments, which 'even if peripheral to the actual governance of institutions (classroom election and the like), incorporate basic elements of democratic practice' (Weinstein, 1991, p. 18). The former is a cognitive approach to integrating knowledge and values, whereas the latter places emphasis on reinforcing practice and theory. While these two approaches are different, both aim to develop informed citizens through the development of intellectual capacities which provide a grounding for active citizenship. Underlying this aim is the assumption that not only is there certain political knowledge that can be attained, but also that it is desirable that such knowledge should be reinforced in schools.

Pedagogically, increasing knowledge of the structure and processes of government is not a simple matter of students taking on board particular facts and applying these to their lives. Rather, it relies on a normative approach to education. Knowledge of the structures and processes of government cannot be separated from institutional and cultural values which are informed by a country's social and political history. For example, in a pluralist society, multiculturalism and reconciliation make the inclusion of an historical dimension contentious, as the values in the syllabus and curriculum documents are not always inclusive—shared by the predominant group but marginalising others—and, hence, formal institutional knowledge has limited effect on the potential of informed political participation unless taught critically, and if not taught critically it can become a model of cultural transmission through the hidden curriculum. This has implications for the development of student capacity for self-correction 'by creating tensions between the centrality of appeals to past practices in making political judgments, and contemporary or future reassessments in light of the inadequacy of such practices as measured against the demands of nonrepression and nondiscrimination' (Weinstein, 1991, p. 18). Non-repression and non-discrimination are identified by Amy Gutmann (1987) as 'principled limits on political and parental authority over education' (p. 44). Non-repression is the principle of preventing the use of 'education to restrict critical deliberation of competing conceptions of the good life and the good society', and non-discrimination is the principle of preventing the denial to anyone, 'an educational good on grounds irrelevant to the legitimate social purposes of that good' (pp. 44–45). Both principles are necessary for critical thinking and deliberation, which are essential for self-correction and, therefore, democratic correctiveness. Political education itself is inadequate for developing the capacity for correctiveness essential for a functioning democracy.

Critical thinking as a citizenship competence

To avoid these problems, some civics and citizenship programs emphasise the reinforcement of civic literacy, an approach to learning aimed at developing a broad range of knowledge, skills, and attitudes that are prerequisites for political understanding (Wringe, 1984, p. 97). Typically, less emphasis is placed on political competence; stressed are procedural principles that underlie democratic attitudes, a focus on political issues rather than on political institutions, or the skills required to influence group decisions and how to do so in an appropriate democratic way. According to this view, both content and skills are necessary for the reinforcement of civic literacy, but concentration should be on skills not content, for without skills 'there may be knowledge about the institutions but no methods of evaluating their worth' (Maitles, 1997, n.p.). Ultimately, content and skills must be closely linked for the development of political awareness, an essential component of civic literacy and vital for social responsibility and political engagement. This aim is to provide citizens with a skills base that enables them to investigate public issues by detecting bias, analysing evidence, weighing up sources, and drawing conclusions (Maitles, 1997, n.p.).

This approach stresses the importance of thinking critically as a citizenship competency, which requires 'paying attention to the development of the epistemological beliefs of students; promoting active learning; a problem-based curriculum; stimulating interaction between students; and learning on the basis of real-life situations' (ten Dam & Volman, 2004, p. 370). Learning to think critically is crucial for democratic citizenship, as citizens today have available to them large amounts of information, both solicited and unsolicited, that they need to assess for reliability and usefulness. Increasingly, countries around the world have responded by promoting the inclusion of a 'critical' component as a reform measure to strengthen civics and citizenship education, variously referred to as critical citizenship education, critical pedagogy, and critical civic literacy. The aim of critical thinking approaches to citizen engagement is to provide opportunities for students to critically evaluate the principles, values, and processes that underlie democratic institutions and systems of governance. Rather than superficial discussion of particular facts (political education), behaviours (character education) or values (values clarification), emphasis is on the underlying concepts that those particular facts, behaviours, and values reflect. The purpose is to develop not only an informed citizenry but an active citizenry able to participate responsibly as members of their society. What is crucial is that education develops in students a degree of social understanding and judgement so that they have the capacity to think intelligently about public issues that matter to them.

Learning to think critically is vital for citizenship competence, so that citizens can participate critically in the social and political practices of the communities to which they belong. Therefore, emphasising civic literacy to develop critical citizenship is a step in the right direction. From a social constructivist point of view, participation plays a key role, for 'to further the critical competence of students it must provide them with the opportunity at the level of the classroom and the school to "observe, imitate and practice" critical agency' (ten Dam & Volman, 2004, p. 375). As learning through participation involves reflection, '[t]he quality of the participation can be improved by reflection', but the learning contexts must provide students with opportunities so that they 'can make sense of and hence have a feeling of responsibility to participate critically in the practice in question (identity development)' (ten Dam & Volman, 2004, p. 375). However, as we noted in Chapter 2, a shift away from emphasising values to emphasising 'techniques of teaching skills' is not a shift toward value neutrality (Denton, 1963, p. 1). A more robust understanding of critical thinking cannot be reduced to its cognitive or logical functions (e.g., critical thinking as informal logic or recognising fallacies). Indeed, this narrow instrumental conception is very misleading, as critical thinking 'is a matter of thinking and feeling empathetically with others, of engaging one's imagination, of having access to a wealth of facts about the possible effects of alternative actions, of discerning patterns of meaning in experience, of looking at the world from different perspectives' (Nord, 1995, p. 346). These components of critical thinking are integral to the teaching of thinking as are the skills themselves.

A broader criticism is that there is an assumption behind this approach, which is common to the others described above, and indicative of education for democracy generally, namely, that students should be initiated into the established traditions and institutional practices, and that gradually they could adapt their ability to think critically to novel situations or to challenge some practices that may no longer be rationally defensible. Moreover, while the emphasis is on developing democratically minded citizens, the focus is still on (1) disciplinary citizenship, (2) the preparation of students to function effectively as future citizens, and (3) the citizen as liberal individual. Although an adequate theory of education for democracy must include a place for improving thinking skills, it would also be a mistake to de-emphasise or deny altogether that democracy is an educational process itself. It is this that distinguishes education for democracy, whereby learning is seen as developing students' intellectual and social capacities, whether a set of values, a body of knowledge or civic skills, for future citizenship, from democratic education, which emphasises citizenship itself as a learning process, thereby offering a broader conception of civic literacy.

Democratic education

How does democratic education differ from education for democracy? While, like education for democracy, the primary goal of democratic education is the achievement of an educated citizenry, unlike education for democracy, its emphasis is not on promoting the competencies considered necessary for civic participation in the political, social, cultural, and economic institutions of the democratic society in which they live. In this sense, education for democracy is mere preparation for students to function effectively as future citizens; a preparation for future living, not a process of living, in the Deweyan sense of education. Democratic education is an educational ideal that recognises democracy as both a goal and a teaching method. According to this view, young people also have an integral role to play in *shaping* democracy, and democracy is an educational process and not something to educate toward.

Ideally, civics and citizenship education should be synonymous with education itself, established as a comprehensive *whole-school approach to education*, rather than as a discrete learning area, to facilitate a holistic understanding of democracy as a mode of associated living. But such an ideal would require a radical reconstruction of education. For example, emphasis would be on collaborative inquiry and experiential education, such as place-based and project-based learning; a flexible interconnected curriculum, rather than a structured curriculum comprising discrete subjects or learning areas, to facilitate trans-disciplinary learning experiences; untimed syllabi so that students are not assessed according to uniform year-level curriculum expectations or stages of development; an alignment of curriculum, teaching and assessment; and emphasis on practices rather than on skills and knowledge.

Arguably, a radical reconstruction such as this is unlikely to be forthcoming in the foreseeable future, although elements have made their way into educational practice. We will discuss inquiry-based leaning and place-based education in chapters to follow, but for our current purposes we will concentrate on current education policy. To this end, an *integrated approach to education* is an effective strategy, characterised by the following steps: (1) integrating or embedding civics and citizenship education across the curriculum to inform the content of core discipline-based curriculum subjects and multi-subject learning areas (thematic studies), (2) encouraging students to make links that can develop both broad and deep civic knowledge and understandings that will empower them as active citizens, (3) increasing student engagement and participation, and (4) and fostering a school ethos, culture, and environment. For both, the whole-school and integrated approaches, the defining feature of democratic education is the inseparable, interconnectedness of civics and citizenship and education broadly speaking.

Historically, two models of democratic education have emerged—freedom-based education and communication and deliberation. Both are rhetorically influential but limited in practice due to their seemingly incongruence with conventional methods of schooling. One model emphasises content, self-regulation, and progressivism, and the other is concerned with process, and communicative and deliberative capabilities.

Freedom-based education

The last century saw an upsurge in the promotion of education reform, and what became known as progressive education. Progressivism is underpinned by the belief that the aim of education is to change school practice, a view that can be traced back to Rousseau's *Emile* (1762), his treatise on education. Rousseau argued that children must develop their own manner and dispositions, and that teachers should let children be 'free' to develop naturally, thus, reducing any factors that may harm their growth. No consideration was to be given to the instruction of morality or ethics *per se*; children had to learn from their own mistakes. In short, Rousseau placed no importance on the teacher's role as instructor, shifting the emphasis directly onto the child's own activity, discovery, and increasing self-awareness. Essentially, progressive education is rooted in the idea of *freedom-based education*, that children are naturally curious, have an innate desire to learn, and, hence, must be free to decide what they study, and how and when they study what they have freely chosen to study (Clabaugh, 2008; Morrison, 2008). This kind of education places a great deal of trust in students to pursue their own leaning, and in the process to become more mature, self-disciplined, and motivated, and recognise the intrinsic value of learning.

Progressive education is also linked to the Swiss education reformer Johann Pestalozzi, and the German educator Friedrich Froebel, but most notably influenced by Dewey's writings on democracy and education. Although he was an early proponent of progressive education, Dewey never aligned himself to the movement and, in fact, distanced himself from it. But it was his principles that schools should reflect the life of the society and that the process of upbringing and teaching is an end in itself that shaped the progressive movement in the U.S.A. and other parts of the world. In practice progressivism advocates a curriculum that follows the interests of students and emphasises active learning and deep understanding. While it can be loosely said that Dewey advocated some sort of progressivism, the theoretical underpinnings of the progressive education movement, especially the relationship between education and democracy, are too vague to resemble his democratic conception of education.

Although the progressive education movement could hardly be considered a unified movement, the progressive experiments in the 1960s and 1970s, including free schooling, open schooling and de-schooling, were inspired by democratic concerns to make education less hierarchical and authoritarian; less ordered by formal rules, laws, and administrative regulations, and more centred on the interests of the students, for example, by placing emphasis on self-regulated learning and student-centred pedagogies. Later, proposals for education reform indicated a commitment to the restructuring of social relationships in schools, which gave students, parents, teachers, and principals greater political control over educational decisions. However, to a large extent, progressivism in the U.S.A., and in many other countries, was discredited for being unclear about the relationship between democracy and educational methods, in particular 'the process of upbringing and teaching as an end in itself' (Englund, 2000, p. 306).

Nevertheless, one model of education commonly seen as an exemplar of progressive education is the freedom-based education/democratic school model. According to this model, students must be left uncoerced to pursue their interests, and schools must embody decision-making structures that facilitate and foster meaningful participation by members of the school community, which 'can take multiple forms, ranging from the micro level of within-class democracy to the more-ideal macro level of whole-school democracy, and within each level, a number of different democratic practices can be enacted' (Morrison, 2008, p. 53). Although, restructuring efforts have been more rhetorical than actual, this progressive model of democratic education provides not only opportunities for students to participate in decision-making or school governance, but also purports to enhance their abilities to self-regulate their roles within community life through learning and sharing. As the history of progressive education shows, few schools actually practiced school democracy in the full sense of the term, insofar as all functions of school management, curriculum, and the pedagogical relationship between teachers and students were fully democratised. Indeed, to varying degrees, progressive schools would concentrate their attention either on freedom-based education or school democracy and incorporate elements of the other or treat both as two sides of the same coin, or even as synonymous. Mostly, schools were less permissive, leaving administration mainly to professionals with varying degrees of input from students and parents.

This account of democratic education has been mistakenly identified with vulgar interpretations of progressivism. However, it is more accurately described as closely linked to progressivism in the U.K. and, particularly, the Scottish educator Alexander Sutherland (A.S.) Neill's renowned Summerhill School, a progressive boarding school in Suffolk, England, established in 1921 and currently run by Neill's daughter, Zoë Readhead. Neill (1960a, 1960b, 1992) took a unique approach to theorising about education. His biographer, Jonathan Croall (1983), spoke of his 'anti-academic philosophy of education' (p. xiii), while others, such as Fred Hechinger (1970), thought he was 'willing to sacrifice brain for heart' (p. 41). Indeed, Neill's approach to education was very different from that of other educational pioneers of his time and sparked huge controversy. He believed that students needed to be given freedom, which, for Neill (1960a), also included freedom from adult control to permit them to be self-regulated. By self-regulation he meant that the child has a right 'to live freely, without outside authority in things psychic and somatic' (p. 105) and 'should not do anything until he comes to the opinion—his own opinion—that it should be done' (p. 114). Neill's aim, therefore, was to stay in the background and compel the children into running their own school.

Summerhill exemplifies a very permissive self-regulating democratic school. The community of students and staff make their own laws, which pertain to situations that arise from community life. Some commentators claim the social control at Summerhill to be based on the democracy of the Athenian model; others maintain it is the educational principles set out in Rousseau's *Emile*. Just which model describes Summerhill best is a moot point. Neill shared Rousseau's belief in non-interference (although he insisted on not having read Rousseau); that freedom exists only when students govern themselves in an environment where they are able to learn and play at will. In addition, he incorporated therapeutic measures, advocating the view that childhood and adolescence could be used to create emotional wholeness and personal strength. He postulated that freedom was desirable not only because it enables children to be natural, but because it empowers them to escape repression, hostility, and guilt. To this, Albert Lamb, editor of *The New Summerhill*, added:

> Neill thought that once this wholeness had been achieved children would be self-motivated to learn what they needed academically. The key to this growth was to give children freedom to play for as long as they felt the need in an atmosphere of approval and love. The children were given freedom but not licence; they could do as they pleased as long as it didn't bother anyone else.
>
> (in Neill, 1992, p. x)

A very liberal notion of freedom. In sum, Neill believed that if children were given freedom—to develop naturally without pressure, removed from fear and coercion by adults—that it would create a happier childhood, allowing self-regulation to begin and for independence to be established, and, thus, for children to accept personal responsibility for their own growth.

Summerhill was not the only prominent progressive school to experiment with freedom-based education or school democracy in the 1920s. In 1927, Dora and Bertrand Russell attempted an educational and social experiment at Beacon Hill School, in West Sussex, England. From 1932 to 1943, the school became exclusively Dora Russell's project, although it had always been more her project. Dora Russell (1980) summed up the school's achievements as a place where democracy was the key principle, and each child was defined as 'a unique individual who belongs, not to the State, or even to his parents, but first of all to himself' (p. 211). It set out to educate children 'to grow up into harmonious adults at peace with themselves and others and so able to work creatively as individuals and, by mutual help, in the community at large' (p. 211). While not attracted to Rousseau's naturalism, the school adopted some progressive methods to which Rousseau himself would not have objected. For example, classes were not compulsory, manual work was encouraged, student self-government was instituted, and the principles of liberty were instilled.

An early Australian example of a democratic school, which emphasised social reform within a self-regulated learning environment, was Koornong School in Victoria. Founded in 1939 by Joseph and Janet Nield and described as an environmental laboratory that brought together progressive education and progressive architecture in a bush setting where '[s]pace and place became key elements of an educational venture' (Goad, 2010, p. 731), Koornong was anything but conventional. Impressed by Summerhill as a model of progressivism, the Nields incorporated many of Neill's ideas. Participation in school governance was a central feature, and the meetings were thought of as plays about the school's social life; the enactment of actual relations conducted within the school. Beyond the school's activities, students were given the opportunity to observe and to take part in the creative activities of the adult world.

A contemporary model, considered the equivalent of Summerhill, and the most famous example in the U.S. of a democratic school that practices freedom-based education, is the Sudbury Model school, founded in 1968. There are currently more than sixty schools that operate independently around the world that identify themselves with Sudbury. While there is no regulated definition of a Sudbury Model school, they share many similarities with other democratic schools underpinned by freedom-based education, namely, de-emphasising classes, no imposed curriculum and students have complete responsibility for their own education, age-mixing, and autonomous democracy. Other notable schools that practice democratic schooling to varying degrees include Pine Community School, Brisbane Independent School, Village School, and Currambena School in Australia; the Democratic

School of Hadera in Israel; Neue Schule Hamburg in Germany; ALPHA Alternative School in Canada; Tamariki School in New Zealand; and Lumiar School in Brazil.

The claim that students ought to govern themselves, to be able to learn or play at will, has been heavily criticised (see Benda, 2007; Bettelheim, 1970; Langer-Buchwald, 2010; Punch, 1976). Many critics of democratic education are either cautious of, or antagonistic towards, school-governance schemes intended to liberate students through progressive practices, such as student participation in the development and evaluation of educational practices, the curriculum, and the life of the school community. It is not evident that freedom-based education, self-regulation, and participation in school-governance are sufficient to foster an educated citizenry competent to participate in democratic societies. Democratic education requires more than churning out decision-makers. Students must be capable of examining and appraising the principles by which they choose to live, so that not only will they be better equipped to deal with the ongoing economic, political, cultural, and social issues that citizens typically must deal with in their local and greater communities, but also to circumvent social crises. By doing so, they will have learned how to examine and appraise institutional and social practices that are likely to contribute to such issues or perpetuate social crises. However, school-democracy, as practiced by Summerhill and other 'free schools', at most, promotes a superficial understanding of moral reasoning as it needs to be connected to deliberation and conscious effort in decision-making as integral to the democratic process of building community to empower students, and, thus, for them to share responsibility for its growth and development. To achieve this, the task of the teacher requires more than staying in the background or sharing equally in educational agenda-setting and decision-making, as decisions, which are not the product of educative development, can lead to the perpetuation of routine, unthinking habits, including collective norms and values. A related criticism, then, is that participation in the self-governing community of schools like Summerhill, was largely therapeutic—for example, as a place 'where happy children learn', 'where children have a childhood' and 'where children have a voice and are heard'—while neglecting to account for that which is necessary to participation in democratic life, namely, developing students' deliberative and communicative capacities, which requires teacher-facilitated classroom dialogue. Lacking such an education, students are ill-equipped to deliberate on matters that affect themselves and others. Students must first learn how to consider the good of their community along with their own personal good before they can make effective decisions on real issues. This is to say, before they can accept full responsibility of citizenship, students must acquire the skills to integrate their personal goals with the goals of society, to 'habitually weigh the claims of society against those of self-interest' (Burgh, Field & Freakley, 2006, p. 57). Two models of participation in school governance that have attempted to bridge this gap are Kohlberg's *Just Communities* and Dewey's *Laboratory School* at the University of Chicago.

The two key aims of Kohlberg's just community method are the promotion of moral development and the transformation of the 'moral atmosphere' of the school into a moral community. At weekly meetings teachers and students engage in the deliberative process of sharing and critically examining reasons (which develops judgement and decision-making skills), and are each entitled to one vote, to determine the rules and norms which guide their common life, and to decide on school policies. The purpose is to build a sense of school community by focusing on achieving as much consensus as is practical to identify with the community and to develop collective norms and values (Kohlberg, 1985; Snarey, Reimer & Kohlberg, 1985). The just community method is, therefore, a community-building approach to character and civic competence, the promotion of democratic values, and increasing moral reasoning. To some extent, the way Kohlberg pursues school democracy in just communities avoids the criticisms levelled at Summerhill and other schools based on the principles of freedom-based education. Nevertheless, as the just community approach to moral reasoning is steeped in developmental stage theory, it faces similar criticisms to those raised earlier regarding the teaching of values through moral dilemmas, normative assumptions about the central role of universal norms in moral reasoning, and its commitment to the view that each stage of development needs to be reached before learning occurs, contrary to sociocultural theory that social learning precedes development (see Vygotsky, 1978; see also Chapter 2).

Dewey was also involved with experimental schools and education reform. He believed that the classroom should be a social enterprise in which all students can contribute, and all are engaged in communal projects. Between 1896 and 1904, he was involved in the Laboratory School at the University of Chicago, where, in Dewey's (1956) own words, students experienced a 'miniature community, an embryonic society' (p. 18). Amy Gutmann (1987) describes it as a model of democratic education. However, she points out that Dewey's characterisation of the school as a miniature democratic community is misleading. Students did not have the same freedom or influence as teachers over matters of curriculum and the structure of the school. They were, nevertheless, encouraged to engage in collective deliberation and decision-making. Regular classroom council meetings were held, and younger students were given the responsibility of carrying out important tasks. Dewey was elusive over which internal democratic structures corresponded to those of a democratic society. For example, teachers had much more authority than democratically elected representatives. However, while the school's internal democratic structures were more democratic than almost all schools in the U.S.A., it was, as Gutmann points out, an 'embryonic democratic society because it elicited a commitment to learning and cultivated the democratic virtues among its students, not because it treated them as the political equals of its teachers' (p. 93). We will return to the Laboratory School in the next section in greater detail.

Democratic schools do not need to be democratic in the same way as democratic societies, that is, they do not need to resemble the political institutions and practices of decision-making or incorporate basic elements of democratic decision-making practices. Indeed, they cannot since schools by their very nature also educate students in the practices of democracy. So, while students cannot expect to have the same citizenship rights as adults, by the same token, it would be inconsistent with democratic practice if they were denied 'both individual and collective influence in shaping their own education' (p. 94). While young children particularly are not ready for full citizenship, they, like all students, have to be prepared for citizenship, or more precisely, *practice citizenship*. So, for democratic education to be not contrary to democratic practice, a considerable degree of democracy within schools is desirable, if not necessary. But the question of just how much democracy is necessary requires further investigation as 'we lack enough evidence to say how much internal democracy is necessary to cultivate participatory virtues among students' (p. 92). Weinstein (1991) argues that '[w] hether student participation in school governance is theoretically motivated by developmentalism or by pragmatist approaches, it seems clear that children have neither the responsibility for making actual school policy decisions, nor information and deliberative competence adequate to the task' (p. 24).

Critics, such as Weinstein, are mistaken in their views that the arguments against participation in school-governance, as practiced by freedom-based education schools like Summerhill and developmentalist accounts of democratic education, necessarily also apply to pragmatist accounts of democratic education, and specifically to Dewey's philosophy of education. There is more to Dewey's theory of education and the way he put it into practice at the Laboratory School than meets the eye. That Dewey understood democracy as a mode of associated living, and not as a system of government, needs to be considered when interpreting his claim that the school should be a miniature democratic community and embryonic society. Instead of school-governance and freedom-based education, an alternative approach to democratic education is purposeful student engagement in dialogic inquiry and practicality; the construction, testing, and application of knowledge to concrete situations so that these situations are reconstructed into meaningful experiences. In the next section, we discuss the connection between democratic education and practicality. But, to conclude here, we cannot stress enough that democratic education places no obligation on those seeking democratic reform to introduce measures in the way that, say, Neill did in Summerhill. Likewise, it should not condemn the inclusion of student participation in school-governance *per se*, provided its pedagogical purpose is to actively engage students in reflective thinking and thoughtful action (both essential features of informed practice integral to active democratic citizenship). For this we once again turn to Dewey.

Communication and deliberation

The second sense in which the term democratic education is used refers to an education wherein emphasis is on the development of students' deliberative capabilities and attitudes, those essential for the social dimension of democracy. This account of democratic education, which relies on a pragmatist interpretation of Dewey's educational point of view, recognises the importance of education as communication 'where different perspectives are brought into ongoing meaning-creating processes of will-formation' (Englund, 2000, p. 312). Like Neill, Dewey also understood the importance of participation, but a significant intellectual difference is that he also recognised that the development of corresponding attitudes for democratic engagement requires effective communication. Mentioned earlier, for Dewey (1916), education is a process of living and not a preparation for future living. As his concern is with democracy as a mode of associated living, the purpose of education is the perpetuation of social life which, he says, is identical to communication. Thus, developing students' deliberative capabilities and attitudes for democratic engagement is not preparing them for the future, but engaging them in conjoint communicative experience, thereby continuously leading into the future—the constant 'reconstruction or reorganization of experience which adds to the meaning of experience, and which increases ability to direct the course of subsequent experience' (p. 76). This is what Dewey referred to when he spoke about democracy as a mode of associated living, and it is here that we find Dewey's connection to democracy and his democratic conception of education, which distinguishes it from school-governance models of democratic education.

Unfortunately, Dewey's educational theories have been variously misconstrued. As we have already noted, he has been connected to the progressive education movement, yet his ideas differ in so many ways from those who call themselves progressive, both in Dewey's time and since then. Dewey, himself, distinguished his Laboratory School from other schools labelled progressive and insisted that his focus was primarily on 'the social phase of education' and not on the complete liberty of individuals, as were progressive schools based on freedom-based education. Rather than being '"child-centered" in a way which ignores, or at least makes little of social relationships and responsibilities', the school was 'community-centred'. Dewey held that 'the process of mental development is essentially a social process, a process of participation' and that the aim was to develop students' abilities to 'live in cooperative integration with others' (Dewey, 1936, p. 467). Moreover, he did not ignore the importance of academic content, as he insisted that teachers have subject-matter expertise, albeit the curriculum was not organised according to traditional subject divisions. Dewey's approach to democratic education provides a model of *democracy as inquiry*, as well as being an educative process, and as such, has much to offer with regards to democratic education. It is important, therefore, to note Dewey's contribution to the formulation and evolution of this model of democratic education, particularly his 'experimentalism with an emphasis on the principles of experience, inquiry, and reflection' (Giles Jr & Eyler, 1994, p. 79). Indeed, Dewey is recognised as a precursor to, and as being highly influential in, the development of experiential education. First and foremost a philosopher, in Dewey's writings on education we see that philosophy *is* the theory of education, and together with his use of theories in psychology, he developed a philosophy of education in which students are directly involved 'with the problematicity of whatever subject matter they are attempting to study' (Lipman, 2004, p. 7).

Confusingly, the term 'experiential education' has served as an umbrella for any model that is considered 'hands-on learning', 'learning by doing', or 'learning through experience'. It becomes difficult to distinguish between those educational practices that retain Deweyan roots and those adapting a much broader idea of experience as central to the educational process. Nevertheless, Dewey's experiential learning has influenced many prominent models and practices in schools which, themselves, provide contexts and frameworks for learning. Typically, these are used as supplements to traditional teaching and curriculum and are a combination of community service with stated learning objectives. Examples are place-based education also known as pedagogy of place and place-based learning, community-based education, service learning, laboratory and clinical learning, education for sustainability, environmental education, outdoor education, and vocational education. The term experiential education has also been used interchangeably with 'experiential learning', which, although a general concept of learning that has a place under the methodologies of experiential education, focuses on the individual learning process and practical issues related to the learner and the learning context. Experiential education, on the other hand, is a philosophy of education and is, therefore, a broader concept, one that informs the methodologies and pedagogies of educational practices such as those mentioned above. What remains at the core of experiential education, in the way Dewey intended, is purposeful engagement with learners in which pedagogy and physical experience must be combined with reflection to develop students' capacities to contribute to their communities.

Dewey's theory of experiential education is articulated in *Education as Experience* (1938), in which he argues that an idea must be tested, and final judgement withheld until it has been applied to the intended situation. Through reflection and reasoned judgement, the consequences that ensue from the testing of ideas are evaluated, and only then do the inquirers establish meaning. In other words, the practical testing of ideas becomes an integral part of the inquiry process; it is essential for the facilitation of the Deweyan ideals of thinking, community, autonomy, and democratic citizenship that it intends to facilitate (Bleazby, 2004, 2006, 2013; Thornton, Graham & Burgh, 2021). Dewey's Laboratory School was, thus, an attempt to incorporate 'practicality' as part of the educative process. Designed as an experiment in collapsing the theory/practice relationship, he did not, however, provide teachers with explicit guidelines or detailed instructions on how or what to teach but, instead, provided them with general principles for teaching practice and the development of curriculum. As mentioned previously, Dewey applied his conception of the scientific method as inquiry to his method for collaborative problem-solving. For this, he turned to the psychological concepts: self-activity and self-creation. He considered 'curiosity, action, and experience as essential conditions of learning', and treated students as active agents who, together, construct 'reality in continuous interaction with their environment', ideally, 'by experiencing real life situations at first-hand' (Knoll, 2016, p. 1). In addition, Dewey introduced the concept of a *problem* as arising from, what Michael Luntley (2016) describes as, 'a disruption to experience but where that disruption is not presented within the conceptual resources already available to the learner' (p. 8). The importance of disruption is in its ability to 'unsettle the learner' and, consequently, engage them as inquirers and challenge them to open-up to 'new experiences and new concepts, otherwise no real learning will take place' (p. 8).

So, for Dewey, problem-solving is more than merely equipping students with the knowledge and skills to solve problems, such as providing students with a pre-set task to be solved by simple means-ends analysis. Instead, he viewed problem-solving *as* learning, whereby inquirers intellectualise a sense of unease into a problem as a source of extending cognition. This sense of unease is 'the rhythm of loss of integration with the environment and recovery of union' (Dewey, 1934, p. 15), which provides the basis for students to inquire further, to seek out information that will help them to resolve questions for which they are curious. Without any disruptions—when human habits are in equilibrium with their environment because no perplexity appears—there is no impetus for inquiry. Once our experiences become unsettled, reflective thought is provoked and inquiry begins. Inquiry, in the Deweyan sense, therefore, occupies an intermediate and reconstructive position between disequilibrium and equilibrium. It is a continuous interaction of collaborative engagement in active reflection to deal with a perplexing situation, and imaginatively testing alternative scenarios that inquirers envision acting upon which have emerged from deliberation, 'till some suggested solution meets all the conditions of the case and does not run counter to any discoverable feature of it' (Dewey, 1933, p. 197). Inquiry, therefore, is a process of moving from an unsettled situation towards a settled situation.

When Dewey attempted to put his method of inquiry into practice at the Laboratory School, he proposed that the curriculum should be fundamentally reconstructed. Instead of allocating time for traditional subjects, the curriculum centred on *social occupations*. Dewey (1900) defined an occupation as 'a mode of activity on the part of the child which reproduces, or runs parallel to, some form of work carried on in social life' (p. 82). In the Laboratory School these were represented by occupations such as cooking, textile work, and shop-work; constructive activities that represented fundamental human activities and involved analysing materials and processes. However, Dewey made a distinction between the educational use of occupations and training in preparation for a trade or other work.

> The fundamental point in the psychology of an occupation is that it maintains a balance between the intellectual and the practical phases of experience. As an occupation it is active or motor; it finds expression

through the physical organs—the eyes, hands, etc. But it also involves continual observation of materials, and continual planning and reflection, in order that the practical or executive side may be successfully carried on. Occupation as thus conceived must, therefore, be carefully distinguished from work which educates primarily for a trade. It differs because its end is in itself; in the growth that comes from the continual interplay of ideas and their embodiment in action, not in external utility.

(p. 82)

The occupations not only allowed students to identify with their tasks they also integrated subject matter and, thus, students integrated knowledge and experiences through thinking and doing to reconstruct their understanding of their environment. This is no accident on Dewey's part, as he persistently critiqued philosophies founded on dualistic divisions, those 'that divide hand from mind, body from world, knowing from touching' which permeate discourse 'around issues of education and the child' (Anthamatten, 2012, p. 27). For Dewey, habit and habitat do not function separately, nor are they in a linear causal relationship or one and the same (i.e., the organism is neither at the mercy of the habitat nor is it, as some holistic views would have, the habitat itself). The two are in a continuous circuitous relationship and, therefore, the task of education is to coordinate experiencing and learning by facilitating meaningful connections between individuals and community, and humans and the environment (Dewey, 1981).

The role of the teacher then becomes one of shaping and directing experiences through facilitating collaborative learning experiences centred on practical problems and activities that reproduce typical situations of social and communal life. To this end, teachers were expected to:

provide the materials and the conditions by which organic curiosity will be directed into investigations that have an aim and that produce results in the way of increase of knowledge, and by which social inquisitiveness will be converted into ability to find out things known to others, an ability to ask questions of books as well as of persons.

(Dewey, 1933, p. 40)

Through Dewey's concept of occupations, teachers at the Laboratory School provided students with concrete situations to encounter 'logically organised bodies of subject matter: chemistry, physics, biology, mathematics, history, language, literature, music and physical culture' (Tanner, 1991, p. 102). Thus, traditional discipline-based content and skills were not ignored but learned *through* occupations, guided by the students' own interests, not by the logical organisation of the subject matter, thereby achieving curriculum synthesis as well as bringing a cultural role to inquiry to make their experience more meaningful and challenging so 'that it arouses in the learner an active quest for information and for production of new ideas' (Dewey, 1938, p. 79).

Dewey's emphasis on the social dimension of democracy—the practice of associated living—demands a culture of collaborative deliberation for effective citizen participation in social and political decision-making regarding matters of public affairs. This is reflected in his curriculum centred on social occupations, which provides a way of developing the cooperative intelligence necessary for the kind of democratic communities he envisaged for social democracy. We add to this that such communities of inquiry are crucial for the democratic correction of social and political institutions to which Plumwood refers. Deweyan classrooms function as 'microcosms of democracy not simply because they are self-governing groups but because their modes of self-regulation and self-correcting can be carried over from the smaller groups to the more massive societies' (Lipman, 1998, p. 25). Participation in school-governance, like cooking, textile work, and shop-work, is also a case of the educational use of occupation; it, too, is a mode of activity which reproduces, or runs parallel to, some form of work carried on in social life. Like all occupational work at the school, the emphasis was on collaborative deliberation and, thus, on democratic practice, all of which contribute to democratic citizenship and civic literacy.

A comparison between Neill's Summerhill and Dewey's Laboratory School highlights the distinct differences in their approaches to democratic education. At one end of the continuum, we have a democratic school that fosters self-regulation, freedom, and school-governance, and at the other, a model committed to experiential education that emphasises communication and deliberation to infuse direct experience with the learning environment and content. If we judge which of the two schools was more democratic solely on individual freedom and self-regulation, then Summerhill was more internally democratic, albeit not without constrains. However, the educational advantage of Dewey's approach to democratic education is that he believed that 'school, as an intermediate institution between the home and society, should give the child an opportunity to a participating and contributing member of a community' (Tanner, 1991, p. 104). Together with the integration of practical learning that emphasised the principles of experience, inquiry, and reflection to synthesise curriculum, he was able to develop a strategy for increasing civic literacy as social and intellectual growth towards self-governance. Self-governance, as the term is used here, is not to be confused with school-governance. Rather, it is engagement with the design and implementation of solutions to social problems that affect not only the members of the class, but also members of the greater community. In other words, the school becomes a place for the continuous reconstruction of experiences that increase students' abilities to direct and control their lives as democratic citizens, which impacts on the greater community—an intermediary for social reconstruction.

Under Dewey's definition of democracy, the quality of democracy is reliant upon the quality of the communication among members of the community, without which decision-making would be haphazard and, consequently, democracy as a system of government would be ineffective.

Dewey also viewed education as a necessity of life—whether done consciously or unconsciously, well or poorly, it is unavoidable, we learn no matter what. Education must, therefore, centre on collaborative deliberation so that the individual and the community come together as a community of inquiry. Dewey's implementation of experiential education at the Laboratory School emphasises the importance of inquiry as a collective method of transmission, transaction and transformation that is necessary for the continual reconstruction of experiences and knowledge. Through this process students experience real social change, which is much more fundamental to democratic citizenship than mere participation in internal school democracy.

Much has been written about the Laboratory School and its shortcomings regarding putting theory into practice (e.g., Durst, 2010; Gutmann, 1987; Knoll, 2016; Tanner, 1991, 1997). Our concern is not with the everyday organisation of the school, analysing the classroom practices of teachers shared in the weekly reports, or on how Dewey needed to modify his expectations. The school was, after all, an experiment, which underwent ongoing evaluation to improve curriculum and pedagogy. Our immediate concern is with how any of the approaches outlined in the chapter can inform civics and citizenship education, develop civic literacy, and provide a framework for education today. Bearing this in mind, Dewey provides a sound basis for education in a democracy, one that directly addresses identity formation as democratic citizenship that is achieved through curriculum synthesis, communication as the basis of community, and education as both a social and intellectual process.

Conclusion

At this juncture, we take pause to review our discussion so far and ask: What is democratic education and how can it be achieved? Dewey's educational philosophy and practice stands head and shoulders above the rest for the reasons we have given here and in the previous chapters. To recap, education has as its primary role identity formation, including the process of national identity building. This is so because identity formation is unavoidable as it is achieved through teaching methods, classroom content, education policies, and national curricula, as well as the hidden curriculum. Dewey is correct that learning is an inevitable outcome of all activities, whether we unwittingly accept that which has been transmitted through communication or grapple with it when engaged in inquiry. As Dewey would tell us, our habits shape our habitat which goes on to shape our habits. Formal education must, therefore, play an active role in shaping citizen identity, not as a pre-given social and political identity shaped by current political discourses that have been historically transmitted from generation to generation, but shaped by collaborative inquiry that is an exemplar of social democracy. Dewey's theory of experiential education focuses attention on the relationship between schooling and life, both inside and outside the classroom, which is vital to democratic citizenship, as students develop their social and intellectual capacities to engage in collective self-correction.

The capacity to engage in self-correction goes beyond what is usually seen as requisite knowledge and skills for civic literacy. Typically, civic literacy focuses on knowing how to stay informed, understanding government institutions and processes, and developing the skills to exercise the rights and obligations of citizenship at local, state, national, and global levels. However, civic literacy is also, to reiterate Barber words, 'the competence to participate in democratic communities, the ability to think critically and act with deliberation in a pluralistic world, and the empathy to identify sufficiently with others to live with them despite conflicts of interest and differences in character' (in Westbrook, 1996, p. 125). Whereas the various approaches to education for democracy discussed above are focused more on knowledge and skills, and self-regulating models of democratic education, such as Summerhill, fail to meet Barber's criteria as their attempts are limited to internal school governance, Dewey's theory of experiential learning certainly is a contender to meet Barber's criteria. This is important as the focus of identity is not on disciplinary citizenship that permeates official policy documents, including curriculum documents that draw on Western values and liberal notions of citizenship, but on Delanty's notion of cultural citizenship which acknowledges citizenship as a collective learning process.

It is crucial, therefore, that a pedagogy for democratic citizenship draws on Dewey's conception of social democracy as a community that emphasises collaborative deliberation and experiential education. However, to fully implement Dewey's ideas into practice, not only requires a radical reconstruction of education policy, but a radical social and political change to convince policy makers and politicians that such changes are crucial to strengthening democratic practices. A small step towards such change, as stated earlier, would be to embed a civic literacy dimension across the curriculum to inform the content of core discipline-based curriculum subjects and multi-subject learning areas. Essentially, this would 'loosen up' the curriculum as Dewey intended, where the focus is not on the logical structure of the curriculum but on the coordination of experiencing and learning by facilitating meaningful connections, thereby achieving curriculum synthesis.

To achieve a Deweyan curriculum synthesis through cross-curriculum integration, we need to reconceptualise Dewey's ideas on practicality so that the principles of experiential education can be infused into the curriculum. For this task, we turn to Matthew Lipman, who argued that philosophy should not only be the general theory of education, as Dewey thought, but also that the practice of philosophy should be *the methodology of education*. Thus, the next chapter is devoted to philosophy for children, an approach to education that has as its pedagogical framework the community of inquiry, which lays out guidelines for teaching practice. For Lipman, the community of inquiry is a community of philosophical inquiry; a model for community-centred, inquiry-based pedagogy that is an exemplar of democracy in action. As such, philosophy for children provides a basis for our proposal for a place-based democratic education.

Note

1 The nine values identified in the *National Framework for Values Education in Australian Schools* are: (1) care and compassion, (2) doing your best, (3) fair go, (4) freedom, (5) honesty and trustworthiness, (6) integrity, (7) respect, (8) responsibility, and (9) understanding, tolerance, and inclusion.

4 Educational philosophy

Introduction

There is a proliferation of literature on the merits of philosophy having the potential to be an effective educational strategy for enhancing democratic ways of life, such as cultivating democratic communities (Burgh, 2003a, 2003b, 2014; Burgh, Field & Freakley, 2006; Lefrançois & Ethier, 2010; Saint, 2019; Venter & Higgs, 2014). Philosophy's effectiveness in this area is evident in the recommendations for the need for pedagogy and curriculum that promotes thinking to reinforce knowledge, strengthen autonomy, and contribute to civics and citizenship education that resonates from the 2007 UNESCO study, *Philosophy: A School of Freedom*. The report endorses teaching philosophy to promote the development of a critical citizenry, placing emphasis on 'putting concepts and ideas into perspective' through reflection and developing 'each person's skills to question, compare [and] conceptualise', which are requisite for 'an open, inclusive and pluralistic, knowledge-oriented society' (p. ix). Also of note is the emphasis on philosophy as having a liberating function (e.g., Glaser, 1994; Sharp, 1993; UNESCO, 2007), particularly its role in fostering autonomy and the development of social and intellectual capacities and dispositions needed for active and informed citizenship (e.g., Bleazby, 2006; Burgh, 2010, 2018; Cam, 2000; Glaser, 2007; Gregory, 2004; Kennedy, 2017; Lipman, 1998; Sharp, 1991; Vicuna Navarro, 1998). To thoroughly explore philosophy's potential, we need to think about the philosophical and educational basis for developing the kinds of curriculum materials and accompanying teaching practices that will enable students to engage in a culture of collaborative deliberation associated with democratic citizenship.

The world is perpetually changing, cultures are changing, and communication is changing. Knowledge seems, therefore, to be in a constant state of flux. In a nutshell, we live in world of uncertainty, or more accurately, more people seem to be uncertain about the world. Pivotal in addressing these matters is the discipline of education. However, education cannot turn to itself for an understanding of the complex relationship between epistemology, pedagogy, deliberative communication, and identity formation. For

DOI: 10.4324/9781003098089-5

such an understanding, education requires philosophy to examine the philosophical assumptions that underpin educational theory and practice. By the
same token, academic philosophy is not always suitable to the task. Moreover, philosophy of education may seem far removed from the world of most
practitioners, or the discipline of education may be viewed by philosophers
as merely a concept open to analytic dissection. Of course, not all philosophy
of education is like this, and increasingly philosophy of education is playing a
practical role in how education functions. We, therefore, take a critical look
at philosophy for children, an educational philosophy that provides us with a
pedagogical framework for our Deweyan influenced proposal for democratic
education. By educational philosophy we mean philosophy functioning
educationally, whereby philosophy is the methodology of education, specifically the integration of philosophy into classroom practice (Lipman, 2004,
pp. 6–8). This is not to be confused with philosophy of education, which is
philosophical reflection on the nature, aims, and problems of education and
includes philosophy of teaching. Educational philosophy, simply put, is the
practical role that philosophy plays in education.

Philosophy for children is an approach to education that focuses on
self-correcting dialogic inquiry. Its pedagogical framework is the community
of inquiry, an exemplar of democracy in action. The community of inquiry
is intended to develop students' social and intellectual capacities and dispositions, through adult mediation between the culture and the child, to
improve the relationship between deliberative judgements and democratic
decision-making. The pedagogy informs the method of classroom practice,
which is the practice of philosophy. Although philosophy is traditionally considered an activity not suitable for children,[1] philosophy for children can
engage in genuine philosophical inquiry provided it is offered to them in
ways suitable to their abilities and interests (Lipman, 1988, 1991; Lipman,
Sharp & Oscanyan, 1980). It has gained much support and has already been
established in a variety of different educational settings, including schools,
colleges, and universities in many countries worldwide with promising
results, which makes it extremely important, particularly as an effective pedagogy aimed at educational reform, as well as for the development of civic
literacy.

This chapter provides an overview of the theory and practice of the philosophy for children approach to education. But it is more than just an
overview; we offer some analysis of what we see as tensions among its proponents. Both provide a context for our proposal for democratic education in
Chapters 5–6. Included in our overview and analysis is an explanation of the
inter-relationship between curriculum and pedagogy. We, then, introduce
the narrow-sense and wide-sense conceptions of the community of inquiry
as a way of understanding what is meant by converting the classroom into
a community of inquiry. We explain how the narrow-sense community of
inquiry, as a pattern or stages of inquiry informs the specific teaching method
for fostering philosophical discussion, and the wide-sense scholarly community of inquiry, as an epistemological and methodological approach to inquiry

as originally described by Peirce, function both separately and together. The wide-sense conception must be treated as the organising or regulative principle of scholarly communities of inquiry and as a classroom-wide ideal for the reconstruction of education. This principle, in turn, must inform the narrow-sense community of inquiry as it provides the pedagogical guidelines for classroom practice, as its effectiveness for converting the classroom into a community of inquiry requires more than a specific procedural method of stages of inquiry for teachers to follow. We continue with a discussion on the dual role of the teacher as facilitator and co-inquirer in mediating between the two conceptions of the community of inquiry.

At this point, we look at three different interpretations of Dewey's educational theory and practice and argue that the phrase 'converting the classroom into a community of inquiry' makes sense only if we understand the community of inquiry as underpinned by a reconstructionist and pragmatist interpretation. Without such an understanding of the relationship between the two conceptions of the community of inquiry to guide the larger aims of an education that supports democratic ways of life, the role of the teacher remains unclear. However, while our analysis leads us to conclude that extending philosophy as the general theory of education to philosophy as the methodology of education is the strength of philosophy for children, a re-evaluation of experiential education is required. To make meaningful connections requires more than connecting student's experiences to curriculum materials; it requires being immersed in real-world situations, like the Laboratory School. However, we argue that it needs to go beyond school occupation work or traditional service learning in the community. To this end, we call for an integration of what Jennifer Bleazby (2013) calls social reconstruction learning, which involves students engaging in communities of inquiry to reconstruct real social problems and facilitate democratic citizenship. It is to this end that this chapter will aim.

Philosophy for children

Developing students' critical thinking skills to prepare them for active and informed citizenship in a democracy is listed as a desirable aim of education on many curriculum and syllabus documents. Philosophy is often claimed to be the 'go to' discipline for developing such skills. This view mistakenly places the educational value of philosophy as tantamount to critical thinking— inference, analysis, evaluation. Lost is Dewey's vision of thinking *as* inquiry; a kind of knowing in action. Inquiry is both critical and creative; a dialogic interplay that lends itself naturally to classroom discussion elicited from students' curiosity that can provide a natural basis for learning. It is this, not critical thinking *per se*, that has the greatest pedagogical potential to develop an inquiring society. Indeed, this narrow instrumental conception of philosophy as merely a thinking-skills program is very misleading, because 'it immediately marginalises the social, ethical, aesthetic, affective and political components that are as integral to the teaching of thinking as the skills themselves' (Splitter & Sharp 1995, p. 3). Educationally, it is vital that we do not sever these ties, lest we provide students with a model of humans as epistemic subjects, bearers of knowledge seeking logical connections, rather than as ethical agents who are aware of their ecological relatedness with others and their environment (Laverty, 1994, p. 73). Such relatedness, or more precisely, interrelatedness, is prevalent in the theory and practice of the community of inquiry, which has a long history that dates back to Charles Sanders Peirce, an American pragmatist philosopher, logician, mathematician, and scientist whose original formulation is grounded in the notion of communities of disciplinary-based inquiry engaged in the construction of knowledge. However, its use as a pedagogical framework for classroom discussion owes much to Matthew Lipman, who, with Ann Margaret Sharp, developed what is known as 'Philosophy for Children'.

Philosophy for children began in 1968 when Lipman started writing *Harry Stottlemeier's Discovery*. This was the first in a series of philosophical stories-as-text for children and adolescents, each of which came with a teacher's instruction manual. Thus, the two fundamental components of Philosophy for Children are the curriculum materials and the methodology[2] of the community of inquiry (both of which will be discussed in more detail below). Lipman and Sharp believed that Philosophy for Children was not only a way to reconstruct philosophy as a pedagogical framework for classroom practice, but a way to reconstruct education itself toward social reconstruction, that is, towards the creation of an inquiring society.

> Unlike others experimenting with 'pre-college philosophy' at the time, who saw schools as a place to do philosophy with young people, Lipman and Sharp saw doing philosophy as an ideal of the education al experience, even capable of transforming education more broadly.
>
> (Gregory, Haynes & Murris 2017, p. xxvi)

However, it was not until 1974 when Lipman and Sharp became co-founders of the Institute for the Advancement of Philosophy for Children (IAPC) and in 1975 conducted the first professional development workshops for teachers that Philosophy for Children began to spread. Today, not only is it recognised by UNESCO (2007) but acknowledge by many philosophers of education and practitioners (e.g., Nussbaum, 2010) as an exemplary educational philosophy that is used in school classrooms around the world. Philosophy for Children has been adapted variously to school classrooms, whole-school philosophy initiatives, school extension programs, community programs such as philosophy in public spaces, adult learning, higher education, and a multitude of informal educational settings in over 60 countries across the globe. However, the philosophy for children movement is far from unified, growing in diversity as it adapts to places.

Philosophy for Children (also written as P4C) now refers to a sub-discipline of philosophy with its own history and traditions. Due to different educational needs and social, cultural, and political contexts, a diverse range of approaches and practices have developed. These include the Community of Philosophical Inquiry (CoPI) method developed by Catherine McCall that emphasises rigorous logical argumentation, and the Continental Community of Inquiry by Matthew Del Nevo (2002) in which students concentrate on original philosophical texts. Subsequently, the term 'philosophy for children' (lower case), also referred to as 'philosophy with children (PwC)', 'philosophy with children and adolescents', 'philosophy for young people', and 'philosophy for/with children (Pw4C)', is often used to capture these diverse approaches, which includes Philosophy for Children (upper case). Alternative approaches not influenced by Lipman include Socratic Dialogue by Leonard Nelson (1965), which focuses on critical philosophy, following the thinking of Immanuel Kant and Jakob Fries, and Oscar Brenifier's method of Socratic maieutics. What all these school philosophy approaches to education have in common is that they aim to engage school students in philosophical dialogue. We will use the term 'philosophy in schools' as a general term to capture the diverse range of approaches that use philosophical inquiry as a classroom strategy, but when referring specifically to the IAPC program, we use 'Philosophy for Children' (upper case) or 'philosophy for children' (lower case) when referring to the philosophy for children movement (i.e., teaching practices influenced by Lipman and Sharp's philosophy of education).

Megan Laverty (2014) observed that the 'philosophy in schools' movement, globally, has expanded and diversified in response to curriculum developments, resulting in an increase in the production of teaching guides and the development of web-based resources, further theoretical scholarship and dissertations, and much needed empirical research. Philosophy and philosophy of education journals regularly publish articles and special issues on pre-college philosophy. In addition, specialised journals have been established, organisations founded to further the aims and objectives of philosophy in schools, and now '[t]here are more opportunities for undergraduate and graduate philosophy students to practice and research philosophy for/with children in schools' (p. 1). It should be noted that philosophy for children, as an international educational and philosophical movement, has had the greatest impact on teachers, schools, curriculum, and educational policy.

Research by educational psychologists and philosophers suggests that the pedagogy of philosophy for children, namely, the community of inquiry, is an effective educational strategy for students to learn about and engage with the world in new ways through pursuing philosophical questions together (Matthews, 1980, 1984; Pritchard, 1985). Gareth Matthews (1980) provides examples of very young children's philosophical puzzlement and argues that such evidence is contrary to Piaget's observations which failed to see the philosophical thinking manifest in the children he studied. The community of inquiry, thus, has the potential not only to be an effective pedagogy to develop students' civic mindedness by developing new sensitivities for living in a democracy but also for thinking about democracy (Burgh, 2010, 2014, 2018; Dombayci, 2014; Echeverria & Hannam, 2017).

In addition, there is ample evidence, supported by many international research studies, on the effectiveness of the community of inquiry in school classrooms. According to Stephan Millett and Alan Tapper (2012): 'In the past decade well-designed research studies have shown that the practice of collaborative philosophical inquiry in schools can have marked cognitive and social benefits. Student academic performance improves, and so too does the social dimension of schooling' (p. 546). An analysis of 18 studies concluded that 'the implementation of P4C led to an improvement in students' reasoning skills of more than half a standard deviation' (Garcia-Moriyon, Robello & Colom, 2005, p. 19). Keith Topping and Steve Trickey's studies concluded that the practice of collaborative philosophical inquiry produces increases in measured IQ, sustained cognitive benefits, and clear performance gains in other school studies (Topping & Trickey, 2007a, 2007b, 2007c; Trickey & Topping, 2004, 2006, 2007). In Australia, recent studies have attempted to show to what degree philosophical inquiry in the classroom has been successful (Millett, Scholl & Tapper, 2019). These studies have demonstrated the potential for collaborative philosophical inquiry to foster pedagogical transformation (Scholl, Nichols & Burgh 2009, 2014, 2016), more effective learning in the science classroom (Burgh & Nichols 2012; Nichols, Burgh & Kennedy, 2017b), and the potential for cognitive dissonance during students' experiences of inquiry to be transformed into the impetus for the acquisition and improvement of social and intellectual inquiry capabilities and thinking behaviours across the curriculum (Nichols, Burgh & Fynes-Clinton, 2017a; Burgh, Thornton & Fynes-Clinton, 2018).

The empirical evidence, so far, points to philosophy for children's effectiveness in increasing learning outcomes in a wide range of areas. Moreover, it has gained attention from both scholars and classroom teachers alike, and it has been promoted in educational and professional contexts and implemented in diverse and divergent classroom practices across school subjects. Philosophy for children, therefore, is an exemplar of educational philosophy, which provides an effective framework for our proposal for democratic education. As a theoretical framework for practice, the educational merit of philosophy for children is that it is an inquiry-based, community-centred approach to teaching and learning through philosophy; a teaching methodology in the tradition of reflective education in which good thinking and its improvement is central. Reflective education expressly puts thinking at the heart of teaching and learning, by fostering good habits of thinking. It is a tradition in which not Plato but 'Socrates, most famously, stands at the beginning' and more recently 'it was Dewey who carried the torch' (Cam, 2008, p. 163). Indeed, as Lipman (2004) tells the story, 'Philosophy for Children is built unapologetically on Deweyan foundations' (p. 8).

However, Lipman questioned Dewey's commitment to reflective thinking when he 'discovered aspects of his philosophy that he treated too lightly, even superficially' (p. 3). As previously explained, Dewey wanted to reconstruct the theory/practice dualism, yet '[n]owhere in his writings does he refer to the practical use of philosophy in education' (p. 6). But upon closer observation he observed that 'implicit in Dewey's writings are pedagogical guidelines, which would be applicable to any curriculum, even to those that had not yet been invented, like educational philosophy (i.e., philosophy functioning educationally, like Philosophy for Children, not to be confused with the philosophy of education)' (p. 7). For Dewey, philosophy is *the general theory of education*, whereas Lipman thought philosophy must also have 'a hand in the construction of all theory, including education' but specifically that '*the practice of philosophy is the methodology of education*' (p. 6).

The problem, as Lipman saw it, is that while Dewey insisted on overcoming the theory/practice dualism by students undertaking practical activities through engaging in social occupation work, he did not think to involve students participating in philosophy as a part of the inquiry process to reconstruct their experiences and knowledge, thus, diminishing his own attentiveness to reflective thinking. Conversely, and ironically, Lipman himself failed to see the importance of experiential education in the way Dewey's Laboratory School did. The two approaches, we hold, fit naturally together. Later in the chapter, we discuss Bleazby's notion of social reconstruction learning as a way of bringing together both Lipman's and Dewey's theories. In the next section, we discuss Lipman's use of philosophical stories-as-text, followed by a discussion on the community of inquiry, both of which are his contribution to overcoming the theory/practice dualism.

The curriculum

Lipman originally wrote a series of purpose-written philosophical stories-as-text (aka 'novels') for children and adolescents, and with Sharp, and other colleagues at the IAPC, developed accompanying instruction manuals that include discussion plans and exercises aimed at developing the philosophical themes contained within the stories. Together, the novels and manuals make up the IAPC curriculum. The use of the term 'curriculum', as Laurance Splitter (2003) notes, is important, as the novels and manuals are 'not just an unstructured collection of philosophical stimuli' (p. 45). Neither are the materials intended to impart knowledge like traditional textbooks. According to Sharp (2017a), whereas traditional philosophical texts attempt 'to present philosophy in a logical and comprehensive manner devoid of experience', the philosophical story-as-text attempts 'to motivate children to inquire into philosophical concepts and philosophical procedures in a way that is directly related to children's experience' (p. 18). The stories, in which children discover and explore the ethical, aesthetic, epistemological, and ontological assumptions of their thinking about issues or the meaning of their own experiences, become stimuli which children, rather than only adults, have control over; 'it is their story and they use it to set an agenda for discussion and philosophical inquiry' (p. 18). The stories are meant to embed philosophy into everyday conversations in issues with which children are familiar. But familiarity can also prompt puzzlement when children bring their own experiences and interpretations of the familiar into the classroom and discover that they differ to the experiences of others.

Lipman (2014) claimed that when children and adolescents are in a state of puzzlement or wonder, provoked by suitable narratives, they find motivation to reason through such an experience in a group setting, for alone 'they find their experience problematic or incomplete, and must join forces with one another if they are to pursue understanding successfully' (p. 12). In this way, they develop 'a tendency to emulate the modes of thought and utterance they find in them' (p. 12). According to Lipman, '[t]he corpus of Plato's writings provides a plethora of such models' (p. 12). Whilst the IAPC stories are not written in dramatic form, as Plato's written dialogues were, they do bear some similarity to their ancient counterparts in offering narratives rich in reasoning of the kind that facilitates dialogue. The narratives act as a model of philosophical practice by depicting child characters engaged in philosophical dialogue with other children and adults. Each of the novels contain the following features:

- A collection of ideas that form the 'spine' of the novel, around which the story is connected.
- The characters are children, with whom the students can identify, who are willing to think and discuss ideas.
- The characters communicate through dialogue and other activities that model the processes of a community of inquiry.
- The dialogue between the characters displays higher-order and reflective thinking characteristic of philosophical dialogue. (Splitter, 2003, p. 42)

Lipman intended the novels to be more than stimuli to provoke philosophical thought and discussion. From an educational point of view, a crucial difference between the novel as a philosophical story-as-text and other stimulus materials, such as children's literature, is that the former 'not only aims to provoke students to raise philosophical issues or questions for discussion, but is also constructed in such a way as to show them how to go about answering such questions and issues' (Cam, 2015, p. 42). The constructed narratives give students a model of philosophical practice through which they 'can learn how to explore recognisably philosophical content in philosophical ways' (Cam, 2015, p. 42). With support from a philosophically trained teacher, students can move between the ideas and situations contained in the story and their own ideas based on their interests. In doing so, Lipman believed that students would internalise and transfer these habits of learning across the school curriculum and, with practice, beyond the classroom into their own communities.

In addition to the novels, the exercises and discussion plans contained in the instructional manuals aid teachers in developing and deepening the discussions based on the wonder the stories provoke; to develop students' understanding of the ideas and concepts through thinking together and connecting them to their own experiences.

> As the conversation brings one or another philosophical notion into focus, the teacher is able to draw upon the resources of instructional manuals which provide discussion plans, reasoning games, and other philosophical activities, so as to lend further structure and direction to the discussion, with the aim of converting the classroom eventually into a community of inquiry.
>
> (Lipman, 2014, p. 10)

It would not be inaccurate to say that the story is intended to be the child's window into the philosophical tradition, and the manual the teacher's.

Lipman and Sharp agreed that the curriculum materials and community of inquiry pedagogy are inextricably linked and provide a model for philosophical practice for teachers and students alike. As Lipman (2004) firmly believed that 'there is no aspect of Dewey's pedagogy that is explicitly rejected or that is not reflected in the Philosophy for Children approach to elementary school education' (p. 8), we can safely assume that he thought Dewey would have approved of the concrete application of philosophy as 'filling in the gap' he had neglected regarding experiential education, namely, the practice of philosophy as the methodology of education. Dewey, of course, used social occupation work to connect experience and synthesise the curriculum, but the activities students performed when engaged in such work functioned as stimuli for thinking and inquiry. Lipman thought that the philosophical stimuli would meet Dewey's requirements, provided there is resonance with the students' own experiences and is accessible to them.

> For Dewey, every classroom session should begin with a cognitive/ affective experience that prompts students to reflect upon it, and to be prepared to reflect upon that process of reflection. In the redesign of philosophy, thinking has been given the highest priority, and it is precisely this concentration upon thinking that makes philosophy invaluable to education.
>
> (Lipman, 2014, p. 11)

It should be noted that Lipman and Sharp were adamant that the use of the materials requires extensive professional development. Nevertheless, there is contention between those who think that the philosophical stories-as-text have greater benefits especially for novice teachers, others who think they are integral to teacher professional development, and still others who think that the quality of training for teachers is the most important factor and that effective stimuli can be found in picture books, children's stories or other appropriate material, provided they can provoke philosophical discussion (albeit some materials may be philosophically richer than others).[3] Opinion is divided, but Sharp's (2017a) view is clear.

> Even though some might believe that approaching philosophical issues through traditional literature is easier than working from these purpose written novels and manuals, I suspect that it is more likely to be the other way around. In most countries, teachers are not prepared in the art and craft of philosophical inquiry. To explore the philosophical dimension of literature, and teaching children to do the same, requires an expertise that cannot be taken for granted, especially given the complexity of a good piece of literature.
>
> (p. 21)

Sharp's words also point to the overriding question of how best to make philosophical progress in the classroom. The answer is neither simple nor straightforward. While it could be argued that the original Lipman philosophical stories-as-text are 'the gold standard for Philosophy for Children story materials' (Cam, 2017, p. 120), the history of philosophy in schools in Australia has shown that of equal or greater importance is the adaptation and production of philosophical resources to fit the culture and political climate (Burgh & Thornton, 2017).[4] Many countries are now producing classroom materials, with philosophers and teachers 'constructing, publishing and piloting philosophical stories for children' (Sharp, 2017b, p. 33). Sharp's belief that the purpose-written story-as-text, epitomised in the IAPC curriculum, is necessary for both teacher education and philosophical progress in the classroom, remains pertinent and continues to be debated in the literature on philosophy in schools. However, an affirmative answer to either side of the debate relies on empirical evidence. As studies comparing the use of materials that follow the format of the original IAPC curriculum and offer the kind of continuity Lipman and Sharp advocated with other purpose-written materials and existing children's literature have not yet been undertaken, the matter cannot be settled. But this does not affect the broader claims that have been made on the benefits of philosophy for children, as the studies cited earlier indicate.

The community of inquiry

The community of inquiry brings together the pedagogical, social, and cognitive elements essential for the facilitation of collaborative dialogic inquiry. The class becomes a community of people who inquire cooperatively and collaboratively in a self-reflective and critical manner about issues of interest to all of them. The participants 'follow the inquiry where it leads and collaboratively engage in self-correction' (Sharp, 1993, p. 57). To convert the classroom into such a community of inquiry is to invite students 'to become aware of themselves as thinkers who make judgements based on reason and criteria' (Splitter, 1991a, pp. 13–14). The community of inquiry is characterised by:

- inquiry aimed at knowledge and understanding,
- intellectual risk-taking and self-correction,
- cooperation, trust, tolerance, and respect,
- a shared sense of puzzlement and wonder,
- student-centred dialogue,
- participants accepting responsibility for their own views, and
- students learning to think for themselves (as opposed to thinking by themselves).

In the community of inquiry, participants share their experiences by thinking and talking about ideas that interest them. The basic arrangement for philosophical inquiry is class discussion, which is student-centred rather than teacher directed. Under the conditions of Vygotskian learning, with guidance from the teacher who facilitates discussion and models the procedures, the class will gradually take on the characteristics of a community of inquiry. The teacher's role is that of a facilitator[5] and co-inquirer (rather than an all-knowing expert or imparter of information) who is responsible for the form of the discussion rather than the specific subject matter. In other words, the philosophy that takes place is generated by all the participants or members in the community of inquiry. Each member brings their own experiences to the discussion. Consequently, the possibilities for nominating what is philosophically interesting are limited only by the constitution of the group. Students are taught how to think (i.e., the main concern of the teacher is to promote the inquiry process) not what to think (i.e., substantive values are not taught, rather, they are the outcomes of the inquiry process). Students do not only learn about philosophy, but in the community of inquiry they *do* philosophy.

Philosophy provides a way of integrating curriculum, teaching, and learning in terms of improved intellectual and social outcomes. Its effectiveness is threefold. First, it can assist schools, teachers, and curriculum planners to engage critically and creatively with the challenges facing education in modern times. Second, in the hands of an experienced teacher as facilitator, it can engage students in an education with meaning and relevance to everyday life. Third, it provides a guiding ideal for classroom practice in teacher education courses and professional development for teachers. Thus stated, the aims and objectives of current education reforms can be met using philosophical inquiry as structured problem-posing and inquiry-based pedagogy. Philosophical inquiry is also conducive to curricula that are based on integrated, community-based tasks and activities that (1) focus on immediate problems in learner's worlds, (2) equip students as future citizens in a democracy, and (3) are aimed at social action that has significance and value to students as active participants in shaping the future.

One practical outcome of understanding how to think philosophically through collaborative inquiry is that it can assist in the development of critical and creative abilities as well as deliberative communication skills. This is because philosophy fosters the ability to think innovatively and imaginatively, to define and analyse problems, to evaluate opinions, make informed decisions, and to reflect critically on the justifications for decisions. It also fosters the ability to convey ideas clearly and fluently, and to interact with others to work towards a common outcome. By understanding what philosophy has to offer through engaging in dialogue with others, the community of inquirers will not only improve the reasoning skills that are essential for making informed judgement, but they will also develop an understanding and attitude towards democratic citizenship. Lipman has described this environment as converting a classroom into a community of inquiry.

The phrase 'to convert the classroom into a community of inquiry' is commonly understood as the use of philosophy as a teaching method to facilitate inquiry-based, community-centred classroom dialogue. However, it has a broader application, as an ideal for the reconstruction of education as inquiry. The community of inquiry as a specific method for fostering philosophical discussion is typically articulated as five stages of inquiry: the offering of the text, the construction of the agenda, solidifying the community, using exercises and discussion plans, and encouraging further responses (Lipman, 1991, pp. 241–243). The method has been described variously by different authors (Burgh, Field & Freakley, 2006; Cam, 2006; Davey Chesters, 2012; Gregory, 2007) and has been adapted by teachers and other practitioners to suit diverse education settings. However, the five stages of inquiry set out in Lipman's educational theory and practice and implicit in the Philosophy for Children curriculum materials still represents the basic standard upon which others draw.

Briefly, it commences with the students sitting in a circle—or equivalent face-to-face arrangement to allow for equality of position with maximum vision within the group—reading a philosophical story-as-text, or other appropriate stimulus, to encourage wonder. As a group, the students identify problems through the generation of questions based on what each of the students finds problematic. Following on, they offer suggestions in response to a central question by expressing their opinions, exploring ideas, stating conjectures, and generating hypotheses to find possible answers, solutions, or explanations. This leads to the analysing of concepts and use of reasoning to develop arguments, so that they gain a deeper understanding of the problems, issues, or topics into which students are inquiring. The teacher's role is to facilitate the substantive discussion through open-ended questioning and the introduction of exercises, discussion plans, and other classroom activities that compel students to inquire further and to connect their questions with the philosophical questions of the tradition and to re-evaluate them. Only after such a thorough investigation is the community of students ready to evaluate their thinking and to bring their deliberations to a close to indicate that the outcome of inquiry has been accepted provisionally (Freakley, Burgh & Tilt MacSporran, 2008, pp. 6–7).

The term 'community of inquiry', when understood as a specific method for classroom practice, distinguishes it from other approaches to teaching and learning. However, it is more than this. The following passage by Lipman (1991) clearly suggests that his aims for the community of inquiry are far-reaching.

> Thus we can now speak of converting the classroom into a community of inquiry in which students listen to one another with respect, build on one another's ideas, challenge one another to supply reasons for otherwise unsupported opinions, assist each other in drawing inferences from what has been said, and seek to identify one another's assumptions. A community of inquiry attempts to follow the inquiry where it leads rather than being penned in by the boundary lines of existing disciplines. A dialogue that rises to conform to logic, it moves forward like a boat tacking into the wind, but in the process its progress comes to resemble that of thinking itself. Consequently, when this process is internalised or introjected by the participants, they come to think as the process thinks.
>
> (p. 15)

This frequently quoted passage has the role of the teacher and the curriculum conspicuously absent (Sprod, 2001, pp. 152–153). The conclusion, however, emphasises the habituation of students into the thought processes of inquiry (hence the emphasis on internalisation and introjection). This is an obvious reference to Vygotsky's zone of proximal development discussed earlier; the distance between what a student learning a skill can do without the assistance of the teacher or someone with more knowledge or expertise and what they can do when assisted by a teacher or someone more skilled. The teacher's role is to assist the students to attain the required skills until the teacher is no longer needed for the task. Progressively, when the characteristic behaviours of the community are internalised, students are more able to think for themselves. In other words, students intersubjectively work toward autonomy. This constructivist process of inquiry is not restricted to the boundary lines of existing disciplines, and, therefore, provides classroom communities of inquiry with opportunities to practice open-ended inquiry within and across disciplines, not as content, but as fields of ongoing inquiry. As the community comprises both the teacher and the students, inquiry tasks both to follow the inquiry wherever it may lead, even if it transgresses traditional subject boundaries. In this way, inquiry has the potential to reconstruct education.

The following passage by Splitter and Sharp (1995) on the idea that every classroom can be converted into a community of inquiry gives a similar impression to Lipman's quote above.

> We believe that all subjects can be taught as forms of inquiry, although we do not pretend to understand how this transformation might take place for each individual discipline and domain. Adult researchers, academics

and practitioners move in and out of the communities of scientific, religious, historical, literary and artistic inquiry that are associated with their work. What we are proposing is that by redefining teaching and learning as inquiry-based activities, children and teachers can participate in this process. This redefinition is the key to improving thinking in all students.

(p. 24)

The role of the teacher as facilitator is implied in this passage by Splitter and Sharp and mirrors what Lipman says elsewhere, dispersed throughout his writing. That is, the teacher and the students, like their professional counterparts, can move in and out of various communities of inquiry that are articulated by the curriculum subjects, but whose knowledge base is informed by the knowledge of each accompanying discipline. But, as Lipman points out, it is more than this, because making such connections is also to gain an understanding of how those disciplines are practiced. Dewey, as you may recall, thought this vital to experiential education, hence the Laboratory School's inclusion of social occupation work to synthesise the curriculum by moving between theory (curriculum subjects) and practice.

As our discussion so far illustrates, to convert the classroom into a community of inquiry requires an understanding of the philosophical and pedagogical components of philosophy for children that can provide insight into Lipman's larger aims for the community of inquiry. Teachers, therefore, need more than a *procedural knowledge* of Lipman's five stages of inquiry. They need to have *pedagogical knowledge*; an understanding of the theory and practice of learning that underpins the community of inquiry. The historical development of in-service training and professional development for teachers and teacher-educators (see Poulton, 2019), and the lack of attention to educational philosophy in pre-service teacher education programs in tertiary institutions (see Bleazby & Slade, 2019), has meant that teachers' understanding is usually limited to procedural knowledge and ability, without a thorough understanding of the epistemological and pedagogical principles that characterise the pragmatism of the community of inquiry necessary for the reconstruction of education. Knowledge of classroom practice can be passed on by transmission, which is not good pedagogical practice and can lead to a lack of teacher confidence in modelling inquiry or becoming co-inquirers as the community of inquiry requires, let alone knowing how to proceed with converting the classroom into a community of inquiry. In addition, there has been very little empirical research conducted on the community of inquiry in teacher education contexts (Brubaker, 2016). We will not pursue the vexed question of how to induct teachers and teacher educators into the theory and practice of philosophy for children, as there is already much written on the topic,[6] except to say that our discussion here and in Chapter 6 will provide theoretical beginnings for others to delve into designing and implementing effective programs for preparing teachers to teach philosophy to pre-college students using dialogical, deliberative pedagogy focused on democratic education. Obviously, any professional development and teacher education program would also need to attend to the theory/practice dualism. It is even more obvious, therefore, that we need to thoroughly understand what Lipman intended when he used the phrase 'converting a classroom into a community of inquiry'.

A useful starting point is to distinguish between the community of inquiry as a specific teaching method for fostering philosophical discussion and the community of inquiry as an ideal for reconstructing education. This is a distinction made by Tim Sprod (2001, pp. 152–156), who refers to the 'narrow-sense' and 'wide-sense' community of inquiry. We have already described the *narrow-sense* community of inquiry as the five stages of inquiry (also called the 'pattern of inquiry') characterised by Lipman for classroom practice. Note that the narrow-sense conception describes any educational setting characterised by the stages of inquiry, such as philosophy in public spaces or co-curricular initiatives (see Prior & Wilks, 2019). The term describes the characteristics of a teaching method that can be augmented by other intervention strategies that enhance teaching and learning, including collaborative learning techniques such as paired discussion and small group work, and research and writing. The more difficult task is to explain what is meant by the wide-sense community of inquiry. It would be impractical, and even ineffective, for classrooms or whole schools to be converted into communities of inquiry if this is taken to mean an approach to education in which communal dialogue is the *only* teaching and learning technique. To interpret what is meant by converting the classroom into a community of inquiry as the *wide-sense* classroom ideal for the reconstruction of education, we will need to go back to the origins of the term 'community of inquiry' as a methodology underpinned by pragmatist epistemology that underscores scholarly (i.e., discipline based) communities of inquiry.

Peirce's influence on educational theory and practice permeates the historical development of the community of inquiry educational discourse. However, he was not responsible for coining the term 'community of inquiry'; he used the terms 'community' and 'inquiry', and community of inquirers, but the term does not appear in his writings. It first appeared in an article co-authored by Lipman and Sharp (1978) in the *Oxford Review of Education*. Lipman credited Sharp with reconstructing the Peircean/Buchlerian notion of community of inquiry into a model of educational practice. Together, they extensively developed the community of inquiry as an approach to teaching that transforms the structure of the classroom in fundamental ways. Their starting point was Peirce's notion of community as a method of investigation, a purposive activity of inquiry, experimentation, and collaboration driven by intelligent curiosity that arises from a 'sense of genuine doubt that signals a rupture in consciousness' (Gregory & Granger, 2012, p. 6). It is a self-corrective process where the exploration of ideas and reasoning are publicly displayed and scrutinised, and it is the site for critical discourse in which new hypothesis are generated and subjected to the most rigorous tests the community can devise. When the community comes together in agreement, we can speak of knowledge, truth, and reality as concepts grounded in the community of inquirers *not* in the individual consciousness (Murphy, 1990, p. 12).

To understand Peirce's pragmatist epistemology, we need to go back even further. Peirce (1868) rejected the philosophical position, forwarded by René Descartes, that we can be clear and distinct about our own thinking and hence that reliable knowledge can be gained from introspection. As Pardales and Girod (2006) attest, 'Peirce believed that philosophy had gone awry with its adoption of a Cartesian view of knowledge' (p. 300). In reaction, he posed a radical new theory of truth, one that did not rely on first principles or epistemic certainty. For Pierce, the world external to the mind existed, but was not known independent of the mind. The world he saw was not illusory or a projection of the mind, rather he believed that what we could say with confidence about the world should be tempered with the knowledge that our perspective is human and limited and, thus, is always fallible.

Along with the notion of fallibility came an emphasis on a methodology for arriving at truth within a community. Enter the notion of the community of inquirers. The only truth to be found in belief is the truth agreed upon by a community through a process of inquiry. For Peirce, inquiry meant the process of scientific inquiry, wherein truth is the conclusion we cannot fail to reach through the employment of mutual processes of inquiry, such as experimentation—the results being rendered by the slice of the world in which the experiment is conducted. The community of inquiry serves as both the arbiter of standards and justification for the construction of reliable knowledge. In Pierce's community of inquiry, it is necessary 'to subject our thinking to standards that lie outside of our own interests, concerns, and reflections. In this way, thinking must continually be subject to a community whose standards allow us to correct and revise our ideas in the course of living our lives' (Pardales & Girod, 2006, p. 302).

Dewey followed Peirce down this path of inquiry by adapting scientific inquiry to larger social concerns, and to education generally. Peirce, unlike Dewey, was hopeful that the conglomeration of constructed knowledge over time would lead to a final understanding of truth. Dewey rejected any hope of unification, in favour of a process of ongoing evolution and reconstruction of knowledge. As Maughn Gregory (2002) notes, Dewey's conception of evolutionary pragmatism, as it relates to the classroom, holds 'that none of the disciplines of human inquiry [are] value neutral—that these disciplines have evolved over generations in response to novel problems and opportunities conceived in relation to human purposes, rather than derived rationally from first principles' (pp. 397–398). Here, Gregory echoes Peirce's and Dewey's insistence on the organic evolution of ideas over time, rather than the reductive 'first principle' certitude Descartes derived from his method. Teaching others to understanding this organic process of reconstruction was of the utmost importance to Dewey (1910), who said that 'if there is any knowledge which is of most worth it is knowledge of the ways by which anything is entitled to be called knowledge instead of being mere opinion or

guess-work or dogma' (p. 395). With this understanding of truth and evolution of the disciplines, it is important 'to prepare students to participate in
that reconstruction' (Gregory, 2002, p. 398), not just within the classroom,
but within the broader community over time.

The test for truth or certainty is not an individual endeavour, but as Peirce
(1868) says, it 'requires us to stand upon a very different platform than this'
(p. 140). The community is that 'different platform' from which we can
achieve significant insight or reliable knowledge.

> In science in which men come to agreement, when a theory has been
> broached, it is considered to be on probation until this agreement is
> reached. After it is reached, the question of certainty becomes an idle
> one, because there is no one left who doubts it. We individually cannot
> reasonably hope to attain the ultimate philosophy which we pursue; we
> can only seek it, therefore, for the *community* of philosophers. Hence,
> if disciplined and candid minds carefully examine a theory and refuse to
> accept it, this ought to create doubts in the mind of the author of the
> theory himself.
>
> (p. 141)

For Pierce, reliable knowledge results from inquiry, which is a rational, scientific process. By scientific inquiry Peirce included all disciplinary-based
inquiry (e.g., science, history, mathematics, philosophy). A community of
inquiry, by virtue of its logic and method of investigation, sets the standards
and the justification for the construction of reliable knowledge. It is the
actual community whose members accept the logic and method of investigation that acts as a deliberative jury between doubt and belief about ideas
or hypotheses.

It is easy to see the historical and theoretical connections that led Lipman and Sharp to adapt Peirce's notion of a discipline-based community
of inquiry to an education setting such as the pre-college philosophy classroom. However, the significant differences between the two communities
of inquiry cannot be ignored. Peter Seixas (1993) points to the limits of
the analogy between what he calls scholarly communities of inquiry and
school-based communities of inquiry (p. 306). Whereas scholarly inquirers
are engaged in the construction of disciplinary knowledge arising out of
their own set of problems embedded within specific contexts and history,
students are not able to do what scholarly inquirers do and, thus, the flow of
knowledge can only be unidirectional (p. 313). Students do not have input
into the scholarly communities of inquiry. What they receive through the
curriculum, textbooks, and the teacher 'is a transformed version of historical
products, which appear to have a different epistemological status from the
work of historians' (p. 314), and other discipline-based inquirers, such as
mathematicians, scientists, philosophers, linguists, and social scientists.

Even if the focus is on the structure and method of scholarly inquiry,
rather than on the knowledge generated, to achieve the necessary abilities to

engage in scholarly inquiry, as Pardales and Girod (2006) explain, students must 'learn, value and begin to practice a common set of procedures and activities that are typical of a community of inquiry' (p. 308). Thus, school-based inquiry has a different focus than that of scholarly inquiry. Unlike scholarly inquirers, students are not engaged in inquiry voluntarily, they are not necessarily practised inquirers before they enter school, and they do not, at the outset, represent the shared values of scholarship and participation. In virtue of its function as an educative activity, a school-based community of inquiry emphasises teacher-facilitated inquiry where mutual respect and concern for all participants are paramount, and progressively 'as the community becomes more skilled and begins to gain confidence, the teacher takes a less active role in the inquiry' (p. 304).

On this account, in formal education settings the narrow-sense community of inquiry is restricted to the procedures of the school-based community of inquiry (i.e., the pattern of inquiry that guides discussion) which seemingly differ from the scholarly communities of inquiry. To add to the list as to why the analogy does not hold, it can be argued that scholarly communities of inquiry are conducted over global sites through a combination of many activities, which do not always involve sitting in a circle or communication between members of the community, and in some cases require work to be done in isolation before consulting again with the community. These inquiries are conducted by international communities of experts whose tasks include keeping abreast of current research, for example, working in small research teams engaging in solitary experimentation, attending conferences, and consulting with other experts in the field as well as allied fields. Yet, despite the seeming disanalogy, it cannot be ignored that the social aspect is also vital to such an inquiry. Sprod (2001) highlights this in his description of scientific inquiry.

> What we call 'scientific objectivity' is not a product of the individual scientist's impartiality, but a product of the social or public character of scientific method; and the individual scientist's impartiality is, so far as it exists, not the source but rather the result of this socially or institutionally organized objectivity of science.
>
> (p. 154)

There are also other products of such a community of inquiry, for example, methodologies, conventional standards, conceptual schema, and interpretations of mathematical formalisms. These products are the result of communications in which other experts in the profession participate, including raising questions, suggesting and exploring alternatives, exploring flaws in data, methods and analysis, giving reasons, identifying assumptions, and other procedural aspects of inquiry, which all happen informally in the form of conferring with colleagues, and formally at conferences or in journal publications. As Sprod says, '[i]n this part of the scientific community of inquiry, the parallels to the discussion stages of the classroom narrow-sense community of inquiry are strongest' (p. 154).

So far, we have seen that in a school-based community of inquiry students cannot really engage in the kind of wide-sense community of inquiry Peirce spoke of until they learn, value, and begin to practise a common set of procedures and activities that are typical of a scholarly community of inquiry. It would be reasonable, therefore, to favour an interpretation of the school-based community of inquiry as a place to build the skills of inquiry which act as a foundation for scholarly inquiry whereby content is 'enlivened and enriched by the ongoing process of inquiry' (Splitter & Sharp, 1995, p. 24). It is a place to initiate students into the knowledge, skills, and dispositions, which are predetermined by the practitioners of the disciplinary areas, that get transformed into the school curriculum so that they come to appreciate that these disciplines are themselves forms of inquiry and 'interconnected in various ways, not entirely unconnected—as the traditional school timetable would lead them to believe' (Splitter & Sharp, 1995, p. 25). This is closer in approximation to the scholarly community of inquiry outlined by Peirce and, therefore, closer to what Lipman, and Splitter and Sharp had in mind by converting a classroom into a community of inquiry as a wide-sense classroom ideal for reconstructing education.

It is noteworthy that the school-based and scholarly communities of inquiry both share the communal and deliberative aspects (i.e., the social aspects Sprod mentions) that are vital to the inquiry process. The community of inquiry, in both cases, sets the standards and the justification for the construction of reliable knowledge. Taking this and other similarities raised above into consideration, we can reinterpret Splitter and Sharp's belief, quoted in the previous section, that 'all subjects can be taught as forms of inquiry' in the following way: The wide-sense ideal for reconstructing education informs the theoretical framework of the community of inquiry, and when applied to the classroom provides pedagogical principles and guidelines for the process of students moving between the classroom community of inquiry and the discipline-based inquiries of adult researchers, academics, and practitioners, and, thus, converting the classroom into a community of inquiry by redefining education (or specifically, teaching and learning) as inquiry aimed at social reconstruction.

Thus, an effective way to deal with the seeming tension between the two senses of the community of inquiry is to make a distinction between the community of inquiry as a specific *teaching method* for fostering philosophical discussion in the classroom and as a *pedagogical framework* that describes the ideal of education as inquiry. The wider-sense conception in an educational setting is a statement *about* education, which has its foundations in Lipman and Sharp's reconstruction of the community of inquiry that draws heavily on Peirce, and, therefore, contains preconditions which act as pedagogical guidelines for teaching methods and classroom practice characterised by the stages of inquiry. These educational preconditions are grounded in an epistemology of community as reflective equilibrium. This equilibrium is suitably described as fallibilistic because the community is constantly open to new ideas, to revision, to improvement, and most of all to self-correction.

Rejected in practice is the search for foundational knowledge and absolute truth, replaced by the interplay between equilibrium and disequilibrium that is necessary to dialogue (we provide further discussion on this interplay in relation to the role of doubt in inquiry in Chapter 5). In terms of usefulness as a description of what teachers should be striving for in classroom practice, the wide-sense conception of inquiry serves the purpose of giving us a broader understanding of dialogue as a collaborative, reflective process, with reconstruction as its outcome.

To facilitate effective reconstruction in the classroom, teachers need to be aware of the relationship between the theoretical framework of the community of inquiry (wide-sense conception) that provides pedagogical principles and guidelines and the specific teaching method for fostering philosophical discussion (narrow-sense conception). A teacher versed only in the practice of Lipman's five stages of inquiry is unable to engage in effective inquiry as they lack a full understanding of the theory and practice of learning in a community of inquiry. In addition, without a thorough understanding of the potential blocks to inquiry that prevent deliberative communication, teachers will be ill-equipped to undertake the reconstruction of education that the wide-sense community of inquiry calls for. We will return, in greater detail, to the role of the educator in the next section.

One last, but important, word before we move onto the next part of our discussion on the dual role of the teacher in inquiry. Sprod (2001) cautions against conflating the narrow-sense and wide-sense conceptions of the community of inquiry. The conflation of the meaning of the term 'converting the classroom into a community of inquiry' to mean, on the one hand, 'a specific method for fostering philosophical discussion and critical discourse', and, on the other hand, the 'ideal for the transformation of education', he says, 'is a confusing and unnecessary one' and, thus, he recommends that the 'concept of converting into a wide-sense community of inquiry ought to be marked by a different phrase' (p. 156). His caution deserves consideration in terms of retaining the meaning of the narrow-sense community of inquiry as a teaching method, but whatever term we choose to substitute for the wide-sense conception, the teacher must understand the relationship between the two meanings. In the absence of another term, the two meanings can be separated by their function, which allows teachers to understand why, how, and when to move between the two communities. Whilst we, perhaps, should not conflate them conceptually, for the community of inquiry to achieve what Dewey and Lipman intended, teachers need to be active in both by mediating between them (Gregory, 2002; Seixas, 1993).

Teachers, therefore, should not lose sight of the wide-sense conception as it informs the methods used in teaching practice by being aware of the theory and practice needed to reconstruct education. After all, Lipman's task for the community of inquiry is to develop students' social and intellectual capacities and dispositions to engage in deliberative communication, which is done through adult mediation *between the culture and the child*. This brings us back to the broader implications of the community of inquiry. Recall

Lipman's emphasis on the practice of philosophy as the methodology of education. For Lipman, this is the impetus for the reconstruction of education as inquiry. To achieve this educational ideal, the community of inquiry's theoretical framework provides the pedagogical principles and guidelines for classroom practice to create meaningful (collaborative-constructivist) learning experiences. This includes, first and foremost, taking into consideration theories of learning, which for Lipman are provided in the pedagogical principles set out in his theoretical writings for the reconstruction of education.

The dual role of the teacher

The wide-sense conception of the community of inquiry, as we've seen, can be viewed as both the organising or regulative principle of scholarly communities of inquiry and a classroom-wide ideal for the reconstruction of education. The two are, of course, connected as they share the same constructivist epistemology and methodology and, thus, teachers need to know how they function as they are 'responsible for structuring the learning experiences of the classroom members' (Seixas, 1993, p. 312). The community of inquiry is a reflective pedagogy that has, as its core, authentic learning as self-correction. It is, as Gregory (2002) notes, a constructivist pedagogy as it engages 'students in processes of inquiry in which they construct their understanding of a topic by means of investigation, application, experimentation, and most importantly, through dialogue with teachers, experts, and other students' (p. 400). Crucial to the process is that students are immersed in problematic aspects of their experience to enable them to engage more meaningfully with these experiences. The community of inquiry, by activating students' interests in learning through their own active intelligence in developing and testing their own ideas and hypothesis as a group, and engaging in self-correction, their experiences, including their habits of thought, feelings, and actions, are reconstructed as more meaningful and can be viewed as a form of self-directed identity formation, as opposed to assimilationist pedagogies.

Central to the practice of engaging students in collaborative dialogue is an appreciation of the philosophical implications of students' philosophical discourse and sensitivity to the immediate concerns of classroom practice. Thus, an important factor for teaching in a community of inquiry is a skilled philosophical facilitator, which Gregory (2008), defines as a teacher 'who listens to children with a sensitive ear; who thinks and feels carefully, and is transparent in doing so; who is procedurally rigorous but is comfortable with ambiguity' (p. 9). Equally important is an awareness of the interplay between philosophical inquiry and the disciplines that inform the subject matter of the curriculum—to think of these disciplines also as fields of ongoing inquiry. Such thinking requires a reconceptualisation of the teacher's role.

Gregory (2002) meets this challenge by calling 'for teachers to mediate between communities of students and communities of experts, by being active participants in both' (p. 403). He refers to Seixas' (1993) claim that the teacher's subject knowledge 'entails a bridge between communities' that extends outward to scholars in the disciplines (experts) 'in one direction and to students in another' (p. 316). Nevertheless, Gregory (2002) acknowledges the asymmetry in the positions of the participants in each community of inquiry, specifically the pedagogic role of the school-based community of inquiry that is absent in its scholarly counterpart. To bridge the gap, he provides an account of six important similarities, which we summarise here: (1) the teacher's role like the expert is to construct the experience and knowledge of others into a meaningful experience, (2) there is a dialogue between the participants over new ideas, (3) both the teacher and the experts listen to and are open to the ideas of others, (4) the participants must follow the argument where it leads, (5) the inquiry is a form of meta-level inquiry or meta-dialogue, and (6) summative evaluation is used to preserve the standards of the norms that remain intelligible and valuable (pp. 403–407). These similarities are crucial to reconciling the problem of the teacher's role in a community of inquiry with education toward disciplinary-based standards, 'so long as learning is understood as an appropriation of predetermined standards that involves student self-correction and self-verification' (p. 407). This requires, first and foremost, that constructivist pedagogy in the form of the community of inquiry is seen 'as an apprenticeship in self-correction, in which the students' capacity to construct and verify new knowledge for themselves within a discipline becomes increasingly informed by the norms of that discipline' (p. 407).

Gregory describes this kind of 'apprenticeship' as students gradually gaining proficiency in the processes and tools of inquiry that enable them 'to perform interpersonal correction such as noticing one another's fallacies, building on one another's examples and interpretations, evaluating one another's arguments, and replicating one another's experiments' (p. 408). This interpersonal feedback requires teachers to work within students' zone of proximal development so that gradually less teacher intervention is necessary—an indication of students' disciplinary maturity. The process of collaborative interpersonal correction eventually 'gives rise to a more significant feat: collective self-evaluation by students of both the outcomes and the procedures of their inquiry' (p. 408). Together, the student self-evaluations and teacher evaluations 'signals the readiness of such a classroom community to embark on student/teacher co-inquiry within a discipline on some realm of experience' (p. 408). Formative assessment is not external to this process but is part of the process itself, for which the aim is to 'prompt students to rethink and inquire further' (p. 408).

The upshot of reconceptualising the teacher's role in a community of inquiry is that the teacher takes on a dual role. The teacher is a co-inquirer who engages in the problems, both epistemological and methodological, of the scholarly community of inquiry, and a facilitator of classroom discussion focused on dialogue and intellectual self-correction aimed at reconstructing the experience and knowledge of students into a form that is meaningful to their lives. To these ends, the teacher needs to ensure there is 'dialogue between proponents of new ideas (including methods and values)' that includes 'a complex process of inquiry that might involve discussion, investigation, and experimentation, depending on the discipline and the nature of the new ideas' (p. 403). As we pointed out earlier, to fulfil these roles, teachers not only need to be skilled philosophical facilitators, but also have an appreciation of curriculum subjects as disciplinary fields of ongoing inquiry, in order to mediate between the two communities and to ensure that the classroom inquiry proceeds in the same manner as the scholarly inquiries.

On to our final point, which we touched on earlier: the interplay between the teacher as co-inquirer and facilitator. Recall, as a constructivist pedagogy, the community of inquiry is committed to following the inquiry where it leads, rather than the teacher leading inquiry within the confines of existing discipline boundaries or toward predetermined outcomes. The teacher's pedagogical responsibility is, therefore, significant; to navigate between the narrow-sense and wide-sense communities of inquiry, which demands that they have knowledge of how both inquiries function, independently and together, in a classroom that fosters philosophical discussion.

The teacher's role is associated with (1) accredited membership to the teaching profession and responsibility for teaching towards the standards of what students are expected to learn, (2) pedagogical ability, and (3) discipline-based knowledge in one or more curriculum areas of study (e.g., history, geography, mathematics, science, humanities). In the first instance, teachers are responsible to meet the standards of the school, professional teaching bodies, and the state. Ultimate responsibility rests with teachers to meet the educational standards set, including summative evaluation, which 'gives the teacher, the school, and the profession unilateral evaluative authority over the student' (p. 407). In this capacity, teachers in schools other than progressive school, such as Summerhill, have authority external to their pedagogical role and, therefore, there exists a power imbalance between the teacher and the students. Students are expected to meet educational standards, some of which may serve no pedagogical purpose whatsoever, but nonetheless the teacher, as a member of the profession of teaching, must apply the standards expected of them by parents and the state. An analysis of this role is beyond the scope of the book. We mention it here only to indicate that teachers face challenges regarding their autonomy in their capacity as members of a profession subject to education policies and other regulations. These are matters of education reform that have bearing on the implementation of democratic education and need to be considered. We note these restrictions here as they can affect teachers' autonomy in their roles as pedagogues and professional members of their scholarly community.

As an accredited member of the teaching profession, teachers also have their own pedagogical expertise. As Gregory (2008) notes, teachers bring many 'advantages to the role of facilitator of children in philosophical dialogue' (p. 11). They have expertise in classroom management, developing rapport with the students, conducting group conversations, and one of more curriculum areas to assist students to 'make connection between philosophy and the other disciplines' (p. 11). Such expertise provides teachers with the skills and knowledge to create supportive learning environments. However, as mentioned earlier, Gregory also claims that '[p]erhaps the most important factor is the skilled philosophical facilitator'; a teacher who listens to students 'with a sensitive ear; who thinks and feels carefully, and is transparent in doing so; who is procedurally rigorous but is comfortable with ambiguity' (p. 9). What we can take from the list of skills for the facilitation of a community of inquiry is that the pedagogical role is primarily a procedural one, with teachers responsible for the structuring of students' learning experiences into a form that is meaningful. The teacher initiates students into the methods of inquiry, develops their appreciation of fallibilism, with the goal of reconstructing students' experiences and knowledge through self-correction. Put another way, the teacher's role as facilitator of the inquiry process 'lies in turning discussion to the best educational advantage' (Cam, 1995, p. 41).

While, procedurally, facilitating dialogue is not a simple matter of 'following a checklist or rehearsing a script (Gregory, 2007, p. 60), Lipman's stages of inquiry are generally followed, although teachers have variously adapted them in practice. According to Lipman, teachers do not present themselves as an authority on any subject or as an all-knowing expert (Splitter, 1987, p. 5). It is not their role to settle disputes over differences of opinion, nor is it their role to express their views as having more weight than that of the students. Because the process of discussion is communicative, and in a Deweyan sense educative, any stifling of dialogue creates obstacles to open-ended inquiry, including teachers who present themselves as experts on the content of the subject. This does not mean that teachers should not express their own views during discussion. What it does mean is that they should exercise caution when doing so and present their view as another perspective *alongside* the students' views. This brings us to our next point: the role of the teacher as co-inquirer.

The role of co-inquirer requires teachers to draw on their knowledge and expertise associated with the community of scholars in their discipline (e.g., history, geography, mathematics, science, humanities), alongside the role of facilitator, to make philosophical connections between curriculum content that might otherwise go unappreciated. As a co-inquirer, the teacher needs to be sensitive to the content, as well as to the context, of the discussion. In this role, the teacher is actively engaged in the inquiry with students, but, unlike the students, is a participant already initiated into the discipline(s). However, the teacher's task is not to impart facts, but to engage students in the discipline(s) as fields of inquiry. Simultaneously the teacher is responsible for facilitating the process of inquiry—the procedural aspects of discussion that Lipman initially detailed in his five stages of inquiry. In other words, the teacher mediates between the school-based and scholarly communities of inquiry by actively participating in both. In doing so, the teacher strikes a balance between encouraging students to be conscious of the procedures of inquiry and allowing them to think for themselves.

It might appear that responsibility for the development of the community of inquiry should rest solely on the shoulders of teachers. But this would be a mistake. Initially, teachers will have greater input into modelling the inquiry process, but over time all participants will become more aware of where the discussion *is*, where it has *been* and where it is *going*. An ideal community of inquiry will evolve into a self-directing and self-correcting community, with direct interaction between the participants as they collaboratively explore the issues raised throughout discussion and facilitate its progress. Eventually students may, themselves, become, members of a scholarly community of inquiry as professionals with expertise in their field of inquiry. As Gregory (2002) writes:

> Students begin as outsiders to a discipline, unable to practice its norms, so that experts in the discipline are not obliged to justify their knowledge to them. However, the better students learn the discipline, the more experts are obliged to engage with them, to give their judgments serious consideration. At some point the students may *become* experts.
>
> (p. 405)

We are not suggesting that the only purpose of the classroom community of inquiry is to ensure all students become 'experts', although it is one of them. Rather, Lipman's quote is intended to illustrate 'growth' in the community of inquiry over time, which has impact and can provide benefits for its participants, and thereby to the greater communities of which they are a part. The teacher is both facilitator and co-inquirer who is a 'witness to the growing maturity of the students, whose reasons are more and more like the kind that experts could use to correct themselves [i.e., scholarly community of inquiry]' (p. 405).

To recap, the wide-sense community of inquiry, as practiced by scholars in discipline-based inquiries, not only produces knowledge that finds its way into curricula but provides the epistemological and methodological framework for the reconstruction of education. To convert the classroom into a community of inquiry, the school-based community of inquiry—a specific teaching method for the facilitation of philosophical dialogue—must be driven by the pedagogical principles Lipman and Sharp adapted to education that were derived from the scholarly, discipline-based communities of inquiry. This requires teachers to not only have a procedural understanding of how to facilitate philosophical inquiry, but to also understand their dual role as co-inquirers to mediate between the two communities of inquiry. Whilst teachers are not fully-fledged members of the scholarly communities, insofar as they are not usually engaged in the methodologically diverse inquiries of scientists, historians, mathematicians, and other knowledge-producing disciplines, they are accredited members of the teaching profession and have familiarity with the knowledge and methodologies currently warranted by the disciplines that inform curriculum content and textbooks—typically through teacher preparation programs, in-service and professional development, journal subscriptions, and membership to teaching associations[7] that represent their subject specific domain. Together with their pedagogical ability, this makes them unique in moving between both communities and to be able to facilitate student learning through self-correcting open inquiry to 'close the gap' between the two communities. In this way, they *are* converting the classroom into a community of inquiry as the boundary between classroom and the greater community becomes more fluid. As scholarly communities of inquiry also inform and are informed by professional, social, and political institutions that make up the greater community, converting the classroom into a community of inquiry as the reconstruction of education is also the impetus for social reconstruction—it is, as Lipman says, an exemplar of democracy in action. The relationship between pragmatist theory, reconstruction, and democratic education is further explored in the next section.

A reconstructionist and pragmatist interpretation of the community of inquiry

An understanding of the wide-sense conception of the community of inquiry as both an organising or regulative principle of scholarly inquiry and a class-wide ideal for the reconstruction of education assumes a certain interpretation of Dewey's general theory of education. Although Dewey's thoughts have been variously interpreted as progressivism, reconstructionism, and neo-pragmatism (Englund, 2000), we argue that converting a classroom into a community of inquiry makes sense only if his general theory of education, which informs the pedagogy of the community of inquiry, is taken to have elements of reconstructionism and neo-pragmatism. This is crucial for an understanding of the theory and practice of converting a classroom into a community of inquiry and the dual role of the teacher. So, we examine the three ways Dewey can be interpreted and what the implications are for each. We argue that neither is sufficient, and that both the reconstructionist and pragmatist account is required. In this way, the interpretation is congruent with democratic education as communication and deliberation, which in turn informs what it means to convert a classroom into a community of inquiry as a process of reconstructing education.

Progressivism is underpinned by the belief that the aim of education is to change school practice. As previously indicated, Dewey distanced himself from the progressive education movement. In spite of this, his theories are still important and relevant to progressive educators today, especially his understanding of the process of upbringing and teaching as an end-in-itself, articulated as 'since growth is the characteristic of life, education is all the one with growing; it has no end beyond itself' (Dewey, 1916, p. 53). For many progressivists, this means that schools should reflect the life of the society as a way of preparing students for active participation in a democratic, global society—typically the schools are self-regulating, self-governing schools, and follow the principles of freedom-based education. So how can progressivism inform our understanding of the phrase 'converting the classroom into a community of inquiry'? The wide-sense conception of the community of inquiry as both a regulative principle of scholarly inquiry and a class-wide ideal for the reconstruction of education could be interpreted simply as pedagogy for changing school practice. But this is hardly informative as it tells us nothing about how progressive pedagogy or teaching methods can bring about such changes, especially as the progressive movement has been somewhat vague about methods and how they might achieve education reform. As it is uninformative and, therefore, provides no principles or pedagogical guidelines, we move onto reconstructionism.

Both progressivism and reconstructionism share a concern for education as change. Whereas progressivism is directly aimed at schooling practices and curriculum to develop individual capacities, reconstructionism emphasises the societal role of the school through its use of democracy as the reference point for schools to develop the participatory capacities and dispositions in students to ensure the ongoing development of society. Seen in this way, reconstructionism views schooling as contributing 'to the development of pupils' interest in societal questions by focusing on possibilities for everyone understanding the kind of issues involved in such questions and opportunities for discussion of controversial questions offering' (Englund, 2000, p. 307). It advocates education as an instrument for change; a view that can be traced back to Dewey's fundamental concern that school and civil society needed attention to strengthen democracy. Democracy in its social form, as a mode of associated living, could only be obtained through a civil society in which citizens have the social and intellectual capacities and dispositions for deliberative communication to form public opinion. Dewey (1916) highlights this: 'Since education is a social process, and there are many kinds of societies, a criterion for educational criticism and construction implies a *particular* social ideal' (p. 105). Reconstructionism, then, is concerned with the reconstruction of civil society as the root of democracy, which has as its beginning point the reconstruction of student thinking, or more broadly, the reconstruction of education. To speak of converting the classroom into a community of inquiry can now be interpreted as fostering students' capacity to form opinions about democratic ways of life; to encourage experimental intelligence and plurality as a way of reconstructing society via education. The method to bring this about is the narrow-sense community of inquiry, but the pedagogy that underscores this method is one of reconstruction. Reconstructionism, therefore, brings the narrow-sense and wide-sense conceptions of the community of inquiry closer together, insofar as both share in the aim of transforming society. But it does not tell us how to convert the classroom into a community of inquiry. For this, we need to also incorporate a neo-pragmatist interpretation.

Dewey reveals pragmatist convictions when he says '[t]he two points selected by which to measure the worth of a form of social life are the extent to which the interests of a group are shared by all its members, and the fullness and freedom with which it interacts with other groups' (p. 105). According to Thomas Englund (2000), seen from a neo-pragmatist perspective, these words emphasise the importance of communication (p. 137). We will take the liberty to embellish on Englund's claim and emphasise collective communication to highlight the importance that Dewey placed on communication as communal dialogue. Democracy is just one side of the Deweyan education coin; the other, as we noted previously, is to be accomplished through effective communication, not just among its citizens, but also among experts in the disciplines and political representatives. This is achieved through education as communication as social life is communicative.

Neo-pragmatism is best understood as emphasising Dewey's attention to dissolving the public/private dualism by stressing the inseparable connection between private and public interests, which, as we discussed in Chapter 1, is severed in classical liberal theory with the private sense of identity (the individual with private interests) and the public citizen (with collective responsibilities). In doing so, he provided the epistemological justification for democracy as a form of communal deliberation. Dewey's attempt to dissolve the public/private dualism was to create a public philosophy (Englund, 2000, p. 308), whereby democracy is a communicative and argumentative consensual process of citizens testing diverse ideas in open and reflective inquiry. Neo-pragmatism, or what is generally referred to as the pragmatic renaissance, has, placed emphasis back on the pragmatism of Dewey and highlighted the importance of his predecessors, especially Peirce. This has allowed for an emphasis on Dewey's notion of communication, which is present it his educative ideal of communal dialogue as being identical with social life. Democracy's legitimacy, therefore, does not rest on an external, pre-political authority (i.e., universal or absolute foundations), but on procedural justification of intersubjective communication and shared practice (see Barber, 1996; Dahl, 1996; Gutmann, 1996; Rorty, 1996).

If we account for both the reconstructionist and the pragmatist interpretations of Dewey's general theory of education, then the phrase 'converting the classroom into a community of inquiry' becomes more informative. We reiterate our previous claim. To convert the classroom into a community of inquiry is to foster in students the capacity to form opinions about democratic ways of life; to encourage experimental intelligence and plurality as a way of transforming or reconstructing society (reconstructionism). But it is also accomplished through education as effective communication which is exemplified by communal dialogue (pragmatism). The method to bring this about is the narrow-sense community of inquiry, but the pedagogy that underscores this method is a combination of reconstruction and pragmatism. It is an educative ideal that moves between the classroom and civil society. This perspective explains social integration as a 'communicative and argumentative consensual process' (Englund, 2000, p. 310) that is an ongoing educative process. It also explains the pedagogical directive of the wide-sense community of inquiry in relation to the narrow-sense community of inquiry, insofar as they share in the aim of reconstructing society through communicative action. Both senses of the community of inquiry have as their requirement an educative role, albeit the role of the facilitator in the narrow-sense conception of the community of inquiry rests with the teacher to cultivate the dispositions of the students with the aim of a wide-sense classroom-wide ideal for the reconstruction of education, whereas in civil society the communicative task is distributed among all citizens whereby citizenship becomes a cultural learning process. This also applies to the professional and expert communities of inquiry where the community also has an educative role to play, including scientific and other scholarly communities in which dialogue itself allows open communication among professionals and between professions, as well as with the greater community.

Accordingly, for this account of the community of inquiry to be effective it must integrate experiential education as a practical component with communal inquiry to facilitate learning outcomes which may lead to social reconstruction. There might be a temptation to say that the curriculum materials, if in the hands of an experienced teacher, can make real-world connections between the students' experiences, the fictional characters, and the philosophical concepts under discussion. Even without the philosophical stories-as-text or teacher manuals, it is not unreasonable to assume this can happen, although without the didactic purpose of the novels and teacher manuals, the onus is solely on teacher training and professional development. Nevertheless, Lipman's integration of philosophy into the curriculum and pedagogy does not fully appreciate Dewey's notion of communal inquiry as social reconstruction. In his admission that philosophy for children owes a debt to Dewey, Lipman says that 'his suggestions as to how it could be used would have been invaluable' (p. 8). So, before we bring this chapter to a close, we offer some suggestions of our own, commencing with Bleazby's (2013) social reconstruction learning 'to incorporate the practical, active dimension of inquiry' (p. 159).

A Deweyan reconstruction of philosophy for children

In her book, *Social Reconstruction Learning: Dualism, Dewey and Philosophy in Schools*, Bleazby (2013) stresses Dewey's commitment to reconstructing the theory/practice dualism that was demonstrated at his Laboratory School 'where students learnt through undertaking practical, "hands-on" activities like sewing, building, gardening and so on' (p. 154). As our discussion in Chapter 3 illustrates, Dewey's emphasis on practical learning was central to his approach to experiential education. While the Laboratory School has received much scholarly attention, this has not generally been the case with proponent of philosophy for children. Bleazby's work on what she calls 'social reconstruction learning' is, therefore, a welcome critique of Lipman's '*substantive* criteria upon which Philosophy for Children insists', and of 'the *pedagogical* criteria upon which Dewey insists' (Lipman, 2004, p. 6). We share Bleazby's (2013) concerns that '[w]hile Lipman reiterates Dewey's rejection of theory/practice dualism, Philosophy for Children (P4C) does not involve students participating in the same type of active transformation of their environment as a part of the inquiry process' (p. 154). She goes on further to say that not only is philosophy for children's 'lack of practicality inconsistent with Lipman's pragmatism, but it is educationally problematic'

(p. 154). The failure of philosophy for children to overcome the theory/practice dualism, she says, 'undermines its commitment to foster reflective thinking, active citizenship, democracy and a pragmatic attitude that is essential for living a meaningful life' (p. 154).

It is puzzling why Lipman, like Dewey, rejected the theory/practice dualism, but unlike Dewey, the pedagogy and curriculum materials Lipman developed 'do not include the type of hands-on, practical problem solving activities that students were engaged in at the Laboratory School' (p. 156). Rather than students actively reconstructing their learning environment, as we have seen, a philosophy for children class involves 'the shared reading of a narrative, containing philosophically puzzling ideas, followed by a classroom communal inquiry initiated by student questions and responses to the text' (p. 156). While the expectation is that the ideas, methods and solutions the students have developed in their communities of inquiry will result in the reconstruction of their experiences and, thus, their behaviours, there is no requirement to apply them to real-world problems as part of the inquiry process.

> For example, they are not required to identify real cases of injustice in the school (e.g., bullying) or wider community (e.g., Third World poverty) and take action to transform the unjust situation in some way. While some P4C teachers probably do use P4C as a launching pad for such transformative action, this is not a standard feature of P4C pedagogy and curriculum.
>
> (p. 157)

To Bleazby, this demonstrates that philosophy for children 'has not fully overcome the problematic theory/practice, mind/body, thought/action, abstract/concrete dualisms inherent in traditional education and epistemology', as the reconstruction of experience requires the simultaneous use of concrete, abstract, practical, theoretical, experiential, reasonable, emotional, and imaginative capacities (p. 157). Curiously, Lipman (2003), himself, writes that '[s]tudents would think better if they could be provided with conditions that would encourage the application of their thinking to the world in which they lived' (p. 208). Yet, his call for converting the classroom into a community of inquiry entails mediating between the narrow-sense and wide-sense conceptions of inquiry—one way to achieve this is for students to engage with real-world issues of importance to them. As Lipman intended that the reconstruction of students' experiences transfer beyond the classroom, surely this involves testing and applying ideas to students' experiences in the local communities. Bleazby (2013) is correct to say that '[d]ialogue, as important as it is, does not constitute transformative action, application or changed behaviour' (p. 157). Indeed, the original IAPC curriculum 'avoids substantive issues of immediate concern to students by creating a totally artificial environment, rather than one that uses real cases, as the basis for discussion' (Burgh, Field & Freakley, 2006, p. 101). Students may relate to the fictional characters in the narratives of the novels, but the characters are decontextualised. It seems that Lipman relies on students transferring their experiences, as if they will naturally flow from classroom discussion into their lives outside of school, rather than giving them actual experiences of prob- lematising situations within the context that they occur.

A related concern that Bleazby (2013) raises is that 'by not requiring students to go out into the greater community and engage in transform- ative action, P4C perpetuates the dominant belief that students are merely future citizens, incapable of positively contributing to their community' (p. 158). This is contrary to Dewey's (1916) position that hinges on 'the idea of continuous reconstruction of experience, an idea which is marked off from education as preparation for a remote future' (p. 80). Moreover, fostering autonomy and active citizenship is one of philosophy for children's stated goals (Lipman, 1988; Splitter & Sharp 1995; Sharp 1991). By not taking the community of inquiry outside of classroom discussion and the world of fictional characters, Lipman undermines his own claim that the community of inquiry is an exemplar of democracy in action. As Bleazby (2013) puts it, Dewey's 'notion of democracy that P4C embraces necessitates intercultural inquiry. The classroom Community of Inquiry must engage in inquiry with diverse communities beyond the classroom in order to be democratic in this sense' (p. 159). Failure to do so leads to another problem Bleazby identifies:

> Since P4C participants do not have to take action, there is nothing to really stop them from going around in circles, endlessly criticising, reject- ing arguments and opinions and settling for relativism. Questioning and being critical is good but not if it merely leads to indecisiveness, a lack of practicality, a constant search for perfect solutions or a failure to come up with positive theories and ideas that enable transformative action.
>
> (p. 160)

Her solution is to introduce service learning to philosophy for chil- dren. She uses the term 'social reconstruction learning' to capture Dew- ey's notion of experiential education to differentiate it from traditional approaches to service learning and to capture 'the critical, collaborative, reciprocal, inquiry-based and transformative action that characterises the critical approach' (p. 179).

Experiential education, as a philosophy of education, has found its way into various practical approaches to learning; for example, it might involve scientific experiments, productive labour, or a kind of service learning, usually work experience or community service activities. Service learning is the most common of these; Dewey's interdisciplinary theme of social occupations being an early historical example that still provides a theoret- ical foundation for service learning today. Typically, students engage in community service to provide them with intellectual skills such as criti- cal thinking or civic learning outcomes such as cultural self-awareness or ethical decision-making. Service learning can also include making positive contributions to the local community. However, not all service learning is compatible with the aims of philosophy for children. As Bleazby notes, traditional service learning 'is politically conservative and prioritises the student's educational needs over the needs of the community', while critical and social justice approaches concentrate on 'bringing about genuine social change and reflects a more progressive political ideology' (p. 154). Put another way, traditional service learning focuses on charity, or a service offered to the community that 'is not actually intended to transform problematic or unjust social structures or conditions', with the aim of alleviating the symptoms, rather than transform the root causes of social problems as critical service learning aims to do (p. 163). The latter account, she says, is congruent with a pragmatist conception of the community of inquiry, which emphasises deliberative communication, and is consistent with Dewey's conception of communal inquiry as a process of constructing and applying ideas that aim at real social change.

The critical or social justice approach to service learning has come under criticism for several reasons: (1) students may take action that is ineffective or detrimental to the community, (2) there is a lack of attention to explicitly teaching or scaffolding of inquiry skills, (3) it lacks clear procedural guidelines for fostering collaborative communities needed for social reconstruction, (4) it could lead to political indoctrination, and (5) it is not always suitable for children and adolescents. Not all the criticisms are warranted, as Bleazby explains (pp. 176–180). These criticisms are due partly to undeveloped theoretical foundations, resulting in confusion over the aims, objectives, and methods, as well as the different meanings the term 'service learning' carries, which in practice results in variations in its nature and quality. Further confusion arises because Dewey has frequently appeared as a significant figure in the history and literature of service learning. This is not surprising '[g]iven Dewey's emphasis on reflective action, experiential learning, and connecting schools to the wider community', although 'Dewey himself did not explicitly recommend that students engage in community service as a regular part of their schooling' (p. 162). Nevertheless, these criticisms do point to some weaknesses in the theory and practice of critical service learning. Hence, Bleazby prefers the term social reconstruction—which has its theoretical roots in Dewey's notion of education as the continuous social and personal reconstruction and reorganisation of experience—to indicate how it differs from both traditional and critical service learning approaches that are theoretically incongruent. Taking this approach, she proposes that philosophy for children 'can be much improved through incorporating critical service learning', and that it 'can help critical service learning overcome some of its problems', and, thus, both 'are mutually dependent' (p. 155).

The importance of classroom communities of inquiry having opportunities for open-ended inquiry within school curriculum subjects that can connect to their real-world experiences cannot be overstated. We spoke earlier of Dewey's idea that common and productive practical activities, when properly used, would connect students to the school curriculum and engage them in communal activities via firsthand experience. Such activities have the potential to incorporate student participation in community development projects, as well as social and political activities to facilitate an understanding of the process of self-correction and, therefore, have the potential to bring about social change. By applying their inquiry skills to actual situations students purposefully reconstruct their social–cultural environment. In this sense education has the potential to extend beyond the classroom and the school. It requires members of the school community to understand the connection between themselves as active members of the community, the school of which they are a part, the greater community, and responsible decision-making. The school and the community to which it belongs becomes a microcosm of a greater deliberative democratic community.

Social reconstruction learning focuses on Dewey's aim (as discussed earlier) to synthesise curriculum though theory (curriculum content, including traditional subjects) and practice (practical learning as experiential education). As Bleazby writes:

> Dewey believed disciplinary content should be taught as knowledge, skills, methods and values that were constructed in response to everyday problems—namely, the problem of how to more effectively interact with our social environment. Hence, the reason that in Dewey's school children would learn geometry in order to build a functioning garden shed; biology in order to effectively grow a kitchen garden; chemistry in order to dye fabrics for a garment; and so on.
>
> (p. 183)

Dewey's position stemmed from his dispute with philosophy's preoccupation with attaining certainty as absolute truths, which has led to its reputation as a discipline dealing in abstractions. The rejection of absolute truths is a key principle of pragmatist epistemology first posited by Peirce (we will discuss this further in Chapter 5) and expanded by Dewey (1970). His proposal for a reconstruction of philosophy situated philosophical problems back to where he thought they belonged, within the sociocultural conditions from whence they originated, 'in order to be relevant to present human affairs' (p. xxiii). Under such conditions, doing philosophy becomes a form of social reconstruction. Here, we see Dewey compare the two ways of doing philosophy:

> Instead of impersonal and purely speculative endeavours to contemplate as remote beholders of the nature of absolute things-in-themselves, we have a living picture of the choice of thoughtful men about what they would have life to be, and to what ends they would have men shape their intelligent activities.
>
> (p. 26)

Dewey's omission to reconstruct philosophy for the school curriculum is especially surprising, as Bleazby (2013) has noted, 'given that the other disciplines included on the Laboratory School curriculum had to be similarly reconstructed so as to draw out their concrete, social, practical, imaginative and emotional aspects' (p. 185). While Lipman did set forth to rectify this oversight, 'his approach to teaching philosophy lacks the valuable practical dimension central to Dewey's curriculum' (p. 185).

Social reconstruction learning requires the integration of philosophy and service learning which is informed by 'clear pedagogical procedures and curriculum content that can actively foster the communal inquiry necessary for effective social reconstruction' (p. 188). To do this, the community of inquiry needs 'to be extended to include relevant members of the community who would be considered equal participants in the classroom inquiry' (p. 181). A social reconstruction curriculum would ideally be cross-curricular and sustainable over a school term or year. It needs to start with a broad issue, and link to key philosophical concepts, which have educational and practical benefits, thus, providing students with opportunities to identify real-world examples or case studies to investigate (p. 185).

> Starting with a broad topic also maximises the options available for taking transformative action. Students need to know from the outset that they are expected to undertake transformative action as a part of the course. This means they can be considering and evaluating possible problems they could tackle throughout the course, allowing them plenty of time to approach relevant community members or organisations that they must engage in communal inquiry with.
>
> (p. 185)

A crucial aspect of social reconstruction learning, therefore, is that the community of inquiry 'must constantly move between philosophical texts and theories and analyses of concrete social problems or case studies, with the overriding aim of articulating the causes and nature problem and identifying some possible transformative action that may be taken' (p. 187).

While there are a multitude of ways to engage students in a social reconstruction curriculum, its implementation, whether at a classroom or whole-school level, depends on the educational context, and 'on the age and abilities of the students, as well as the local community and resources available' (p. 188). Much also depends on 'the way dominant school structures and educational ideas can impede such teaching', and how prepared teachers are 'to adapt such educational ideas, implement them gradually and partially, and constantly justify and explain the value of these ideas and practices because colleagues may perceive them to be unorthodox and even dubious' (p. 189). As an example of social reconstruction learning and how philosophical content can be made relevant to social issues, we offer the following case study of an inner-city state primary school in Brisbane, Australia (Burgh, Field & Freakley, 2006; Hinton, 2003; Hinton & Davey Chesters, 2013; White et al., 2019).

The school was funded through Federal government money available for 'social justice', which was used to reinvent the school, including the addition of whole-school philosophy and environmental programs. The teachers underwent extensive and ongoing in-service programs for teaching philosophy and creating links between the school community and the wider community, as well as academics and teacher-educators in philosophy for children. The learning that takes place is within a practical learning context ('real-life' learning as it was referred to by the principal and staff) (Hinton, 2003, pp. 50–51). As part of an extensive environmental education program, the students were involved in various educational and practical activities, such as frog and compost worm breeding, and growing and selling vegetables. They worked with the local council to revegetate the banks of the creek next to the school, as well as collected water samples from the creek and graphed their findings to determine the health of the waterways in Brisbane. The school also has a permaculture garden and rainforest area, and together with the creek, these sites were used by teachers to develop activities which, through philosophical inquiry, were integrated into science, English, mathematics, environmental studies, and other subject areas. In addition, an environmental education resource person was employed by the parents and citizens (P&C) association to plan with teachers and work with classes.

> On one occasion some of the older students noticed many dead fish in the creek. They wrote to the local councillor, the *Courier-Mail* (the state's daily newspaper), the local newspaper, the Department of the Environment, and their member of State Parliament. They received a response from the council and the local newspaper ran a front-page news story. A representative from the Department of the Environment informed the students that traces of chemicals used for termite control were found in the samples and that a number of possible contamination sites were located. They were also visited by Anna Bligh, Member of Parliament for South Brisbane and at the time Minister for the Environment, to whom they presented a petition signed by most of the students in the school. This petition was subsequently tabled in parliament and appeared in Hansard, the official record of Parliamentary proceedings.
>
> (Burgh, Field & Freakley, 2006, p. 204)

Following on, the school collaborated with a school in Osaka, Japan, where students from both schools investigated the health of the creek next to their respective schools, thus, extending the program internationally.

In conjunction with integrating the curriculum with philosophy and practical learning, the school uses purpose-written philosophical resources, although they preferred the Australian produced material rather than the IAPC curriculum (e.g., Cam, 1993, 1994, 1995, 1997, 2006). The principal and staff have also developed and published their own material, in collaboration with philosophers and educators in philosophy for children (Cam et al., 2007; Davey Chesters et al., 2013). The use of philosophical short stories, teacher resource/activity books, and other stimuli, combined with the practical activities, to synthesise the curriculum, illustrates well the integration of theory and practice using experiential education, which is informed by clear pedagogical procedures and curriculum content to foster the communal inquiry necessary for effective social reconstruction. Students engage in philosophical discussion and the practical testing of ideas, not just in the classroom but with the school community and their local communities. Their learning involves the identification of social and environmental issues and problems and the subsequent development and implementation of real solutions. Students are involved in social reconstruction because they bring about real social change.

Before we conclude the chapter, we wish to draw attention to another aspect of social reconstruction learning that deserves attention. Because social reconstruction learning takes place inside and outside of the classroom, and pedagogically not only moves between theory and practice, but between two different learning environments—*places* in which learning occurs—it can gain additional educational and practical benefits by incorporating place-based education or reconceptualising it as primarily a form of place-based education, rather than service learning. How the teacher and students understand 'place' will affect how they approach problems in the context of social reconstruction learning. We, therefore, propose that place-based education can provide them with educational and practical opportunities to explore the notion of a 'sense of place'—how they perceive a place, which includes place attachment and place meaning (Kudryavtsev, Stedman & Krasny, 2012). In Chapter 6, we will revisit place-based education and argue that, not only can it be improved through incorporating social reconstruction learning, but also that place-based education can extend social reconstruction by aiding in the development of ecologically minded identities by attending to the human/nature dualism, and, thus, making both *place-responsive* pedagogies. We will also revisit the case study to illustrate how this would work in practice.

Conclusion

To pull together the threads of our discussion, the words 'the relationship between epistemology and pedagogy' come to mind. The influences of Peirce's pragmatist epistemology, Dewey's pedagogical ideas and characterisation of democracy, and Vygotsky sociocultural learning theory, which resonate in the theory and practice of philosophy for children, illustrate that Lipman was convinced of the importance of epistemology and learning theory for education. Dewey, who 'drew parallels between how experts construct new knowledge through inquiry in disciplinary fields, and how students learn through their own active inquiry in and out of school' (Gregory, Haynes & Murris, 2017, p. 101), was particularly influential. He provided the pedagogical principles and guidelines for the reconstruction of education that make social reconstruction possible. Lipman's aim of converting the classroom into a community of inquiry, therefore, demands an understanding of the relationship between epistemology and pedagogy that provides grounding for philosophy for children.

It is true that teachers can conduct communities of inquiry and provide students with meaningful experiences, even with only basic practical knowledge of Lipman's stages of inquiry. Empirical studies also show that such classroom communities of inquiry can result in intellectual and social benefits (see Garcia-Moriyon, Robello & Colom, 2005; Millett & Tapper, 2012; Millett, Scholl & Tapper, 2019). However, our contention is that the aim of social reconstruction demands much more. As an institution of liberal democracy, education needs reconstruction for it to be an agent of social renewal rather than reproduction. We need to turn our attention to the wide-sense community of inquiry to provide insights into the relationship between epistemology and pedagogy, so as to better inform the narrow-sense community of inquiry.

To reiterate, the wide-sense conception of the community of inquiry is the regulative or organising ideal of pragmatist epistemology that underscores all discipline-based inquiry (e.g., the sciences, social sciences, geography, history, mathematics). It also provides pedagogical principles or guidelines (e.g., fallibilism, doubt, collective deliberation, warranted assertions) for implementing the narrow-sense conception of the community of inquiry, a teaching method of five stages of inquiry in the classroom. This is crucial for converting the classroom into a community of inquiry otherwise the method remains rudimentary (e.g., sitting in a circle, providing philosophical stimulus, constructing the agenda, solidifying the community, using exercises and discussion plans, and encouraging further responses) without the wide-sense understanding of how to pedagogically navigate fallibilistic epistemology. Moving between the facilitation of inquiry (procedural) and the curriculum content (substantive), which are the subjects informed by the different discipline-based inquiries, requires the teacher to also be a co-inquirer with the students, to move between the two communities. To do so teachers need to be aware of the difference between the knowledge constructed by the scholarly inquiries that finds its way into textbooks and the actual discipline-based inquiries engaged in ongoing investigations where new knowledge could arise. Teacher's awareness or lack of awareness of this tension becomes a model for students. In other words, teachers need to be aware of the distinction between, for example, science that produces knowledge as a product and science as a form of inquiry.

In the next chapter, we focus on pragmatist epistemology to highlight the importance of genuine doubt as a felt experience that provides an experiential component for the cultivation of fallibilism, which Peirce named as both a principle and an attitude, necessary for the creation of self-correcting communities of inquiry. This can be seen as a vital component of experiential education that is essential for social reconstruction, and which has implications for teachers, as it provides a characterisation of the teacher as someone who can navigate between the roles of facilitator and co-inquirer, someone who is epistemically capable of letting doubt guide self-correcting dialogue.

Notes

1 Plato tended to restrict philosophy to mature students on the grounds that it made younger people, including children, excessively contentious. This view, although not popular among philosophers today, was echoed by Tony Coady who, while generally positive about the philosophy for children movement, cautioned that 'philosophy can easily create smartarses out of bright kids. ... If introduced to people who are still immature, it could have a bad effect' (in Slattery, 1995, p. 21).

2 For an analysis of the community of inquiry as a methodology see Kohan & Costa Carvalho (2019).

3 For further discussion see: Burgh & Thornton (2017), Cam (2015), De Marzio (2011), Gazzard (2012), Glaser (2019), Lipman (2014), Sharp (2017a, 2017b), Splitter (2003, 2019), Wilks (2019).

4 See also: Burgh & Thornton (2019c), Part II: Books into Ideas: Laurance J. Splitter (Ch. 6), Jennifer Glaser (Ch. 7), Susan Wilks (Ch. 8), Tim Sprod (Ch. 9), Philip Cam (Ch. 10), and Clinton Golding (Ch. 11).

5 'Facilitator', as we use the term, does not refer to someone who makes an action or process easy or easier. The teacher, as a facilitator, works within the zone of proximal development to make collaborative work possible, but is also an integral part of the learning process. In the philosophy for children literature, the role of the teacher as facilitator has been described variously. For example, as 'a teacher-as-improvising-philosopher', meaning 'composing in the moment one's own way of thinking, being sensitive to, and affirming difference, and being a teacher in process' (Kohan, Santi & Wozniak, 2017, p. 259), and as self-liberator and enabler of 'epistemic justice in order to ensure perspectival multiplicity, multiple identities, and the legitimization of difference characterized by pedagogy of search' (Kizel, 2021, p. 1).

6 Some proponents of philosophy for children, such as Lipman, favour extensive teacher training programs and stress the importance of the philosophical stories-as-text and discussion plans and exercises in the teacher manuals, which should be used in conjunction with teachers immersing themselves in communities of inquiry, mediated by a philosopher. There is a range of views, from requirements that teachers should have a background in philosophy to teacher in-service professional development led by teacher educators who, themselves, have had no formal qualifications in philosophy, except for minimal in-service training. See: Çayır (2018), Daniel (1998), Davey Chesters & Hinton (2017), Gazzard (2012), Gregory (2008), Lipman (1987, 1988, pp. 151–159), Lipman, Sharp & Oscanyan (1980, pp. 207–215), Splitter (2014).

7 Subject teaching associations have active members in the teaching profession and academic disciplines and, therefore, provide opportunities for members of the two communities of inquiry to engage in discussions, research, and collaborative projects, and attend and participate in conferences and professional development. Subsequently, subject teaching associations can 'exert considerable influence on curriculum development' (Hilferty, 2001, p. 6).

5 Knowledge construction and knowledge exclusion

Introduction

Lipman's tenure as a professor at Columbia University opened his eyes to his students' lack of capacity to wonder, to think critically, and to grasp the basic tenets of critical thinking. Lipman and his colleagues came to the following conclusion:

> Many adults have ceased to wonder, because they feel that there is no time for wondering, or because they have come to the conclusion that it is simply unprofitable and unproductive to engage in reflection about things that cannot be changed anyhow. Many adults have never had the experience of engaging in wondering and reflecting that somehow made a difference in their lives. The result is that such adults, having ceased to question and to reach for the meanings of their experience, eventually become examples of passive acceptance that children take to be models for their own conduct.
>
> (Lipman, Sharp & Oscanyan, 1980, p. 31)

These words are as relevant today as they were in 1980. Children grow up, become adults, and unquestioningly transmit their habits onto the next generation. Without wonder, the cycle continues.

In *The Myth of Sisyphus*, Camus (1977) writes that we 'continue making the gestures commanded by existence for many reasons, the first of which is habit' (p. 13), and that the repetition occurs because we 'get into the habit of living before acquiring the habit of thinking' (p. 8). Camus is in like-minded company with pragmatists like Peirce, from whom Dewey, Lipman, and his colleagues heavily borrowed. They all rejected the idea of the human ability to acquire certainty in the quest for absolute truth. Peirce understood that navigating a world of uncertainly is a collaborative endeavour that requires working with uncertainty. An uncertain world is one in which we must, as Dewey said, see life as communication and communication as education,

DOI: 10.4324/9781003098089-6

so all life is education—a social democracy as an associate mode of living. Camus (2001) called this a true democracy, which, he says, presupposes

> that no truth in its realm is absolute and that adding many human experiences each to the other represents a more precious approximation of the truth than a coherent but false doctrine. Democracy does not defend abstract ideas or a brilliant philosophy. It defends democrats, which presumes asking them to decide how best to guarantee their defense.
>
> (p. 14)

In other words, democracy relies on, Camus thought, the modest citizen who 'recognizes that his efforts possess characteristics that are in part risky and that he does not know everything' (p. 13). Consequently, 'he recognizes that he needs to consult others, to complete what he knows with what they know' (p. 13), and in doing so, 'through the confrontation of their ideas stand the best chance of adopting the best tactics' (p. 14). We will return to Camus later in this chapter, but for the moment suffice it to say that his 'modest democracy' requires an active and informed citizenry, which, in turn, requires civic literacy in order to consult with others to make the most prudent decisions in a world of uncertainty.

We live in a media-driven environment that has exacerbated the erosion of public trust in science, where the scientific method is poorly understood and undermined by vested interests, and where uncertainty itself generates an inability to make decisions that will impact on future generations. Amidst this, environment scientists vie with uninformed politicians, 'influencers', climate denial think-tanks, and powerful corporate interests for the public's attention regarding the impacts of climate change. Amidst the environmental and economic uncertainty and increasing distrust in politicians to govern effectively, is it any wonder that many adults find it 'unprofitable and unproductive to engage in reflection about things that cannot be changed anyhow' (Lipman, Sharp & Oscanyan, 1980, p. 31). It seems that many adults have, indeed, ceased to wonder, and in doing so, have ceased to question why things are the way they are, to imagine how they could be otherwise, and how they can act to break habits, their own and others, towards the creation of new conscious habits centred around human and environmental flourishing.

Lipman and his colleagues shared the view on the need for education to maintain children's sense of wonder, and their propensity for spontaneous questioning, as central to developing social and intellectual capacities and dispositions for active citizenship and to bring about an inquiring society. If we apply the words of Lipman and his colleagues to classroom practice, we can draw the conclusion that students' interests, curiosity, and sense of wonder are dependent on the teacher's philosophical wonder and, therefore, we cannot expect good philosophical discussion when such wonder is absent. Like Lipman and others, we also think that the reconstruction of education is crucial to preventing a dearth of 'wonder being transmitted from generation to generation' (Lipman, Sharp & Oscanyan, 1980, p. 31).

Wonder is closely related to the concept of doubt in pragmatist epistemology—inquiry implies wonder, and the purpose of inquiry is the settlement of doubt. As both these concepts are crucial for a practical understanding of converting the classroom into a community of inquiry, we need to go back to Peirce's pragmatist epistemology of fallibilism and the role of doubt in establishing inquiry. A successful community of inquiry must be open to self-correction (or more precisely, democratic self-correction), which entails the cultivation of doubt as a precondition for genuine inquiry, so that the students follow the argument where it leads rather than to a predetermined conclusion for which the epistemic grounds have not been questioned. Teachers, therefore, need to question their own understanding of the world, so that they, themselves, are disposed to being perplexed or inquisitive about the content of the classroom materials, thereby stimulating student-oriented discussion. In this way, teachers become exemplars of wonder that students take to be models for their own conduct. Without wonder, we perpetuate the passive acceptance of that which Lipman and his colleagues speak. But there is, we will argue, another dimension to a lack of wonder, namely,, a lack of recognition of our own prejudices, which, in turn, perpetuates epistemic disparities among members of the community of inquiry. Thus, education's task is to maintain students' sense of wonder that is essential to begin genuine inquiry and vital for developing collective epistemic awareness in the classroom, as we will show.

This chapter will, therefore, focus on the community of inquiry, specifically on the necessity of *felt* genuine doubt as the starting point for inquiry (see Burgh & Thornton, 2016a, 2016b; Legg, 2008). Attention to feeling is an important part of the community of inquiry and offers a way to address some of the concerns raised by feminists regarding philosophy as an adversarial pursuit that historically is underpinned by masculine notions of truth, reason, and rationality. As Bleazby (2013) puts it, 'P4C reconstructs traditional gender stereotypes, which link caring, imaginative, concrete, social, and connected thinking with femininity and abstract, rationalistic and individualistic thinking with masculinity' (p. 139). So, our starting point is to raise the key concerns and responses from feminist writers in philosophy for children, who compare the adversarial conception of philosophy with the Socratic Method, a form of cooperative argumentative dialogue that is found in the practice of the community of inquiry. Unlike the adversarial approach to philosophy, the deliberative nature of the community of inquiry, like the Socratic Method, has doubt as central to inquiry. Both also share the idea of inquiry as the method of learning to think. Moreover, the pragmatist epistemology that shapes the community of inquiry rejects the adversarial way in which philosophy is done. For these reasons, philosophy for children escapes the scrutiny of the critics of the adversarial method. Curiously, the literature on the community of inquiry, and philosophy for children generally, has neglected the notion of genuine doubt in classroom practice, despite the concept having a pivotal role in Peirce's notion of inquiry as a regulative ideal.[1] Therefore, we seek to reinstate the centrality of genuine doubt in line with Peirce's intent.

Re-emphasising genuine doubt as integral to inquiry enables a deeper understanding of the interconnected relationship between wonder and inquiry and how it can inform the practice of the community of inquiry, and ultimately social reconstruction. It is also the initial step towards dislodging the epistemic blocks to inquiry reinforced by the dominant rationality of Western liberal discourses. Such blocks become lodged in the architecture of education and democracy and hamper our individual and collective ability to adapt to new ideas and information, which in turn hampers our ability to correct past and current mistakes and, subsequently, alter our course away from existential threats such as climate change. We argue that drawing an individual's attention to their own prejudices opens a pathway to what Peirce refers to as genuine doubt. With Camus' philosophy in mind, we show how the awareness of prejudice and the role it plays within the community of inquiry is effectively illustrated through the concept of absurdity captured in the image of Sisyphus. The absurd contains theoretical resources that can aid in the development of educational awareness of prejudices and, in so doing, counteract the desire for certainty. The tension between recognising our prejudices and our desire for certainty can be described as lucid reflection, an awareness of the absurd, of holding both beliefs, which is a sustained feeling of doubt that can prompt inquiry. We call this approach to teaching 'lucid teaching' as experience of lucidity comes from an epistemological commitment to the absurd. Teaching that is focused on 'an expansion of the experience of absurdity as a starting point whereby relativity and human limits are rational results of living in a universe devoid of absolutes' (Hodgson, 2004, p. 2).

Both Camus and Peirce align in their thinking on the recognition of the experience of disorientation leading to the need to act on that experience, which dictates a particular method. For Peirce, it is the testing of our experiences of the world in relation to those of others and the reconstruction of paradoxical or contradictory positions to create a habitat in which new beliefs and habits can form. For Camus, it is lucidity, the persistent awareness of the absurd. Lucidity increases the probability of the creation of lucid inquirers and the prospect of a community free from dogmatic certainty and open to constructive and creative dialogue. Whereas Peirce turned to the community of inquiry as a regulative ideal to facilitate the tension between two contradictory experiences, those being genuine doubt and belief, Camus' absurdist thesis, also an acknowledgement of the tension between two contradictory experiences—the comfort of the familiar with the recognition of the contingent—leads to solidarity within the context of existential rebellion. These two positions, from different philosophical traditions, converge with respect to the experience of inquiry, and thereby can provide pedagogical guidelines for fostering philosophical discussion in the classroom community of inquiry.

Whilst our framework of lucid teaching is intended to be instructional for practitioners, it can also inform teachers' understanding of the epistemic dynamics of communal inquiry, and how to mediate between the narrow-sense and wide-sense communities of inquiry. So, we address the question: Can philosophy facilitate epistemic inclusion by converting class-rooms into communities of inquiry that sustain, what Markauskaite and Goodyear (2017) call, 'epistemic fluency', that is, the ability to be 'flexi-ble and adept' with respect to interconnected knowledges? In response, we introduce the concept of epistemic violence, which is a form of harm that has the potential to created obstacles to inquiry. We provide an account of the community of inquiry as peace education because it develops students' intellectual and practical abilities to turn conflict into inquiry, and, thus, a way of directly addressing epistemic violence and improving the quality of the epistemic relationships between participants.

Epistemic harms also occur in the selection of classroom resources. Nar-ratives are not neutral, but are either evaluative and prescriptive, or shy away way from real-world controversy such as sex/gender and race/ethnicity. To deal with these issues, we argue that lucid teaching requires teachers to cul-tivate traitorous identities, someone who resists the epistemic assumptions and institutional practices of the culture to which they belong as a classroom intervention to listen to the voices of those who are outside the dominant narrative and are having difficulty being heard or understood. The purpose is to provide students with opportunities to develop epistemic understand-ing through engaging in multi-voiced dialogues, which can foster epistemic fluidity and inclusion.

Philosophy: Collaborative inquiry or adversarial argumentation?

A great deal of the literature on philosophy for children, on both its ped-agogy and curriculum, assumes that its benefits—for example, the valuing of personal experience and others' opinions, the development of care, trust and tolerance, accountability, and self-correction—feature in philosophical inquiry generally. However, insights from feminist critiques of epistemology and philosophical methods of inquiry, appear to paint a somewhat different picture. Terri Field (1997) succinctly captures this concern:

> Feminists have found fault particularly with the type of knowledge phi-losophers have claimed to have access to (i.e., universal, objective), the method in which this knowledge is said to be attained (i.e., through rea-soning, logical deduction, aggressive argumentation) and the nature of the knower in this process (i.e., value-free, neutral, detached, rational).
>
> (p. 19)

These insights have contributed to critiques which hold that the construc-tion and use of reason and rationality, and their close ties to claims about cer-tainty and absolute truth, especially in the Western philosophical tradition, have silenced women's voices. These challenges also extend to other margin-alised and oppressed groups, which we will address later in this chapter and in Chapter 6. In response, some feminist philosophers have suggested that women develop their own discourse and ignore the philosophical tradition (e.g., Irigaray, 1985), whereas others contend that this tradition must be confronted (e.g., Lloyd, 1984). Concerns have also been voiced by feminist philosophers who have addressed the connections between women, feminism, and philosophy for children. The following question by San MacColl (1994) expresses well their concerns: 'would you wish on women or small girls a practice of philosophy which you yourself have come to see as deeply imbued with disguised, gendered ideals and associations?' (p. 5).

In response, we explore one of the main accusations frequently aimed at philosophy, that it is necessarily adversarial. This is a serious charge as adversarial argumentation 'is commonly driven by a binary understanding of ideas. Claims are either true or false; arguments are either valid or invalid' (Lenz, 2020, n.p.). This view is reflected in the above quote by Field. To be adversarial is to fail to see the importance of 'truth seeking' as a collaborative endeavour driven by doubt and wonder, but to treat such an endeavour as a clash and defence of beliefs. Using the insights of Janice Moulton, who contends that the Socratic Method of philosophy has been confused with the adversarial method,[2] we distinguish between certain features of philosophy that may appear problematic from a feminist perspective and those embedded in the philosophical method that underscores the community of inquiry. It is a matter of importance to respond to these issues as Lipman and Dewey belong to the reflective education tradition that started with Socrates. We argue that Lipman's approach to philosophical inquiry offers much to alleviate the more adversarial and limiting elements of the Western philosophical tradition—although later in this chapter, we raise some further concerns that we argue need to be addressed.

Criticisms of traditional Western epistemology and philosophical methods of inquiry are not restricted to feminist critiques only. One such critic who has devoted a book to the topic is Edward de Bono (1994). He contends that Western thinking is failing because it places too much emphasis on critical analysis, dichotomous reasoning, and ruthless judgements and is, therefore, not designed to deal with change. Much of what he says is reflected in feminist literature on philosophy as an adversarial method. One of de Bono's mistakes, however, is that he uses the term Western mode of thinking interchangeably with the terms 'Socratic Method', 'Aristotelian emphasis on analysis', and 'adversarial method'. He assumes that Western philosophical thinking is necessarily adversarial. While we would agree that in practice this has often been the case, philosophical thinking can be, and is, conducted in a non-adversarial way also.

Moulton (1983) suggests that the Socratic Method has been confused, in philosophy, with what she calls the adversary method. The latter method, she claims, is 'part of the larger paradigm that distinguishes reason from emotion, and segregates philosophy from literature, aligning it with science' (p.163). A feature of this method is that the parties involved in philosophical discussion endeavour to justify (defend) their own thesis (argument), and question (attack) or refute (destroy) the other party's (opponent's) thesis, by reasoned (rational) means, using established standards of evaluation (logic or vertical thinking). The most common way to do this is through posing hypothetical counterexamples whereby 'one needs to abstract the essential features of the problem' and construct an analogy that can 'be considered dispassionately apart from the issue in question' (p.159). This kind of inquiry tends to prioritise the logical structure of the argument over the plausibility of the claims or meaningfulness of the argument when viewed in a larger context. This is not to say that use of hypothetical counterexamples or analogical reasoning is never appropriate. Rather, it is crucial to realise that sometimes the complexity of the issue under discussion needs to be retained to appreciate elements that may be excluded if it were reduced to limiting analogies. Earlier we raised a similar criticism of Kohlberg's use of moral dilemmas in values education.

Similarly, the exclusion of emotion from the reasoning process should not necessarily be something to aspire to in philosophical inquiry. Genevieve Lloyd (1984) has developed a comprehensive analysis of how reason has not only been privileged as a philosophical ideal, but how it has been defined by its very exclusion of women/femaleness/the feminine. Thus, if a woman prioritises reason over emotion, she is often denied her femininity and seen to be as good as a man or, more contemptuously, 'she's got balls'. It is not only women who have been excluded from the sphere of Reason.[3] Slaves, children, the working classes, colonised peoples, and practically every non-white ethnic group have, at some time, been portrayed as lacking the ability to reason. In discussing the separation of reason and emotion in Western philosophy, some feminist philosophers have proposed that emotions may in fact be helpful and even necessary to the learning process. While 'uncontaminated' reason, that is, abstracted from the personal and the particular, has been upheld as a means to attain universal knowledge, critics like Alison Jaggar (1989) and Susan Sherwin (1989) challenge such assumptions. They argue that rather than aspiring to value-free, neutral, or detached theorising, we should take the context in which we think into account. This includes those personal, social, and historical patterns that shape our ways of thinking. Such an approach notes the importance of prejudice, but only in the sense that by recognising it and opening it up to inquiry, we can be called upon to be accountable for our position in the construction and transference of knowledge.

Lipman's approach to philosophical inquiry offers much to remedy the more adversarial and limiting elements of the Western philosophical tradition. Clearly, we should not simply aim to reproduce traditional methods of doing philosophy in the classroom. De Bono (1990) asserts that critical thinking as the complete form of thinking, in the philosophical tradition, can be dangerous because '[t]here is a silly belief, based on misinterpretation of the Greek master thinkers, that thinking is based on dialectical argument' (p. 13). He is more concerned with what he refers to as the practical operation of thinking as a deliberative process. However, doing philosophy need not be limited to narrow conceptions of critical thinking as sequential logical thinking, as de Bono claims. We concur with Lipman (2003) that philosophy itself can incorporate a multidimensional and pluralist approach to thinking; critical thinking that emphasises precision and consistency, creative thinking which uses the imagination to develop innovative ideas and generate hypotheses, and caring thinking that cultivates and appreciates the value of the inquiry process (pp. 197–271). Philosophy does not need to be adversarial and, therefore, is not necessarily a hindrance to multidimensional and pluralist approaches to thinking. The community of inquiry demonstrates a positive direction for philosophical inquiry in respect to participation, relatedness, and relevance to those involved.

A review of the literature on the theory and practice of the community of inquiry reveals that this position has much support. Splitter (1991b), for example, argues against the 'intellectual nit-picker' who spends their time 'carping at other people's arguments', and stresses that 'this kind of characterisation leaves out the productive or constructive dimension of critical thinking which is ultimately of great significance' (p. 90). Lipman (1991) directly cites Moulton's argument against the adversary method as support for his view of a community of inquiry (p. 257). This suggests that he does not identify his position and, by implication, his views on philosophical classroom discussion with the type of philosophical inquiry she is criticising. Instead of possessing a narrow conception of critical inquiry, he maintains that the community of inquiry 'intermixes the critical concern with justice and the creative impulse towards caring. It produces respect for both principles and persons and thereby provides a model of democracy as inquiry' (p. 254). Lipman's comments are also a vindication of the views of the justice and care approaches to ethical deliberation first outlined by Gilligan—recall our discussion of Gilligan's studies on the difference between rights-based ethics (what she calls the justice approach) and an ethics of care. She argues that the former is symptomatic of masculine gender identity and the latter of feminine gender identity. Rights-based ethics, as we have seen, have been criticised by many feminists as inherently adversarial. Having rights sets boundaries between various rights-holders. In the event of disagreement or conflict, the various rights need to be weighed up against each other to allow adjudication upon which rights are stronger.

Another point to make regarding de Bono's views about the adversarial model of philosophy is that he underestimates the power of genuine Socratic dialogue. After all, Socrates' aim was to show people how to think for themselves rather than to gratuitously destroy another person's argument. Moulton (1983) points out that '[u]nlike the Adversary Method, the justification of the elenchus [the method associated with Socrates] is not that it subjects claims to the most extreme opposition, but that it shakes people up about their cherished convictions so they can begin philosophical inquiries with a more open mind' (p. 156). In other words, a better interpretation of the Socratic Method, and by extension reflective education, is that it is concerned with a process of unlearning whereby students systematically question their beliefs to the point of discovering their own ignorance.

From there, students are in a better position to become aware of the presuppositions and principles that underlie their convictions and beliefs. Indeed, Moulton also stresses the importance of the quality of acceptance in the Socratic Method, in terms of finding common ground between inquirers in a philosophical discussion. This is to say, to engage in a meaningful way with others in inquiry and possibly to convince them of alternative views, it makes sense to find premises that both parties can agree with before proceeding. Such an approach assumes a more cooperative and creative attitude to philosophical inquiry than often occurs in practice. Moulton's argument, then, is that Socrates' method has been misinterpreted under the influence of the adversary paradigm and, consequently, 'we have not been able to conceive of philosophy being done any other way' (p.157).

Philosophical inquiry, as deliberative rather than adversarial, provides opportunities to redefine and explore alternative understandings in the classroom. Children and adolescents are still learning about the values and expectations of their peers, social groups and communities, and society at large. By providing them with an opportunity to explore through shared, cooperative dialogue, students, can become aware of each other as persons. This is to say, philosophical classroom practice can allow for the recognition of their fellow inquirers as legitimate co-inquirers in the pursuit and construction of knowledge. The collaboration of reason and feeling (i.e., the idea of experience and the experience in itself), as a way of acquiring knowledge, is invaluable especially in relation to ethical understanding and political decision-making, for it enhances our ability to relate to others and the world; disagreements are seen as contention rather than as competition. In other words, instead of philosophy going to battle until the last idea is left standing, it can be understood as a community in dialogue with the aim of settling beliefs, which are 'provisional judgments rather than firm bases for absolute convictions' (Lipman, 2003, p. 93).

By providing opportunities for students to express themselves in the ways just described, they become aware that there is no privileged domain where philosophy can or should take place.[4] Reasoning is no longer just a cognitive (or as some might claim 'disembodied') process whereby *ideas of experiences* are examined and *experiences in themselves* ignored. Activities that create opportunities for children and adolescents to understand through their own experiences enhance their capacity to relate to, and participate in, the world in different and constructive ways that otherwise may not have been available to them. It could be said that children and adolescents may come to recognise that they have an interesting understanding of 'other'. After all, they could very well be the other in relation to adults (e.g., a special case of the marginalised other as 'incomplete'), and very often are in traditional classrooms (see Kennedy, 1998, 2006, 2012; Kohan, 1995; Murris, 2013, 2016a, 2016b). This has direct bearing on the role of the teacher in a community of inquiry; to be aware of obstacles that prevent questioning and open-ended inquiry, such as epistemic bias and other prejudices, for example, assumptions about gender and race, so that all voices, opinions, and perspectives can be heard. That the community of inquiry rests on a pragmatist epistemology of fallibilism means doubt is at the centre of inquiry. Without doubt, 'the inquiry is susceptible to the epistemic bias and prejudices that too often go undetected. Thus, we turn our discussion now to pragmatist epistemology which rejects both certainty and adversarial philosophy. Indeed, pragmatism embraces uncertainty as the driving force for collaborative communication and deliberative inquiry.

Learning to doubt and doubting to learn

Doubt can be described as a state of hesitancy over whether to accept or reject a given proposition. Peirce thought it to be a peculiar sensation accompanied by the desire to ask questions. It is an irritating quality, like an itch begging to be scratched. Like scratching that gives relief, Peirce thought that doubt gives rise to inquiry as a way to find another kind of relief, to settle upon a belief. So, doubt is pivotal in pragmatist epistemology. To explain this further, we start with Descartes' scepticism and his search for epistemological certainty. We do so because, as we mentioned previously, Peirce had serious doubts about the sincerity of Descartes' doubting. Indeed, he thought that Descartes feigned doubt in order to settle on certainty. However, Peirce's rejection of Cartesian certainty leads to living with uncertainly, which did not disturb him in the same way as it did Descartes. To live with uncertainty meant breaking free from our habits of belief that inhibit inquiry to test if new beliefs suit better the circumstances that brought us into doubt.

   In order to detail these connections, we focus on the phenomenology of inquiry; that is, inquiry that begins with genuinely felt doubt, pointing to a problematic situation to which the inquirer seeks a solution or resolution. We reinvigorate the ideas of Peirce by borrowing the language and concepts of Camus, who has much to offer philosophers of education.[5] We show where Camus and Peirce are congruent in their thinking, insofar as they can inform the educative process of the community of inquiry. We conclude with a discussion on the implications for classroom practice and for the role of the teacher in cultivating collective doubt.

Confronting Descartes

Descartes sits alone by the fireplace. As he listens to the crackle of the logs, he begins to wonder, is there anything about this world we can claim to know with certainty? Not the senses, painters such as Leonardo da Vinci had shown a century earlier that the senses can be tricked by perfecting chiaroscuro, the art of depicting the three-dimensional world in two-dimensional paint. Early science had provided Descartes with a host of other examples, and besides, who is to say that we are not under the influence of an evil demon who delights in fooling our senses, as Descartes himself questioned. But if the senses are fallible, what else might we be wrong about? Is not all knowledge procured through the senses? If our senses cannot guarantee the authority of our thoughts, what can? Descartes' answer to this problem was not what, but who. God being all good was the grantor of knowledge, but before he posited God, Descartes found comfort in his own thoughts.

Descartes was a philosopher, most famous for a quote he never explicitly wrote, *cogito ergo sum*, which roughly translates as 'I think, therefore I am'. The task Descartes set for himself in his *Meditations on First Philosophy* was to look for some bedrock, a foundation on which human certainty could be built. He proposed that we might arrive at this position of certainty through a method of doubting everything. The certainty Descartes settled upon rests on an internalist theory of epistemic justification, rejecting an externalist one. Descartes' search for knowledge was not dependant on the external world, but rather the internal world of ideas. It is Descartes' quest for certainty and theory of knowledge that both Camus and Peirce reject.

While Camus' and Descartes' responses to the problem of existence contrast each other, they share a methodological similarity. To Camus (1991), the absurd is 'a point of departure, the equivalent, in existence, to Descartes's methodical doubt' (p. 8). It is the only certitude to which Camus will consent, yet—and herein ends the similarity—it is not singular like Descartes *cogito*. Rather, the absurd 'is essentially a divorce. It lies in neither of the elements compared; it is born of their confrontation' (p. 33). The absurd is the divorce between the desire to know the world, to find comfort, rest, and reason in it, and the indifference to our desires we find in the world. It is the lack of fit between our human desire to know and our inability to satisfy this desire, a desire that is stymied by what Camus (1977) describes as 'the feeling that all true knowledge is impossible' (p. 18).

In positing the absurd, Camus is rejecting the epistemology of Descartes, for although he thinks all true knowledge to be impossible, he does not doubt everything. He writes: 'This heart within me I can feel, and I judge that it exists. This world I can touch, and I likewise judge that it exists. There ends all my knowledge, and the rest is construction' (p. 24). For Camus, whether there is a transcendental meaning or an ultimate reality, is forever beyond the reach of human knowledge. However, he did not doubt the existence of the world that lay beneath his fingertips. Although we cannot witness existence divorced from our human perspective, this does not mean the world is unreal, a mere representation, but neither does it give us absolute certainty in our conclusions—the truth lies somewhere in-between. Camus (1991) saw the world as ever-changing, uncertain and beautiful. It is not simply a puzzle to be solved but an experience to be lived. The dualism between the rational and the irrational is blurred; feeling and reason must be considered together, and their interplay to be noted.

> Absurdism, like methodical doubt, has wiped the slate clean. It leaves us in a blind alley. But, like methodical doubt, it can, by returning upon itself, open up a new field of investigation, and in the process of reasoning then pursues the same course. I proclaim that I believe in nothing

and that everything is absurd, but I cannot doubt the validity of my proclamation and I must at least believe in my protest.

(p. 8)

Peirce, too, recognised a kind of divorce between humans and the world, in his insistence on the irreducible fallibilism of inquiry, insofar as he thought the world not to be static—a reality of purely unwavering natural law—but a world of continual evolution exhibiting spontaneity. As we discussed in the previous chapter, truth and reality, according to Peirce, are the products of inquiry. However, Peirce is not an idealist, he does not think that the world is only a product of the mind. He thought not only that the external world exists, but also that we come to have the best understanding of it through a process of inquiry with others. Like Camus, he thought that what we can hope to know and consider true is finite and constructed. Whatever exists outside the mind is far too complex to be fully understood by humans, and what we think we know can often be shown not to be the case with the addition of further evidence, hence the need to acknowledge our fallibility. But he did not reject a world independent of minds about which we are able to develop beliefs (Pardales & Girod, 2006). We cannot hope to 'know' in the absolute sense of the word, but we can seek to know as much as possible and the best way to do this Peirce thought, was through the process of inquiry—a systematic procedure for seeking truth he called the scientific method. According to this method, '[t]he opinion which is fated to be ultimately agreed upon by all who investigate, is what we mean by the truth, and the object represented in this opinion is the real. That is the way I would explain reality' (Peirce, 1878, p. 300). The opinion ultimately agreed upon, or 'objectivity in scientific inquiry is a function of collaborative research, mutual criticism, replicated experiments and other social practices' (Laverty & Gregory, 2007, p. 282). Pragmatist epistemology rejects any authority external to the scholarly community of inquiry (or community of experts engaged in the scientific method) as such communities are epistemologically autonomous. Peirce coined the term 'self-correcting':

> to describe how a person's or a community's habits of belief give way, through inquiry, to more adequate beliefs (adequacy measured by the melioration of experience), as opposed to being corrected once and for all by reference to a special class of infallible truths whose genesis is external to the community.
>
> (Gregory, 2002, p. 398)

Unlike Camus, Peirce's (1868) ideas were forged in the meeting of philosophy and science. But like Camus, he also rejected Descartes' *cogito*. Particularly, he objected to the idea that 'philosophy must begin with universal doubt' and that 'the ultimate test of certainty is to be found in the individual consciousness' (p. 140). 'There are', he claimed, 'many facts which Cartesianism not only does not explain but renders absolutely inexplicable, unless to say that "God makes them so" is to be regarded as an explanation' (p. 140). Peirce concluded that 'modern science and modern logic require us to stand upon a very different platform from this' (p. 140). Complete doubt cannot be a starting point, but instead, we 'must begin with all the prejudices which we actually have when we enter upon the study of philosophy', which are 'not to be dispelled by a maxim, for they are things which it does not occur to us *can* be questioned' (p. 140). In other words, Peirce did not believe that anyone could doubt everything simultaneously, because to act in the world requires beliefs about the world and the things we do. Any attempt at universal doubt is not to engage in real inquiry but in pretence or feigned hesitancy; to engage in mere *paper doubt*, which is questioning divorced from the feeling of doubt. Paper doubt lacks positive reasons for doubt, it is without the 'heavy and noble metal' of genuine doubt associated with the desire to question and, thus, leads to self-deception because no-one can ever strip bare of all prejudices of thought. Indeed, Peirce considered Descartes' meditations to be an exemplar of paper doubt. In his own words:

> A person may, it is true, in the course of his studies, find reason to doubt what he began by believing; but in that case he doubts because he has a positive reason for it, and not on account of the Cartesian maxim. Let us not pretend to doubt in philosophy what we do not doubt in our hearts.
>
> (pp. 140–141)

By assuming a position of emptiness, a freedom from prejudices in the form of total scepticism, Descartes failed under Peirce's definition to engage in a genuine inquiry, that is, he failed to both acknowledge and question his own prejudices. We will return to the concept of genuine doubt and to the importance of prejudices for inquiry in the sections to follow.

Unlike Descartes, Peirce did not commit to the view that we could divorce our body from our mind, our experiences from our thoughts and our thoughts from our feelings. He argued that if absolute truth and certainty were to reside in individual consciousness (i.e., introspection), then we should have been convinced with reasoning, rather than require an individual test of certainty akin to that of the Cartesian maxim, which amounts to: 'Whatever I am convinced of, is true' (p. 141). Making individuals absolute judges of truth is tantamount to claiming that metaphysics has reached certainty beyond that of the physical sciences. Indeed, according to Peirce, for any theory of reality to be reliable, requires the rigors of the scientific method, hence his insistence on the importance of a community of inquirers as an active learning community.

> In sciences in which men come to agreement, when a theory has been broached it is considered to be on probation until this agreement is reached. After it is reached, the question of certainty becomes an idle one, because there is no one left who doubts it.
>
> (p. 141)

The notion of people coming together to rigorously test ideas and hypotheses by employing an interpersonal method of arriving at results forms the basis of his notion of the community of inquirers, from which the idea of the community of inquiry derives. Only through a process of externalisation of thought facilitated by such a community are we able to reinterpret and then re-internalise our thoughts, thereby changing our beliefs and by extension our habitual actions stemming from our initial prejudices. In a dialogic setting, what begins as 'interpersonal interaction becomes an intrapersonal cognitive habit' (Reznitskaya & Gregory, 2013, p. 118). The importance of habit is often overlooked. To bring it into focus, we turn again to Camus in the next section.

Whilst we do not wish to make the strong claim that Peirce and Camus share epistemological commitments, we argue that the epistemic ramifications of their shared rejection of Cartesianism is congruent, albeit not without difference. Camus' contribution can aid in understanding the radical nature of pragmatist epistemology and the role of the teacher in cultivating doubt through his appeal to what he sees as the absurdity of the human condition; the human desire to seek clarity and the reality of a word that cannot reveal itself. An understanding of Peirce's and Camus' epistemic concerns, when considered together, offers a richer conceptualisation of the relationship between belief, prejudice, and genuine doubt, which is necessary to propel a rigorous method of inquiry founded on fallibilism. Without such understandings, a community of inquiry remains superficial. For this reason, we further explore their congruencies in the next sections, with the addition of Plumwood's encounter with a crocodile.

Breaking habits: Between a rock and a crocodile's jaws

For Camus (1977), our habits are what give shape and meaning to our lives. He derives this conclusion from the plight of Sisyphus, the figure in Greek mythology who the gods condemned to an eternity of rolling a rock up a mountain only to have it roll back down, then descend after it to begin an endless cycle of repetition of 'the struggle for the heights', an eternity of the same habit. Even faced with this laborious and seemingly futile punishment, this forced upon habit, 'one must imagine Sisyphus happy', as the 'struggle itself towards the heights is enough to fill a man's heart' (p. 111). Walking back down to his rock, he is aware of the life contained in his immediate surroundings. His task he knows is always waiting for him at the bottom of the mountain, and yet with all eternity stretched before him he takes his time reaching it again. On the slow amble down, he cultivates what is left for him to cultivate; the relationship between his senses and his thoughts—he becomes *lucid*.

The wonder Sisyphus finds in 'each mineral flake of that night-filled mountain' (p. 111) was not what the gods had in mind, not part of the task they had preconceived for him; it is his act of self-creation, his art of learning. It is the learning that happens beyond the textbook, beyond the scope of the teacher's intent. A learning centred on the importance of relationships. This form of learning is akin to Camus' notion of lucidity; an understanding of the absurd, the space between our thoughts, feelings, desires, beliefs, and the indifference of the world to them. This space, we argue, is comparable to Peirce's notion of fallibility necessary for genuine doubt, which is the driver of genuine inquiry. In the context of education, lucidity is *the conscious appreciation of the fallibility of our narratives achieved through the cultivation of awareness of our habits and habitat.*

The limitations of Sisyphus's situation mean that his ability to inquire is limited to his experience, that is, the meeting of his thoughts and his senses with the world surrounding him. While the tract of land he could walk, and the scope of external habits he could create, are much more confined than most of us need endure, his experience is not so different to our own. We experience this in the form of repetitions in the course of a normal day, week, month, year—the paths we follow most of the time in our everyday encounters, like waking up at 6:00 am every Monday to Friday to catch the train to work, doing the dishes, brushing your teeth before you go to bed. Unlike Sisyphus, many of us fail to cultivate the habit of developing awareness of our senses; we look but often what we see is influenced by habit, by the familiar, we listen but often hear only the expected (Murris, 2013). Our worldview is shaped through past narratives and the words we hear are given meaning through the unconscious whispers of past stories.

In many ways, by internalising, unquestioningly, the epistemic culture of the community in which we are situated, we play the role of our own gods; we limit the range of our own internal habits, and by extension the habitat in which we co-exist, creating a built environment; one that is not open to change or correction. The structures that we create then go on to limit the habits of future humans, perpetuating the limitations on our intellectual and physical experiences, and in this way, through our collective existence, past, present, and future, 'we' endure the punishment of Sisyphus. Dominic Hyde (2016) explains this in terms of intellectual freedom.

> Intellectual freedom is compromised by the domination of instrumental rationality that sees all as a means to the furtherance of our currently-accepted economic and political structures (the system). They are unexamined ends in themselves, leaving no room for open questioning of the values inherent in and presupposed by these structures and their goals. Our horizons draw in, our Life-world narrows, and we become dominated by a world-view that does not offer or consider possible alternatives.
>
> (p. 2)

We habituate to the built environments, the political, the epistemic, and the physical, and in doing so, we cease to question the history, cause and effects, and reasons for the existence of such structures; that is, we cease to wonder. Camus was witness to some of the world's greatest conflicts, he understood all too well the tendency in people to become habituated to conditions and to lose sight of their initial struggle against the acceptance of such conditions. Meursault, Camus' (1960) main character in *The Outsider* (aka *The Stranger*), mused that 'even if I'd been made to live in a hollow tree trunk, with nothing to do but look up at the bit of sky overhead, I'd gradually have got used to it' (p. 75). Meursault is an example of the passive acceptance that Lipman warns children will follow as a model for their own conduct; the passive acceptance that goes along with a lack of wonder.

To wonder is, in Peirce's words, to remain fallible, and in Camus' words, to become lucid by embracing the absurd. Before we continue, it should be noted that our extended analysis of Peirce and Camus regarding the community of inquiry is a response to Denton's (1967) claim that '[e]ducation, in its institutional form, can justify its existence only to the extent that it implements programs for the development of lucid individuals' (p. 99); to produce the moral individual, 'moral because, in the face of the absurd, he lucidly lives the philosophy of limits' (p. 127). We agree with Denton's claim and add that this would require teachers who are both lucid and understand how to facilitate lucidity in the classroom. By taking Camus' concepts of absurdity and lucidity and Peirce's ideas of genuine doubt and fallibilism, and mapping them onto existing educational frameworks, we offer a new way of thinking about the purpose of lucidity in education—lucid teaching. Lucid teaching can offer an experiential account of mediating between the narrow-sense and wide-sense communities of inquiry essential for social reconstruction and, thus, for the broader framework of democratic education we propose here. Lucid teaching requires that teachers maintain the tension between their dual roles as (1) co-inquirer who has a greater understanding than the students of the (wide-sense) scholarly communities of inquiry that have generated knowledge imported as facts into textbooks and (2) facilitator of the (narrow-sense) community of inquiry as a specific method for fostering philosophical discussion, in which the students do not possess the abilities of the scholarly community. To do this, teachers need to maintain a tension between a feeling of perplexity and lucid reflection. To further explain lucid teaching, we introduce Plumwood and her experience with a crocodile.

Few who have experienced a crocodile's death roll have lived to tell the tale. Even fewer have recognised and explored the resultant discrepancy between their experience and their own privileged conception of how the world does and should operate, as Plumwood did.

> Before the encounter, it was as if I saw the whole universe as framed by my own narrative, as though the two were joined perfectly and seamlessly together. As my own narrative and the larger story were ripped apart, I glimpsed a shockingly indifferent world in which I had no more significance than any other edible being.
>
> (Plumwood, 1999, p. 91)

We all live confined by our narratives, our own stories of the world constructed around our experiences. From the perspective of the crocodile, Plumwood was no more than a meal, nothing more than a piece of meat, such an experience, seeing herself from the outside, from the perspective of the other, crumbled her narrative of familiarity, safety, and superiority. All the habits, values, and meanings she had built up over a lifetime were in an instant trumped by the survival value her flesh held for the hungry crocodile. The boundaries between self and existence, the narratives and routines that sheltered her from knowledge of her mortality, the ultimate end to her personal stories, fell away and she saw in that instance, the cold 'indifference' of the external world.

For Camus (1977), a moment such as this reveals the absurd and 'inaugurates the impulse' of lucidity.

> It happens that the stage sets collapse. Rising, streetcar, four hours in the office or the factory, meal, streetcar, four hours of work, meal, sleep, and Monday Tuesday Wednesday Thursday Friday and Saturday according to the same rhythm—this path is easily followed most of the time. But one day the 'why' arises and everything begins in that weariness tinged with amazement. 'Begins'—this is important. Weariness comes at the end of the acts of a mechanical life, but at the same time it inaugurates the impulse of consciousness.
>
> (p. 18)

As we saw during our earlier discussion of Sisyphus and in the above passage, Camus contends that the shattering of narratives can occur even in the course of a normal day. We do not need an experience as traumatic as Plumwood's to shake us to our core. The normal rhythm of life, the stage sets, and the habits that we all live by can be broken when we ask why. Why do we do what we do? Why do we attribute significance to the sorts of things to which we attribute significance? Why do we value the things we value? These questions are provoked by the beginning of an understanding that things could be other than they are; an encompassing awareness of the contingent and constructed nature of our narratives and resulting habits.

The experience of the 'end of the acts of a mechanical life', as described by Camus, along with Plumwood's encounter as prey to a crocodile, both arise from an existential understanding of a given moment, an understanding that is manifest in Pierce's description of the psychology of inquiry, namely, genuine doubt, which requires one to genuinely *experience* doubt—a persistently irritating quality or state of disequilibrium that drives us to seek satisfaction in a state of fixed belief. It is 'the experiential alarm signalling the need for a revision of one's hypothesis' (Hildebrand, 1996, p. 3). In Plumwood's case, genuine doubt was brought about by the crocodile's teeth, in Camus' a recognition of the ridiculousness of habit was enough to initiate it. But it is not enough to merely begin asking questions, what comes after the why is important. The trick Camus thinks is to sustain the recognition of the absurd, or in Peirce's vernacular, to maintain an attitude of fallibilism.

The shift away from individual certitude to a reliance on scientific method requires an attitude of fallibilism. To Peirce, fallibilism's refusal of absolute theoretical certainty is tantamount to the refusal to set up barriers to inquiry. Hence, his emphasis on the notion of genuine rather than Cartesian paper doubt as that which constitutes the starting point of almost all inquiry. In his 'First Rule of Logic' (1899), Peirce states that:

> Upon this first, and in one sense this sole, rule of reason, that in order to learn you must desire to learn, and in so desiring not be satisfied with what you already incline to think, there follows one corollary which itself deserves to be inscribed upon every wall of the city of philosophy: Do not block the way of *inquiry*.
>
> (p. 48)

Put another way, the first rule is to wonder and to cultivate it enough so that it may prevent other methods of settling doubt from becoming dominant and blocking 'the way of inquiry'. Peirce goes on to list four common points of resistance to inquiry and wonder:

1. absolute assertion,
2. maintaining something to be absolutely unknowable,
3. maintaining that something is absolutely basic, ultimate, independent of all else, and utterly inexplicable, and
4. holding that perfect exactitude is possible, especially that which precludes unusual and anomalous phenomena. (pp. 49–50)

Peirce's account of communal inquiry as the settlement of opinion through the method of science contrasts with other methods of fixing belief, such as 'refusing to consider contrary evidence (the Method of Tenacity), accepting an institution's dictates (the Method of Authority), or the most coherent and/or elegant-seeming belief-set (the A Priori Method)' (Legg, 2014, p. 205). However, cooperation in inquiry is not guaranteed; we cannot, as Peirce points out, assume a 'social impulse' to strive for truth or 'coincide with fact'. In practice, we can use any of these methods to satisfy our desires to quell the irritation of doubt through retaining our own belief or uncritically adopting someone else's belief. A lucid teacher will resist this impulse and help guide their students to do likewise, instead adopting the perspective afforded by fallibilism, 'that no empirical statement is impervious to epistemological challenge' (Powell, 2001, p. 11). Fallibilism should not be mistaken for total doubt or scepticism, which 'can only paralyse action'. Rather, the classroom needs to adopt the 'scientific spirit' which 'requires a man to be at all times ready to dump his whole cartload of beliefs, the moment experience is against them' (Peirce, 1960, 1.55).

Peirce's fallibilism committed him to the view that no belief is immune to doubt and, therefore, that these barriers to inquiry would be disrupted by the onslaught of everyday experience, which eventually would reveal contradictory experiential episodes provoking a state of irritation—the accompanying feeling of genuine doubt—that appears to undermine the basis for our habit. Once felt, our habits no longer command our actions, and we become uncertain as to how to proceed. Plumwood's experience with a crocodile and Camus' description of the revealing of the absurd are illustrations of Peirce's view that experiential episodes can give rise to disequilibrium resulting in genuine doubt, wherein our belief-habits no longer offer us confidence to accept them as an explanation of reality. In the case of Plumwood's experience, her encounter with a crocodile challenged the core of her previously fixed beliefs, first, by bringing about an initial awareness of her prejudices (her belief in her safety and superiority), followed by doubt in the face of the contradictory experience (the crocodiles jaws), subsequently leading to the questioning and conscious re-interpretation or reconstruction of her prejudices factoring in the new experiential information (a process of lucid adaption).

According to Peirce, whenever we experience states of genuine doubt, we are inclined toward ending the accompanying irritation (disequilibrium) and settling into a state of habitual belief (equilibrium) brought about by inquiry (the means by which belief is settled).

> The irritation of doubt is the only immediate motive for the struggle to attain belief. It is certainly best for us that our beliefs should be such as may truly guide our actions so as to satisfy our desires; and this reflection will make us reject any belief which does not seem to have been so formed as to insure this result. But it will only do so by creating a doubt in the place of that belief. With the doubt, therefore, the struggle begins, and with the cessation of doubt it ends. Hence, the sole object of inquiry is the settlement of opinion.
>
> (Peirce, 1877, p. 6)

In this sense, genuine doubt challenges established beliefs, values, and realities. The irritation is extended to the interpersonal within the community of inquiry and acts as stimulus for people to come together to rigorously test ideas and hypotheses to arrive at results.

Genuine doubt is the seed for wonder, accompanied by the desire to learn. The doubt we experience is an awareness of a disruption to our everyday experiences. The wonder that ensues signifies interrogation and exclamation: a 'reflective, self-critical, perplexed wonder' (Toulmin, 1994, p. 77) that exists between sensation and thought. When confronted with the object of wonder, we are drawn into what Dewey calls a problem-solving experience, where wonder yields to a prolonged curiosity or wonder-induced inquiry. This, in turn, leads to a post-reflective situation, namely, the reconstruction of experience and knowledge about the self and the world; a 'process of intelligibility, the path from wonder to surprise, a feeling of newness and attention-seizing freshness to curiosity, prolonged attention, satisfaction' (Fisher, 1998, p. 149). Genuine doubt can be cultivated through the community of inquiry coupled with lucid teaching, where the questioning of reality and knowledge of that reality induces perplexity, intellectual curiosity, and awareness of the fallibility of our beliefs. Such inducement occurs when both the students engaged in inquiry and the teacher who facilitates the inquiry are motivated by wonder. In the next section, we provide a more detailed description of lucid teaching in the classroom.

Experiencing the absurd: Lucid teaching in the classroom

Camus' notion of the absurd can inform discussion on the relationship between the phenomenology of inquiry and the communal processes of reconstructing knowledge. Lucid teaching, we hold, can provide a means to understanding the processes of habituation that lead to inoculation against wonder as an obstacle to genuine doubt, and hence a lack of desire to learn or to inquire, which could lead to a dearth of questioning and wonder. Those physical and intellectual habits that limit our intellectual freedom can cause us to cease to question, and in doing so, we become immune to wonder, that is, resistance to critical questioning, and self-correction. For once problems become familiar, we lose sight of them, we habituate or adapt to them, rather than continue to question and strive to create solutions. The relationship between lucidity and resistance to wonder can be likened to Plato's description of Socrates as gadfly; a relationship of an uncomfortable goad to Athenian politics, which he compared to a slow and dim-witted horse.

Genuine doubt as a spark for lucidity acts as a gadfly; a persistent irritant that challenges our view of reality as well as our established beliefs, values, and socio-political structures. However, it could be argued that there is a difference between Camus' response and the pragmatist's response to Cartesian certitude and absolute truth. Whereas Camus' response relies heavily on the *individual* to address the everyday problems of the historical moment in which he or she lives, Peirce speaks of *communal dialogue* as an interpersonal method for developing beliefs about the world. Seemingly, this gap in their thinking could make them incompatible in terms of a mutual educational process. However, what might seem like Camus' over-reliance on the self as solipsistic hero is subverted by his views on communicative ethics, namely, rebellion as a lived philosophy responding to a situated narrative.

Camus' (1991) rebellion is against the certainty of other and singularity of people's judgements. It is towards blind faith in the certainty of reason that Camus revolts. Such blind faith often leads to extremes of support for a certain way of doing, being, or thinking to the exclusion and detriment of all others. Mary Graham (1999) makes a similar point, if 'one true way is posited, sooner or later individuals or groups are inclined to ideologise it; rigid thinking then follows (or vice versa), and the formation of groups of 'true believers', chosen people, sects, religions, parties etc., cannot be far behind' (p. 113). It is such totalising ideologies that too often lead to conflict and epistemic and physical violence, as we will look at in greater depth in the next section. It is Camus' revolt, his rejection of totalising ideology, that has the most relevance to the community of inquiry pedagogy, in that his method of lucidity has the capacity to tie us together in an appreciation of difference. It is a rebellion that begins with the feeling of absurdity. In Camus' (1977) words:

> Therefore the first progressive step for a mind overwhelmed by the strangeness of things is to realize that this feeling of strangeness is shared with all men and that human reality, in its entirety, suffers from the distance which separates it from the rest of the universe. The malady experienced by a single man becomes a mass plague. In our daily trials rebellion plays the same role as does the 'cogito' in the realm of thought: it is the first piece of evidence. But this evidence lures the individual from his solitude. It founds its first value on the whole human race. I rebel—therefore we exist.
>
> (p. 28)

The feeling of absurdity begins the movement towards the understanding of the absurd. Once absurdity is felt 'the primitive hostility of the world rises up to face us across millennia' (p. 20). It is then that we witness the world stripped of our narratives, as Plumwood did after her run in with the crocodile. We then experience the world without 'the images and designs that we had attributed to it beforehand', and the world then 'evades us because it becomes itself again' (p. 20). Only once we have become cognisant of our experience of absurdity do we begin to understand the absurd; the distance between ourselves and 'the rest of the universe', a distance shared by all humanity.

The concept of the absurd is the negation of the Cartesian first principle of existence. The reflection on this negation leads to the Camus' discovery of first certitude; that of rebellion or revolt 'from which the progress toward positive direction becomes possible' (Sagi, 2002, p. 108), that is, towards the solidarity of suffering and the community of humanity the recognition of the universal nature of suffering can create. In other words, the concept of the absurd subverts Descartes' solipsism, 'placing "we" before "I" and culminating in the concept of solidarity' (p. 1). Such solidarity requires a recognition of the limitation of the other, the ethic of the breath.

> In the absence of ultimate reason, Camus could be said to reason from the breath. With each breath, he understands that his life is valuable, at least to him. Casting his thoughts outward, he understands that while they too breathe, other's lives are valuable to them; he forms his sense of value on that which he deems most fundamental and irreducible: life.
>
> (Thornton, 2019, p. 615)

When we individually rebel against suffering in all its forms, collectively we flourish. Camusian rebellion occurs when an individual accepts the absurd and takes action to minimise shared suffering and to increase shared understanding; when at a given moment, an opportunity to reinterpret life and to construct new meanings or understandings commensurate with other people's abilities to do the same, is realised.

There is still another question that cannot be avoided. If genuine doubt is a necessary condition for inquiry, how can teachers engage students in the educational process, especially those who are not always philosophically open or eager to engage in inquiry, that is, those who are resistant to questioning their own understanding of the world? This question highlights what Wendy Turgeon (1998) calls the problem of the reluctant philosopher, the condition whereby various obstacles—psychological, behavioural, and environmental—prevent students from participating in philosophical inquiry. There is a tendency for the literature to be generally optimistic that philosophical inquiry itself can provoke the reluctant philosopher into dialogue. However, this does not consider the situation of the students within the greater community which itself could be resistant to critical inquiry. Enter the role of lucid teaching, leading to the creation of a lucid community.

An understanding of genuine doubt in Peirce's writings together with Camus' method of lucidity (as revolt) can equip the teacher to act as Socratic gadfly to engage students in questioning and to convert the classroom into a community of inquiry. Genuine doubt bears resemblance to the experience of absurdity within Camus' work; indeed, absurdity can be thought of as the phenomenological awareness of genuine doubt. As it is conceivable that anyone could experience genuine doubt or absurdity under apt conditions, in the absence of such conditions it is the task of the teachers to take notice of potential moments of genuine doubt, such as instances of hesitancy, uncertainty, or disagreement, in order to provoke lucidity. As these moments propagate within the classroom, they create the potential for disequilibrium, and subsequently, communal rebellion essential to the formation of a lucid community. If genuine doubt and the absurd come from within situatedness, we cannot expect students to make the transition from individual existential rebellion to communal rebellion without guidance. The goal is not to immediately push them into critical thinking, but to extend their experience of the imaginative through extending their experience of genuine doubt (Bleazby, 2012). It is the role of the teacher to sustain these moments of awareness in order to develop lucidity; the confrontation with the absurd which is both a physical experience and a logical discovery that the 'absurd is lucid reason noting its limits' (Camus, 1977, p. 49). Lucidity is vital to the functioning of the community of inquiry as it builds on the experience of genuine doubt, introducing an ethical component (i.e., the ethic of the breath) and creating a preparedness to confront what Dewey calls the problematic situation; a situation of uncertainty that is practical and existential in which habitual responses to the habitat (environment) are inadequate for the continuation of ongoing activity that pursues fulfilment through needs and desires.

Developing lucidity through experience of the imaginary extends the metaphor of the gadfly to that of the stingray. Within the community of inquiry, the teacher plays the dual role of gadfly and stingray (see Murris,

2008, 2016b, pp. 181–186). The teacher as facilitator acts as gadfly goading students into 'actively seeking opportunities to be perplexed, numbed and open to change through reflection and self-reflection' (Murris, 2008, p. 671). The characterisation in the *Meno* of Socrates as stingray is that he *makes anyone who comes close feel numb* and unable to speak. Socrates accepts this characterisation provided the stingray also stings itself as he insisted that he be as numb as his interlocutors: 'It isn't that knowing the answers myself, I perplex other people. The truth is rather that I infect them also with the perplexity I feel myself' (in Plato, 1961, 80a–c). This describes the role of the teacher also as co-inquirer. In other words, teachers, both as facilitator/gadfly and co-inquirer/stingray are perplexed. The teacher and the students then act as one self-stinging classroom community, 'rearranging, shifting, displacing and reframing ideas and beliefs' (Haynes, 2008, p. 51). The cultivation of collective doubt then is essential for collaborative dialogue (Burgh, Thornton & Fynes-Clinton, 2018; Fynes-Clinton, 2015; Nichols, Burgh & Fynes-Clinton, 2017a). If we think of the community of inquiry as a life-long learning process that extends beyond the classroom, the metaphor of the self-stinging stingray 'is even more applicable as persistence for reflection and a commitment to having an inquiring mind' (Davey Chesters, 2012, p. 82).

Within the context of the community of inquiry we have described as lucid education, Lipman's novels for classroom inquiry, or any philosophy story-as-text or curricular materials that reflect childhood experience by drawing attention to moments that can create genuine doubt, act as gadfly in the hands of teacher-facilitators, in order to transform the classroom into a fever of stingrays. The novels create a potential disruption to the students' belief-habits. Because the narratives do not always speak for themselves, the teacher must act as a lucid facilitator and co-inquirer to open up moments of potential lucidity. To borrow from Gadamer (2004), these moments expand horizons through the imaginative world. For Dewey this is engagement in intelligent imagination, an 'imaginative process of creating possible means of reconstructing experience' (Bleazby, 2012, p. 99). For Camus (1977), life lived 'turned away from the eternal is but a vast mime under the mask of the absurd. Creation is the great mime' (p. 87), freeing us to lucidly play under the knowledge of an absurd sky. Like two children gazing at the night sky and connecting the stars, turning them into images that create narratives, together they recognise, create, and recreate their shared reality. These historical narratives stay with us as we grow into adults, and, therefore, need to be questioned and explored in order to avoid a society inoculated against wonder.

The communicative interchange between the teacher and students in a community of inquiry is not strictly egalitarian because of the teacher's dual roles as facilitator and co-inquirer. Both roles require teachers to draw on their expertise as (1) accredited members of the teaching profession who have pedagogical expertise, and (2) members of scholarly communities with interests or expertise in curriculum content (subjects such as the arts, mathematics, science, history). Students come to understand that teachers have subject knowledge, but as co-inquirers teachers need also be aware that their expertise and the expertise of their discipline or profession is limited (the wide-sense community of inquiry), and they must also convey or model this limitation in their role as facilitators of a specific teaching method for fostering philosophical inquiry (the narrow-sense community of inquiry). As it is often said, teachers need to assume a position of scholarly ignorance. However, teachers should be careful not to feign ignorance, lest students become sceptical and see such ignorance as paper doubt. As co-inquirers, teachers need to assume a position of genuine doubt to prompt students into their own states of genuine doubt. An effective pedagogy of lucidity requires an acute consciousness of the limits of reason in settling the divorce between belief and reality and ensuring that both teacher and students are aware of potential prejudices.

Prejudice is commonly viewed as an unfavourable opinion or feeling formed without knowledge or evidence. However, as mentioned previously, for Peirce (1868), prejudices 'are things which it does not occur to us *can* be questioned' (p. 140). They are habits of mind or beliefs that guide observation and deduction. Such prejudice at the outset of inquiry comes not with judgement and is, therefore, neither favourable nor unfavourable. Rather, prejudice is a preconceived opinion that acts as a pre-understanding for the topic under investigation but is capable of being subject to critical examination and revised understanding through communal inquiry and self-correction. If, like Peirce, we accept that we cannot begin philosophical inquiry with complete doubt—that we can only 'begin with all the prejudices which we actually have when we enter upon the study of philosophy' (p. 140)—then inquiry does not take place in a vacuum. Instead, it is the engagement of individuals steeped in a social structure of historical customs, habits, and traditions of a community. These historical narratives make up our prejudices, and thereby constitute our being in the world. They 'stay with us as we grow into adults, and, therefore, need to be questioned and explored to avoid a society inoculated against wonder' (Burgh & Thornton, 2016b, p. 12). In a community of inquiry, unsustainable prejudices are jettisoned and enabling prejudices retained through imaginative and meaningful dialogue, careful reasoning, and reflection over time within the same community of learners. It is important, therefore, for the community to engage with each other's narratives, to listen to seemingly oppositional narratives as well as shared narratives, along with the diversity of voices contained within them. Like Lipman's purpose-written philosophical stories-as-text, in which philosophical concepts and philosophical procedures directly relate to children's experiences through the experiences of fictional characters, so too with the community of inquiry, but children *are* the characters in their own narratives directly relating to their own experiences. Indeed, as explained previously, for social reconstruction to occur, students need to engage experientially in real-world activities, not just in the classroom but extended into the local community—this could mean community members being invited into the classroom or students going into the local community. Moreover, as we shall see later, the purpose-written texts do not necessarily directly relate to student experiences as they are decontextualised from political realities. Nevertheless, prior to any judgements, the 'story-telling' needs to be sustained. This can assist the emergence of, or it can cultivate, genuine doubt, not only in individuals but also in the community, which can bring on the need for inquiry and subsequent critical analysis.

We argue that a diversity of prejudices is a necessary starting point for genuine inquiry, for it is only when children and adolescents bring diverse perspectives to the community of inquiry that cooperative intelligence can occur. As Gregory (2005) puts it, '[g]ood inquiry depends on a rich diversity of options—options for beliefs, values and action—upon which the community may apply its procedures of intelligent selection' (p. 269). These prejudices propel the inquiry and produce the outcome. Awareness of the importance of prejudices allows teachers and students alike to look for and expand upon moments of disequilibrium in the classroom, thereby multiplying awareness and experience of the divorce between belief and reality, which is why attention to lucid teaching is crucial as it sustains an awareness of the absurdity to reconcile this divorce through inquiry. Once cognisance of our own prejudices is achieved, we are confronted by these prejudices as barriers to inquiry, and a choice presents itself; either we accept things the way they are and remain confined by our own narratives, or we consent to wrestle with our belief-habits, admitting that they could be otherwise.

A well-formed community of inquiry founded on fallibilism is open to the sensation of genuine, heart-felt doubt 'which really interferes with the smooth working of belief-habit' (Peirce, 1960, 5.510), and subsequently gives a positive reason to move from disequilibrium to equilibrium; that is, to be in a state of inquiry in which we communally struggle to attain a new belief-habit. We are warranted in accepting the result of our deliberations as 'the most reasonable by account of all available arguments and evidence' (Gregory, 2006, p. 166) derived from a rigorous method of intellectual cooperation, but only provisionally, always keeping in mind that even equilibrium is a temporary state bound to evolve into disequilibrium once again in an ongoing repetitive cycle. Unlike the endless repetition of the task the gods had condemned Sisyphus to, each new cycle is a reconstruction of experience, which as Dewey told us, is an evolutionary process of growth; it is education itself.

Effectively, the classroom is converted into a community of inquiry because it becomes a model of the wide-sense communal inquiry of which Peirce spoke, an organising or regulative principle for social inquiry. A defining feature that distinguishes our conception of the community of inquiry from those who are focused on inquiry as solely the improvement of critical thinking, or on the teaching method as stages of inquiry only without an understanding of pragmatist epistemology and its pedagogical principles, is that we emphasise a pedagogical strategy in which teachers understand the limitations of reason. *These limitations are defined by Peirce's irreducible fallibilism of inquiry, but with emphasis on Camus' absurdity, namely, the phenomenological realisation that total clarity or understanding of the world remains out of reach.* Facilitation becomes the facilitation of lucid inquiry with a focus on the development of lucid individuals through autonomous collective inquiry. In practice, the teacher needs to be lucidly aware of moments of hesitation in a community of inquiry. These moments, when facilitated, can create and sustain a tension that pushes students past their comfort zone and compels them to test their belief-habits and accompanying actions. However, for teachers to be genuine in their dual roles as facilitators and co-inquirers they need to experience genuine doubt over the limits of their expertise and the knowledge of their discipline or subject area. Avoiding the temptation to uncritically remove this unsettling feeling through the methods of tenacity, authority, or *a priori* that Peirce spoke of (e.g., by leaping into hope for an unattainable settled knowledge or to move from disequilibrium to equilibrium on impulse rather than by way of a warranted method of fixing belief), requires lucidity, a sustained or studied awareness of the absurd. Such a state is necessary for the maintenance of effective communities of inquiry that are sensitive to epistemic exclusion. One could say, therefore, that a teacher's role is to facilitate an embedded inquiry of the absurd. However, we cannot expect students, especially in the early years of schooling, to be naturally inclined to this state; it must be cultivated.

Keeping all this in mind, the community of inquiry is an ideal educational setting in which students can cultivate doubt by exploring their prejudices, and thereby engage in genuine inquiry. To this end, teacher education programs would need to concentrate on the teacher as facilitator and co-inquirer and emphasise the phenomenology of the community of inquiry, its pedagogical principles, and pragmatist underpinnings. Our discussion here can provide the conceptual and pedagogical guidelines to develop such programs. Meanwhile, there is another matter to attend to. Prejudices can create obstacles to inquiry through epistemic bias, exclusion, and superiority, which is a form of violence that is neither only physical nor psychological but can result in both. In the next section, we put forward an argument that the kind of community of inquiry we described here is a form of peace education.

Epistemic violence and peace education: Turning conflict into inquiry

Genuine doubt, as we have seen, is central to pragmatist epistemology and, therefore, to the theory and practice of philosophy for children. As pragmatist epistemology replaces truth with reflective equilibrium—the process of inquiry that moves from disequilibrium to equilibrium—facilitating a community of inquiry necessitates careful attention to the epistemic nature of inquiry, including obstacles that prevent the flow of inquiry, This is vital, as students bring their habits formed largely by social and political institutions, such as the family, religion, law, and cultural mores, to the classroom (Furlong & Morrison, 2000; Splitter, 1993) and vice versa. It is inevitable that the classroom habitat, as a microcosm of the community in which it is situated, will perpetuate the epistemic practices and injustices of that community, manifested in attitudes, beliefs, behaviours, and actions that can limit the student's ability to learn. The educational task, then, is to create opportunities for students to problematise the very environment they inhabit. To this end, our concern is for peace education aimed at addressing epistemic violence; a form of harm brought about by the presence of a rationality of domination that hinders the development of multi-voiced narratives in inquiry.

The classroom community of inquiry is often viewed as a solution to inequality in the classroom—an intellectually safe environment which allows students to explore, practice, and internalise good reasoning through philosophy so that they can make school relevant to their lives. Traditionally, the teacher's role in a community of inquiry has been variously described as that of taking a 'neutral stance' or a 'position of indifference', or at the very least being 'sensitive to the context of discussion'. However, we argue that it is misplaced to assume that the community of inquiry is a safe intellectual environment in which it is simply a matter of the teacher facilitating the discussion procedurally, letting the argument lead, which Lipman took as the guiding principle for his process of inquiry. For, as Freire (1970) put it,

> the dominant ideology makes its presence in the classroom partly felt by trying to convince the teacher that he or she must be neutral in order to respect the student. This kind of neutrality is a false respect for students. On the contrary, the more I say nothing about agreeing or not agreeing out of respect for the others, the more I am leaving the dominant ideology in peace!.
>
> (p. 174)

Teachers must be aware of the possibility of epistemic exclusion and privileging to be able to detect and disrupt them in order to facilitate a peaceful inquiry (i.e., inquiry sensitive to epistemic practices). We do not consider peace in the negative sense, as the absence of personal or direct violence (e.g., peace due to ceasefire), or the absence of conflict generally. Peace is more than preventing the consequences of an undesirable act from occurring. Hence, we prefer the term peace in the positive sense, as used by peace studies scholars to mean a process of eliminating structural violence, that is, all forms of injustices, discrimination, and unequal access to opportunities (Fountain, 1999; Galtung, 1969; Hicks, 1987, 2004; Jäger, 2014; United Nations, 1999). However, our focus is not on 'eliminating' structural violence, as this not only seems an impossible task, but requires more than educating toward peace. Instead, our focus is on developing students' capacity to respond skilfully to conflict as a way of life and a requirement of citizenship. Specifically, we focus on epistemic exclusion and privileging as a form of structural violence that has the potential to block inquiry. Thus, we concentrate on peace education that prepares students to turn conflict into inquiry, rather than peace education as instilling values of 'fraternity and non-violence' (Gregory, 2004, p. 277). The community of inquiry provides such a framework; however, we argue that it must be facilitated in a way that mitigates the effects of epistemic violence by creating an educational habitat in which multiple ways of knowing can flourish.

Children should be seen and not heard: The impact of epistemic violence

In an increasingly globalised world of shifting cultural narratives that profoundly shape societies and underpin how we conceptualise sex/gender, race/ethnicity, class, sexual orientation, age, ability, and other social categories (i.e., abstract identities defined by physical, social, or mental characteristics), education needs to actively engage with cultural diversity to mitigate the problem of identity prejudices that contribute to the process of 'othering'. Indigenous struggles for recognition, gender inequality, increasingly vocal opposition over asylum seekers, discrimination against ethnic minorities, and marriage inequality, to name but a few, all illustrate such a need. Denzin and Lincoln (2008) argue that there is no separation between education, politics, and morality, 'that all inquiry is both political and moral' (p. 2). Schools engage in epistemic practices through curriculum and pedagogy, which rely on the interpretation or acceptance of knowledge and are, therefore, an integral part of epistemic cultures; cultures of 'knowledge setting' that contribute to and shape society.

Epistemic practices shape our belief-habits through which we make sense of the world. Repetitive interaction with our environment builds our habits. Rightfully or wrongfully, when we enter a new environment, we are likely to see it through the framework of the familiar. A similar process is active when we look at children. We see children not as they are but as we think they should be. This extends to the content of their speech—often we fail to take seriously or value children's knowledge. To counter such practices, teachers 'need to be open to what they have not heard before, and resist the urge to translate what they hear into what is familiar' (Murris, 2013, p. 251). They need to be careful not to dismiss the content of the child's words based solely on the age of the speaker. Such dismissals are evident in the cases of 'teenage activists'—read 'not adults'. Malala Yousafzai who became a global ambassador for the rights of all children, especially girls, to have an education; gun control advocate Emma González; Amika George, an activist who campaigns against period poverty in the U.K.; and especially Swedish climate change activist and initiator of the global school strike movement, Greta Thunberg, all of whom have been dismissed as being used by parents or other adults, or 'set up' as a front for radical groups or 'left-wing propagandists'. For example, Thunberg was criticised by U.S. commentator Dinesh D'Souza who said: 'Children—notably Nordic white girls with braids and red cheeks— were often used in Nazi propaganda. An old Goebbels technique! Looks like today's progressive Left is still learning its game from an earlier Left in the 1930s' (SBS News, 2019, n.p.).

Murris argues that to dismiss the content of the child's words would be to commit epistemic injustice. Miranda Fricker (2007) identifies two kinds of epistemic injustices: testimonial injustice and hermeneutical injustice.

Testimonial injustice occurs when prejudice causes a hearer to give a deflated level of credibility to a speaker's word; hermeneutical injustice occurs at a prior stage, when a gap in collective interpretive resources puts someone at an unfair disadvantage when it comes to making sense of their social experiences. An example of the first might be that the police do not believe you because you are black; an example of the second might be that you suffer sexual harassment in a culture that still lacks that critical concept. We might say that testimonial injustice is caused by prejudice in the economy of credibility; and that hermeneutical injustice is caused by structural prejudice in the economy of collective hermeneutical resources.

(pp. 1–2)

Whilst Fricker is largely credited with beginning what Rachel McKinnon (2016) calls a 'watershed moment' (p. 443) in epistemology, certain minority groups have a long history of producing literature on the topic of epistemic injustice that has itself been subject to epistemic injustice. McKinnon reminds us that 'whose work we engage with is a matter of epistemic justice' (p. 439).

Kristine Dotson (2011) acknowledges the work of Gayatri Spivak, specifically her use of the term 'epistemic violence', to argue that the 'epistemic side of colonialism is the devastating effect of the "disappearing" of knowledge, where local or provincial knowledge is dismissed due to privileging alternative, often Western, epistemic practices' (p. 236). Dotson goes on to argue that 'to communicate we all need an audience willing and capable of hearing us. The extent to which entire populations of people can be denied this kind of linguistic reciprocation as a matter of course institutes epistemic violence' (p. 238). Following Dotson, we further adapt Spivak's (2003) use of the term epistemic violence to escape the unnecessary burden of fairness Fricker's use of injustice carries. Fricker (2007) notes that for 'something to be an injustice, it must be harmful but also wrongful, whether because discriminatory or because otherwise unfair' (p. 151). However, for our purposes, epistemic harm is enough. This is not to say that justice is not something to strive for, or that epistemic injustice is not an extremely useful concept, rather it is to broaden the umbrella to include all epistemic harms.

Our concern is with epistemic violence as the stage prior to epistemic injustice, particularly in the context of the community of inquiry as classroom practice. A form of violence found in speech acts, in systems of rationality, and broadly speaking, in our relationship with others, both human and non-human, and inclusive of our relationship with ourselves. We locate epistemic violence in what Plumwood (1993, 2002) calls 'inferiorization', which is brought about by a particular rationality of domination that dehumanises individuals or groups of humans and environment. Hyde (2016) notes that a rationality of dominance, 'according to which the subjugation of and associated presumed mastery over nature, women, indigenous peoples and the working classes proceeds by a defective kind of "rationality" according to which they are all Other' (p. 5).

The traditional western conception of rationality Plumwood critiques plays a key role in justifying maltreatment visited upon those it relies on and simultaneously excludes from the realm of reason and the category of fully human. These exclusions amount to a denial of humanity, which Plumwood (1993) argues results in the creation of a class of 'others'; humans grouped as non-humans, lumped with animals and nature as inferior to 'naturalize domination' (p. 54). Traditionally, women and minority groups have been predominant in this category. We equate this logic of domination with epistemic violence because it is inherently discriminatory and inclines us to categorise, judge, and treat other humans as less than human due to historical socio-political prejudices. Prejudices based on a system of dualisms 'which permeate [Western] culture, forming a fault line which runs through its entire conceptual system' (p. 443).

Epistemic issues in the classroom

In the classroom, these prejudices appear explicitly or implicitly through dominant narratives; narratives that subjugate others and may come accompanied with feelings and expressions of anger, frustration, disbelief in alternative narratives, or general discomfort. Prejudices also lie in assumptions about communication practices that we take for granted, such as asking direct questions, facial expression, eye contact, and expressing disagreement, all of which are considered acceptable ways of showing respect and making students feel safe in the community of inquiry. However, such assumptions in teachers' daily practices can create cultural tensions. For example, '[i]n Canadian Aboriginal cultures, it is considered rude to maintain eye contact, whereas the dominant discourse in Canadian education is that a person who does not maintain eye contact is lacking integrity and honesty' (Makaiau et al., 2017, pp. 227–228). That we are ignorant of such prejudices requires that we engage with others so that we become aware of them; the possibility of our becoming cognisant of our prejudices and prejudice habits opens when we become aware that we are engaged in dominant narratives. To address this problem pedagogically requires a form of peace education. Hence, we argue for a conception of peace as the ability and disposition to cope with conflict as a democratic community through environmentally and socially embedded inquiry, or as Dewey would have it, through habit and habitat. In a world where peace is never finally achieved, always struggled for, we need an educational process that embodies this struggle. The process needs to allow for multiple ways of knowing and not impede on the intellectual freedom of those who do not fit or support the dominant narrative. Philosophy for children is often said to be an exemplar of inquiry that produces children able to make well-reasoned arguments. However, like the greater community, it is not immune to epistemic violence. Unless care is taken in all aspects of inquiry, choice of materials, facilitation of dialogue, and classroom structure, the inquiry is likely to create students capable of reasoning only within the confines of dominant rationality.

Lipman, Sharp, and others, as we have seen, recommend that philosophical inquiry is best brought about using purpose written stimulus material to create an intellectually safe environment for students by connecting their experiences to those of the children in the stories-as-text to provide a model for doing philosophy. According to Lipman (2014):

> The modelling role of the text is of enormous importance. If our aim is to get children to do philosophy, then the text should provide a model of children doing philosophy. If our aim is to get children to reason together, explore concepts in an illuminating way, build on one another's ideas and strengthen their judgment through thoughtful deliberation, then we must provide texts that depict children doing these very things. If we think it important that children's opinions, values and enactments be well-reasoned, then we should have them read and discuss stories in which fictional children aspire to and work towards precisely these outcomes.
>
> (p. 11)

However, as Darren Chetty (2014) argues:

> Whilst Lipman claims to have "neutralized" the "godlike power of the author" in his philosophical novels, this has been strongly questioned by Kohan (1995), and Rainville (2000 [sic]), both of whom argue that it is not neutral to ignore the foundations of systematic discrimination and the ways institutions have arisen out of and continue to perpetuate the repression of minoritized groups.
>
> (p. 15)

Hell Rainville's (2001) claim is that philosophy for children's 'purportedly neutral approach to philosophical inquiry may unwittingly contribute to the marginalization of Indigenous peoples both in North America and around the world' (p. 67). She observes that: 'I have yet to read a paper in the growing body of Philosophy for Children literature which acknowledges the ways in which our so-called democratic institutions have arisen out of, and continue to perpetuate, the political, economic and ideological repression of Native North Americans' (p. 66). Her concern is echoed by Walter Kohan (2018), who, following Freire's moral condemnation of neutrality, contends that '[e]ducation cannot be apolitical, politically neutral or aseptic' (p. 621). Purporting that education must be neutral, is a way of silencing the Other without admitting a standpoint, hiding behind the mask of neutrality. For these reasons and more, Rainville (2001) argues for 'conscious partiality'.[6]

> 'Conscious Partiality' requires that teachers acknowledge their own (inevitable) biases, as well as the conceptual limitations of their chosen material, while paying particular attention to the political contexts in which education takes place. As a result, Philosophy for Children must

be willing to incorporate historical detail and socio-cultural awareness into any programs which are meant to be truly liberatory.

(p. 67)

Rainville argues that education cannot be ahistorical, that teachers must understand the historical forces that shape the lives of their students, especially those to whom history has been oppressive. Sociocultural awareness is critical for mitigating epistemic violence, as our respective *positionalities*, that is, our standpoint or socio-political location, 'influence how we perceive and understand the world, as well as how our efforts to perceive and understand the world are viewed by others' (Reed-Sandoval & Sykes, 2017, p. 219). The teacher's role as facilitator and co-inquirer demands the capacity to discern the ways in which the students' learning experience in the community of inquiry are influenced by cultural dimensions, as context 'can impact the sorts of questions and discussions generated by children' (Reed-Sandoval, 2014, p. 9). In this sense, the community of inquiry is *place-based*, albeit place mediated through the human, insofar as history and cultural are brought together in the context of students' experiences of self/cultural identity. Students who have been subjected to epistemic violence, and other forms of discrimination, 'become empowered to bring into the philosophical dialogue their own experiences of marginalization especially when their unique contexts are acknowledged and respected' (Elicor, 2019, p. 28).[7] We will speak more on this in Chapter 6.

Murris (2015) adds that the traditional 'P4C curriculum is evaluative and prescriptive (in the sense of what counts as philosophy and what needs to be appropriated by the learners) and therefore normative' (p. 67). Doing away with the characters in the purpose written stories-as-text *frees* children from the normative pressures of aspiring to the ideal 'adult philosopher's child' (p. 63). Further, Chetty (2014) notes that 'the selection of a text will itself steer a discussion, inasmuch that it will make some ideas more likely and others less likely to be explored' (p. 25). In the context of multiculturalism and pluralism, he makes the following point:

> There may be an assumption on the part of P4C practitioners that fantastic tales are a better way of thinking about race and culture than real-life situations. It may be that they offer the comfort of distance or that they encourage a dispassionate approach to philosophising. However, it is questionable who is being comforted here. Are we to assume that children are incapable of serious thought about the real world? Or do these 'race fables' provide some comfort and protection for adults working with children? And if so, do they not set boundaries for what exactly we discuss when we claim to enquire into race?
>
> (p. 25)

It is not enough to create an intellectually 'safe' environment by creating a distance between real-life and the stories-as-text used as stimulus material, we need to also create an environment that allows intellectual freedom to flourish. For, as Chetty argues, 'if we are truly interested in promoting dialogical enquiry, then we must recognise that for marginalized and oppressed minorities, "there is no safe space" (Leonardo & Porter, 2010, p. 140)' (p. 24). Indeed, '[d]espite the frequent references to identity, diversity, justice and equality both with the P4C literature and as conference themes, work that deals explicitly with race/racism remains rare' (Chetty & Suissa, 2017, p. 11). Inquiry derived from purpose written stimulus material that focuses discussion on a kind of rationality of inquiry but does not explicitly address race/racism, could be complicit in perpetuating a rationality of dominance—such as the stories-as-text written by Lipman and alternative materials produced by proponents of philosophy for children, as well as various resources recommended by practitioners. These materials, as Chetty (2014) puts it, 'may still serve to perpetuate rather than interrogate key epistemological assumptions that characterise Whiteness' (p. 16). Classroom resources that act as starting points or stimulus for discussion cannot be absent of culture, power imbalances, history, and other salient features that decontextualise the characters (including race, gender, sexuality, social class), otherwise they become oversimplified in the same way the moral dilemmas that we spoke of do. For Chetty, '[i]dentifying which starting points disrupt and which perpetuate dominant racial (and other) discourses would therefore be a useful task for P4C practitioners' (p. 24).

Christina Slade (1994) focuses on gender differences in language and the use of reasoning, specifically on how the IAPC novels model children's language and the way gender is reflected in the children's talk. She concentrates on *Harry Stottlemeier's Discovery* to address the question of how gender might be treated in a classroom community of inquiry. Unlike Lipman's other novels *Kio and Gus* and *Pixie*, in which the main character's names are ambiguous and reflected in the ambiguity of the conversational style, this is not found in *Harry Stottlemeier's Discovery* which is explicitly written with the principles of reasoning in mind. There is no question; Harry is a boy. 'His role in the text confirms the gender stereotype of males as innovative, analytic and "rational." His friend, Lisa, is involved in his discoveries but typically plays a supporting role or raises objections which are sceptical of the value of the analytic technique' (p. 31). Rather than deal with the complex problem of the onus being on the text to resolve gender stereotyping, Slade turns to philosophical investigation to put power in the hands of students to question the very text they are given as stimulus. She also turns to Lloyd as a source for facilitating discussion through questioning the accuracy of the depictions and whether they should apply. She concludes that the community of inquiry, if aware of gender stereotyping, 'is a technique for avoiding the worst of gender-based miscommunication' (p. 32). However, while this takes the onus off the text, it puts an even greater onus on the teacher to be aware of their own epistemic biases and prejudices.

Whether it is 'rectifying' the text, selecting classroom materials, or careful facilitation of philosophical discussion, teachers need to be aware of the epistemic obstacles that can perpetuate dominant discourses and exclude multi-voiced, communal dialogue. Once again, we cannot stress enough the importance of the teachers' role as both facilitator and co-inquirer, whose expertise is required to move between theory and practice, the text and real-world, which requires an awareness of the epistemological differences between the classroom and scholarly inquiries, and to mediate between the narrow-sense and wise-sense communities of inquiry to maintain an epistemically inclusive learning environment. Lipman's aim, that teachers should convert the classroom into a community of inquiry, demands this, but so too do the following words regarding our assumption about the world.

> We must also be ready to realize that the ineffectiveness of our own approaches may be due to faulty assumptions we ourselves are making— or perhaps even to prejudices we ourselves hold—with regard to the nature of the problem.
>
> (Lipman, 1991, p. 255)

Given our discussion so far on pragmatist epistemology, and the need to cultivate collective doubt to move from disequilibrium to reflective equilibrium, the community of inquiry should be an intellectually 'safe place' only insofar as it seeks epistemic inclusion, not to shy away from real-world controversy, or what Haynes and Murris (2012) refer to as pedagogical 'no go areas'. Indeed, it is necessary for students to take intellectual risks that extend to their own and others' experiences. To facilitate such an inquiry, teachers need to become more aware of their own discomfort and how these can create obstacles to inquiry, to understand that the experiences and ideas the students bring to the classroom are embedded in broader historical, social, and political contexts and, therefore, that there are no simple solutions. They need to practice lucidity, that is, to be epistemically aware while listening and being sensitive to prejudices and moments in the inquiry where identity and positionality need to be understood to mitigate epistemic violence, which might otherwise go undetected where only the dominant rationality is present in the dialogue. In other words, teachers need to listen for any prejudice against someone's credibility as a member of a group, whether sex/gender, race/ethnicity, sexual orientation, ability, social class, or anyone speaking outside the dominant discourse, thus, making it difficult for them to be understood.

To redress these issues, there is need for re-thinking pre-service and in-service teacher education program. An effective program would need to be informed by theory and practice, including the relationship between epistemology and education, the teacher's role in the reconstruction of education, and the role of communal dialogue in constructing identity, whilst keeping in mind that education, itself, is one of the primary institutions for the transmission of dominant rationality and that teachers play an active part in this, either explicitly or through the hidden curriculum. For the remainder of chapter, we focus on the latter and examine the implications of teachers, on the one hand, being an integral part of the transmission of culture and, on the other hand, being expected to be a part of education reform. Liberalism is the dominant rationality in Western-style liberal democracies and, therefore, has social and epistemic privilege as a narrative, including narratives surrounding identity. Managing pluralism and multi-voiced discourses can create tensions in classrooms where the students' lived experiences of social categories (i.e., abstract identities), such as race/ethnicity or sex/gender, are diverse. Tensions can be exacerbated in schools where the student population and the teachers identify, consciously or unconsciously, with the dominant culture and rationality, or in multiracial schools. How teachers facilitate the tensions in a community of inquiry is crucial to identity formation. If teachers relate to the lived experiences of others as imagined through their own cultural positioning or identity, they create obstacles for enabling multi-narratives and privilege the dominant rationality.

Developing traitorous identities

To address the problem of dominant rationality in the classroom, we adapt Plumwood's (2002) notion of 'traitorous identities'— people who belong to the dominant culture yet resist its usual epistemic assumptions and institutional practices. Traitorous identities are created by focusing attention on 'experiences that do not fit the dominant story' (pp. 12–13); experiences that point to the need to revise our 'conception of the self and its relation to the nonhuman other, opposition to oppressive practices, and the abandonment and critique of cultural allegiances to the dominance of the human species and its bonding against non-humans' (p. 205). Traitorous identities that enable some men to act in solidarity with feminists 'in active opposition to androcentric culture, some whites to be actively in opposition to white supremacism and ethnocentric culture, also enable some humans to be critical of "human supremacism" and in active opposition to anthropocentric culture' (p. 205). To be traitorous is to consciously rebel, for the self to be dislocated from the privilege and position of dominance, which prompts action to navigate the boundaries of sameness and difference where there is no certainty—a characteristic of lucid teaching.

Developing a traitorous identity is not the same as playing devil's advocate. Whereas the former is an ongoing learning process that requires genuine doubt, the latter is acting a role for the sake of argument—to express a contentious opinion for the sake of provoking debate or to test opposing positions or arguments—and, thus, is paper doubting. Playing devil's advocate tends to be used in adversarial philosophical argumentation.[8] In a community of inquiry, both are concerned with the epistemic integrity of the inquiry. However, the role of the devil's advocate is to express contention in order to provoke debate or test the strength of the opposing arguments when the dominant opinion in the inquiry is lack dissenting views. The traitorous identity, on the other hand, is aware that such a lack could be due to the marginalisation of certain discourses which is, in turn, due to the marginalisation of certain identities. Thus, they understand epistemology to be the very thing that prevents us from hearing the other, that is, all epistemology is culturally defined. The devil's advocate, lacking such understanding, could fail to recognise the moral, historical, cultural, and social extent of epistemic bias. A traitorous identity, then, is not a disembodied abstract spectator or an insider looking out, but someone who focuses their attention on experiences that point to the epistemic marginalisation brought about by dominant logic and who by listening to marginalised discourses reflects on their own way of seeing, which in part is shaped by their relationship with the dominant culture (see Bailey, 1998; Harding, 1991; Mallory, 2009; Scholz, 2013).

We argue for the development of traitorous identities as a pedagogical intervention for fostering epistemic inclusion to disrupt the privileging of dominant discourses and allow for multi-voiced dialogue. Teachers have a responsibility to their students to be mindful of their own prejudices, to develop their own traitorous identity, which then becomes a model for inquiry. Otherwise, prejudice has a way of seeping into discourse, content choices, and methodology in general; of seeping into the habitat and limiting intellectual freedom. Hence, Dewey's (2010) claim, mentioned earlier, that an 'environment in which some are limited will always in reaction create conditions that prevent the full development even of those who fancy they enjoy complete freedom for unhindered growth' (p. 244). Such freedom requires the inclusion of multiple knowledge systems, not as topics or issues to critique, but as starting points for inquiry. Failing to include varieties of knowledge systems, either through text, or the knowledge of teachers, students, parents, and members of the wider community, fails to interrupt the dominant narrative, leaving it unquestioned—or, to reiterate Freire's words, 'leaving the dominant ideology in peace'. In short, the teacher needs to be aware of the limiting capacity of epistemic violence to create an epistemically inclusive space for the collaborative reconstruction of experience.

The development of traitorous identities, in both teachers and students can be achieved through lucid teaching as a pedagogy for facilitating inquiry. In such an inquiry, the teacher as facilitator and co-inquirer will be aware of the fallibility of narratives to mitigate epistemic violence perpetuated by dominant narratives. To aid in the awareness of dominant narratives, both teachers and students need to be attentive to the phenomenology of the community; to their own felt experiences along with those of others, for example, anger, hesitancy, resistance, silence, silencing. The community of inquiry is guided by an epistemology of revolt, a rejection of certainty, and a universal narrative, to create opportunities to problematise the students' experiences of self and identity. It is, as we said, peace education because students develop the communicative skills to turn conflict into inquiry as a way of life.

It is important for both the teacher and students to resist the immediate desire to pass normative judgement on what they might consider to be undesirable narratives in the community. This is not to say everyone is entitled to their opinion without providing reasons. Harmful speech acts directed at other members of the community should be treated as obstacles to inquiry that hinder the development of a multi-voiced epistemic community, conflict that must be turned into inquiry. If teachers treat such acts a 'no go areas', by silencing the offending student or moving the inquiry away from the topic raised, the deep-seated prejudice underlying the student's comment is unmoved. By ignoring or morally condemning the prejudice, nothing is done to shift the prejudice. Often silencing, which itself is a form of epistemic violence, serves to reinforce the prejudice. Applying the force of normativity to a narrative before inquiry begins not only closes the possibility of the students self-correcting or questioning their prejudices, but also assumes a privileged position within the inquiry, shutting out genuine doubt. This is especially problematic when the normative position taken by the one silencing is itself underpinned by unexamined prejudices.

Recognising dominant narratives acts as a signal for the teacher to assume the role of the traitorous teacher, the Socratic gadfly, and self-stinging stingray who is both facilitator and co-inquirer. The teacher must listen not only to the students' words but also look to the clues that grant access to their phenomenological world (e.g., facial expressions, body language, group interactions) that may indicate potential moments of doubt about their experiences of social identity, or the narrative being expressed. Facilitation of such moments can draw 'an individual's attention to his or her own prejudices' and open 'a pathway to genuine doubt' (Burgh & Thornton, 2016b, p. 166). For as Peirce (1899) put it, to genuinely doubt is to 'not be satisfied with what you already incline to think' (p. 48). Genuine doubt creates a space for the questioning of habits, their underlying beliefs or prejudices, for the examination of their consequences as well as their historical development, allowing for a re-evaluation of the fit between habit and habitat. It offers opportunities for fostering traitorous identities to allow students to question the dominant narrative, to imagine themselves in the position of other and to listen to their narratives. Likewise, teachers as co-inquirers need to pay attention to their own experiences of doubt, and as facilitators of the dialogue to understand where and with whom, to place the onus on the inquiry, in order to listen to the position of other. By understanding and experiencing fallibilism, 'teachers become exemplars of wonder that children take to be models for their own conduct' (Burgh & Thornton, 2016b, p. 172). The intellectual freedom of the teacher becomes a model for the intellectual freedom of the student and vice versa.

Left unattended, epistemic violence will continue to function as prejudices that can manifest in unfair treatment of individuals and unjust structural practices embedded in law, religion, government policy, educational theory, and practice, along with other social and political institutions. Lucid teaching as a pedagogy for inquiry, in which the teacher as co-inquirer takes on the role as traitor to their own identity, gives students the opportunity to reconstruct their experiences by exploring the normative judgements passed on to them through their daily lives, so that they too can become traitorous to the dominant narrative when it epistemically excludes other voices. Further, doing so allows them the intellectual freedom to create their own characters, their own art of learning, in the way Sisyphus did, while his rock was rolling. This provides opportunities for students to develop epistemic understanding of being in the world and the reciprocal relationship between their belief-habits and the construction of the habitat—which we argue *is* the core of peace education. Like education, peace is never finished once and for all, and the prevention of violence is as Camus put it, 'everyone's business', hence the need for a process of peaceful inquiry, a method of turning conflict into cooperative inquiry.

Conclusion

In 1899, Dewey made the observation, that social life had 'undergone a thorough and radical change', driven by the acceleration of industrial society, and as a result, he warned that '[i]f education is to have any meaning for life, it must pass through an equally complete transformation' (Dewey, 1956, p. 49). Radical societal changes have increased exponentially since then, but education has not kept up, resulting in well-entrenched institutional habits that are difficult to change. We now live in an information age which is increasingly filling our lives with technology, which is 'characterized by a continual reorganization of systems which are increasingly interdependent, requiring skills, not routinization, but of collaborative problem solving', and, therefore, 'students need to be taught to value process over product' (Kennedy, 1995, p. 160). We argue that for education to be one step ahead, rather than lagging behind, process needs to be underpinned by wonder and genuine inquiry.

As change in a democracy comes from self-correction, the purpose of education lies in its ability to develop habits that are flexible and open to reconstruction so that the citizens it produces are capable of changing social conditions. So long as education keeps lagging behind, there remains a danger that the citizens it produces are not only ill-equipped to deal with the well-entrenched habits of existing institutions, but do not have the skills or knowledge to correct those habits, hence students need to value process over product. This is why the quote on wonder with which we open the chapter is as relevant today as it was when first written in 1980, 81 years after Dewey's remarks. If many adults have developed the habit of no longer wondering, their behaviour becomes an example of passive acceptance that children and adolescents 'take to be models for their own conduct' (Lipman, Sharp & Oscanyan, 1980, p. 31). The adult as teacher is tasked with becoming an example of someone with flexible habits that are open to reconstruction.

Reconstruction is pivotal to our proposal on democratic education. However, in this chapter, we have spoken of the community of inquiry only as an epistemic community and the teacher as a facilitator and co-inquirer who fosters epistemic fluidity. As we advocate social reconstruction learning the fluidity extends beyond the school into the greater community in which it is situated, which is our response to Dewey's problem of the school lagging behind radical social changes, namely, to develop student habits that are flexible and open to reconstruction so that they have the capacity for changing social conditions. In this sense, the students as participants in the community of inquiry are socially constructed and socially situated beings who develop within local social relationships, institutional practices, cultural norms, and rules. These learning relationships are, therefore, place-based learning relationships. In the next chapter, we explore how place-based education can provide social reconstruction learning with a place-responsive pedagogical dimension and, thus, connect democratic education to ecology.

Notes

1 James B. Schreiber and Connie M. Moss (2002) offer an account of the concept of genuine doubt with respect to teacher beliefs and explain its importance in teacher education. However, they do so without reference to the literature on philosophy for children or Lipman and Sharp's concept of the community of inquiry with its roots in Dewey's pedagogical criteria.
2 We use Moulton's article to differentiate between two different descriptions of philosophical argumentation. However, discussion takes place in a much broader context. For example, Phyllis Rooney (2010) points out that 'there is a level of adversariality peculiar to philosophy that merits specific feminist examination, yet doesn't assume controversial gender differences claims. The dominance of the argument-as-war metaphor is not warranted, since this metaphor misconstrues the epistemic role of good argument as a tool of rational persuasion. This metaphor is entangled with the persisting narrative of embattled reason, which, in turn, is linked to the sexism-informed narrative of the "man of reason" continually warding off or battling "feminine" unreason' (p. 203). For further discussion see: Ayim (1988), Code (1991), Field (1995, 1997), Grimshaw (1987), Harding & Hintikka (1983), Kourany (2009), Rooney (2012).
3 Lloyd identifies this type of reason as 'Reason' (upper case R) to remind us that reason as we know it is in fact narrowly defined.
4 It is a point of contention among some philosophers as to whether reasoning can be expressed through different media, and if so, whether it is, or is not, philosophy. It is sometimes asserted that art becomes/is philosophy and vice versa. For example, in *Art as Experience* (1934), Dewey claimed that it is '[t]o aesthetic experience ... the philosopher must go to understand what experience is. For philosophy like art moves in the medium of the imaginative mind, and ... art is the most direct and complete manifestation there is of experience as experience' (p. 274).
5 Prior to Denton's (1963, 1964, 1967) research, there was a dearth of scholarship on the educational aspects of Camus' philosophy. Since then, there has been a spate of publications (see Curzon-Hobson, 2003, 2013, 2014, 2017; Götz, 1987; Greene, 1973; Hobson, 2017a, 2017b; Marshall, 2007, 2008; Ó Gallchóir & McGarr, 2021; Oliver, 1973; Roberts, 2008a, 2008b), including a special issue of *Educational Philosophy and Theory* (see Vol.45, No.11: Gibbons, 2013a, 2013b, 2013c, 2013d; Heraud, 2013; Roberts, 2013a, 2013b; Roberts, Gibbons & Heraud, 2013), which offer a range of educational perspectives on aspects of Camus' individual works. However, Denton (1964) draws conclusions from Camus' moral philosophy that directly 'bear on the nature and purpose of education' (p. 99). A recent attempt to follow Denton's lead of adapting the tenets of Camus'

philosophy specifically to pedagogy, insofar as the conclusions can offer guidelines for practice, is Weddington (2007). See Thornton (2019) for a response to Weddington's application of lucidity. See also Burgh & Thornton (2016a, 2016b).

6 Rainville cited 'Conscious Partiality' as a term taken from Marguerite Rivage-Seul (1987).

7 Peter Paul Elicor (2021) suggests that a culture-enabling P4wC teacher should have three desired traits: (1) openness to various cultural resources and frames, (2) a sense of critical positionality, and (3) partiality to the culturally marginalised (pp. 12–16).

8 Ross Phillips (1994) asks: 'why should a devil's advocate not be a good servant of the epistemic interests of the community of inquiry?' (p. 15). He offers three suggestions as to why people might be suspicious of using the devil's advocate in a community of inquiry: (1) the regrettable verb 'to play', which he says is spurious and easy to dismiss, (2) misgivings about the appropriateness of the adversarial approach to philosophy, and (3) 'unresolved tensions in idea of the community of inquiry' (p. 15). To take the devil's advocate seriously, he says, one must be sincere not insincere. However, Phillips assumes that insincerity comes with excessive individualism, but '[f]rom the point of view of the community's interest sincerity does not matter. At least logically it does not matter' (p. 20). His response to his own question is that all members of the community of inquiry should, perhaps, be devil's advocates. However, this fails to account for the problem of epistemic violence due to dominant narratives. Traitorous identities position themselves *with* others by listening attentively to mitigate epistemic violence. To be sincere is not necessarily the same as being in genuine doubt which is required to develop traitorous identities.

6 Democratic education as place-responsive learning

Introduction

In 1937, Dewey had this to say about modern society and the educational challenges demanded by democracy:

> One hundred years ago in the simpler conditions of life, when the social group was the neighborhood or the small community, before most of the inventions that have transformed modern society had come into existence—or, at least, before they had made any great impress on modes of living—it was not altogether unreasonable to advance the idea that individuals are born with a kind of democratic aspiration; and that given this innate disposition and tendency, schooling would enable them to meet the duties and responsibilities of life in a democratic society. In the comprehensive conditions of today, such an idea is fallacious. Only as the coming generation learns in the schools to understand the social forces that are at work, the directions and the cross-directions in which they are moving, the consequences that they are producing, the consequences that they might produce if they were understood and managed with intelligence—only as the schools provide this understanding, have we any assurance that they are meeting the challenge which is put to them by democracy.
>
> (Dewey, 1937, pp. 182–183)

Dewey's simpler time was 184 years ago, 184 years of the failure of schools to meet the challenges of democracy. In the terms of our current geologic age—the Meghalayan—184 years seems no more than a pile of sand on a vast beach, however, the effects of those few grains of sand have been so great that many argue we have entered a new age, the age of the human or the Anthropocene. The hallmarks of this age are those that we have already discussed, industrial and technological advances, and the resultant environmental degradation, including climate change, species loss, and environmental injustices, all of which propel a narrative of uncertainty, of intense turbulence, disillusionment, and bewilderment in the face of an increasingly uncertain future. Resultingly, concern for the health of the environment has

DOI: 10.4324/9781003098089-7

become paramount, with human connections to nature seen as increasingly crucial for human well-being and the future health of the planet. All this has impacted on education, especially now that demands for sustainability are gaining increasing attention.

> However, if the push towards sustainability in education is to remain vital and relevant we will need more than a general consensus that this is a good idea. We will need to infuse new eco-centric thinking and values into our schools that will allow students to live and work as citizens in more interconnected ways in the world.
>
> (Tooth & Renshaw, 2009, p. 95)

For education to remain 'vital and relevant', not to lag behind the rapid social, political, and ecological changes that are occurring, civics and citizenship education, environmental education, and sustainability education cannot be separated. Rather, they must be embedded across the curriculum with experiential learning. Attention needs to be on connections between self, others, and place as essential to identity formation in a democracy. For this, we turn to place-based education.

Place-based education (or pedagogies of place) is a community-based experiential approach to education that connects learning and communities in order to increase student engagement, as a way to achieve academic outcomes and student understanding of the world around them. Founded on the idea that the student's local community—including the school grounds, neighbourhood, and suburb, town, or city, as well as the communities within these places, each with their own history, environment, and culture—is one of the primary learning resources for students, place-based education can assist communities in which schools are situated to solve community problems through student involvement, facilitated by teachers who also pay attention to the contextual nature of where the learning experience occurs. Proponents of place-based education have argued for its many putative benefits, such as strengthening connections between students, schools, and local communities (Smith, 2002), reducing student alienation through connected and grounded learning experiences and, thus, also increasing students' appreciation of their local environment (Theobald, 1997; Theobald & Curtiss, 2000), providing opportunities for democratic participation (Sobel, 2004), and fostering ecological literacy (Orr, 1992).

According to Gregory Smith (2002), place-based education shares five common features: (1) local phenomena is the basis for curriculum development, (2) emphasis is on creative learning experiences stimulated by students' questions, interests, and concerns, (3) teachers are facilitators and co-learners who mediate between the school and the community, and (4) community engagement opportunities for learning are increased (p. 539). These features provide place-based education with the potential to overcome the theory/practice dualism that Dewey rejected. This is because place-based education situates learning in the surrounding environments of the school community, which not only extends or supplements classroom practice, but also synthesises curriculum (i.e., integrating curriculum, pedagogy, and assessment with practical learning). However, traditional approaches to place-based education still leave the human/nature dualism untouched. Our concern is that place is treated as the physical space in which the problem occurs, where the emphasis in on solutions to problems that help both the students and the community, instead of also focusing on a 'sense of place' as both contributing to and offering solutions to problems. In other words, a place-based education that is sensitive and responsive to the complexity of the relationship between belief-habits and habitat and, thus, reconstructs the human/nature dualism inherent in some approaches to place-based education.

The literature on place-based education has grown considerably in recent years (e.g., Goralnik, Dobson & Nelson, 2014; Knapp, 2005; Ross, Oppegaard & Willerton, 2019; Russell & Bell, 1996), including a number of critiques, adaptations, and alternatives, such as critical place-based pedagogy which combines critical pedagogy and place-based education (Gruenewald, 2003a), place-conscious pedagogies (Greenwood, 2014; Gruenewald, 2003b), and place-responsive pedagogies (Mannion, Fenwick & Lynch, 2013; Wattchow & Brown, 2011). Some have arisen due to criticisms of the purported neutrality of place in place-based approaches to learning, wherein the emphasis is on the learning objectives achieved through service to the community. For example, David Gruenewald (2003a), who advocates a critical and place-conscious approach, argues that place-based education has the potential to be transformative with the ultimate goal of 'learning more socially just and ecologically sustainable ways of being in the world' (p. 9).

Critical approaches to place-based education that are sensitive and responsive to place can help understand that place 'manifests a way of knowing, and places are often objects of power created to further particular forms of domination based on gender, sexuality, race, age, class, and physical ability' (Cravey & Petit, 2012, p. 102). Indeed, place-based education schools can, themselves, perpetuate dominant discourses. For example, the increasingly popular forest schools have been criticised for being 'rooted in idealized and romanticized notions of nature and childhood' (Nxumalo & Cedillo, 2017, p. 100). Plumwood (2012) notes how such notions of nature contribute to the human/nature divide and exclude Indigenous understandings of Place.

> Wilderness tends to be understood, however, as something that is separate from land that is used, land that supports us. There is a sundering, a splitting in this outlook that differs from an Indigenous understanding of unity of place. [...] wilderness (wildness) was not a special place set apart as sacred in contrast to the profane earth. [...] all the earth was sacred and there was no necessary split between use and respect.
>
> (p. 31)

An understanding of place, therefore, requires more than acquiring theoretical and practical knowledge of communities within places that have their own history, environment, economics, social relationships, political institutions, and culture.

How we understand place is fundamental to understanding the potential of place-based education in giving students a *sense of place*—how they perceive a place, which includes place attachment and place meaning (Kudryavtsev, Stedman & Krasny, 2012). Exploring understandings of a sense of place is also fundamental to developing democratic citizenship. If democracy is a mode of associated living, then citizens belong to the human social world and 'the human social world is embedded in and part of the natural world, with all its complexities, relations and repetitions' (Cole & Somerville, 2020, p. 1). In other words, humans, and all human activities, are part of nature and not separate from other natural phenomena. Not only are we not independent of nature, insofar as we are interdependent and belong to the natural, physical, material world, but the human body is itself an ecosystem. A sense of place is also fundamental to social reconstruction learning and, indeed, to all service or community learning, as work and other activity undertaken with the community is connected to place, and that connection needs to be explored for the reconstruction of experiences to be place-sensitive or ecologically meaningful. As Freya Mathews (2004) notes, 'since making things comes to us as naturally as eating and drinking do, our handiwork itself has as much a claim to be considered part of nature as the handiwork of spiders, insects and marine life does' (n.p.). From this perspective, we cannot separate human activity from the place in which it is undertaken.

In this final chapter, we focus on the importance of place-responsiveness as essential for democratic education. After all, schooling's role in identity formation is more than the development of personal and community identity, it is also about nation-building. As we have already discussed, this is unavoidable through both the school and the hidden curricula. And as we are concerned about *placing* civics and citizenship education as the core of all education and curriculum objectives, attention to place is pertinent as the liberal-democratic nation-states to which citizens belong are inseparable from land and country. So, first up, we introduce place-responsive democratic education. We discuss how place-responsiveness needs to be integrated into social reconstruction learning for democratic education to be committed to dissolving the theory/practice and human/nature dualisms in order to develop democratic and environmental citizenship essential for eco-democracy, a mode of associated living necessary for sustainable living. Next, we provide examples to assist teachers to explore place-responsive approaches to place-based learning: (1) Peter Renshaw and Ron Tooth's documentation of environmental education centres in Queensland, Australia, which illustrates different ways that groups have incorporated it into their teaching and learning, (2) Mary Graham's exploration of Aboriginal Land ethics and her observation of what she calls liberalism's survivalist ethos from the perspective of a Kombumerri/Wakka Wakka person, which illustrates the kind of identity that the non-Aboriginal teacher needs to seek to be traitorous as a facilitator and co-inquirer, and (3) a discussion on how place-responsive pedagogy can be adapted to our earlier example of social reconstruction learning in an inner-city school. These examples also point to the importance of critical Indigenous pedagogies of place. Before we conclude, we look at some of the bureaucratic and political challenges that education reformers should expect when attempting to implement the kind of radical democratic education we propose.

Place-responsive democratic education

To reiterate, missing from traditional approaches to place-based education is a focus on place as the development of a sense of place that is vital to students' formation of identity as ecological citizens (Thornton, Graham & Burgh, 2019, 2021; Thornton, 2022). To achieve this, the human/nature dualism must also be overcome. As we discussed in Chapter 4, Bleazby's (2013) social reconstruction learning reconstructs philosophy for children by integrating it with service learning, a Deweyan kind of experiential learning, but she also draws on feminist pragmatism, ecofeminism, and the community of inquiry pedagogy to engage students in 'philosophical inquiries with their local community with the purpose of reconstructing actual social problems, in order to facilitate independent thinking, imaginativeness, emotional intelligence, autonomy, and active and informed citizenship' (p. 3). This is achieved by identifying and analysing social problems 'in order to develop and implement solutions that will meaningfully transform them', which 'requires students to develop complex inquiry-practical skills and caring dispositions' (p. 158). Thus, reconstruction occurs not only in the students, but also in the society and the individual citizens they assist.

Social reconstruction learning holds potential for the kind of place-based education we propose, as it emphasises Dewey's notion of reconstruction, namely, education as an ongoing re-organisation or reconstruction of experience that increases student's ability to direct and control their lives, rather than acting as a preparation for something else (e.g., being job ready or a citizen); an unfolding of innate knowledge and abilities (nativist or Platonic view of education); a training of mental faculties; the acquisition of knowledge and skills; or the perpetuation of tradition. However, greater emphasis on place is still needed. For example, service learning focuses on experiential learning that is rooted in the local community and synthesises the curriculum through student and school staff involvement in solving community problems—for Dewey the emphasis was on social occupations that integrated subject matter (i.e., curriculum knowledge) and experiences with work carried on in social life. In addition, service learning can also incorporate place-based learning, with attention to the unique history, environment, culture, economy, literature, or art of a particular place. However, attention needs to also be on the ontological relationship to place for social reconstruction learning to become, what Denzin and Lincoln (2008) call, 'a form of praxis and inquiry that [is] emancipatory and empowering' (p. 2); that is 'a reflexive discourse constantly in search of an open-ended, subversive, multivoiced epistemology' (p. 6).

In recent years, Indigenous conceptions of place, which are integral to Indigenous ways of knowing, being, and doing, especially the ontological relationship to Land (Graham, 1999, 2014; Moreton-Robinson, 2015), have been increasingly advocated by Indigenous scholars and non-Indigenous scholars alike. The centring of Indigenous concepts of place in schooling, especially education for sustainability and environmental education, is necessary in order to decolonise mainstream education by interfacing Indigenous and Western epistemologies, values, and philosophy in order to mitigate the epistemic injustices and environmental crises brought about by the domination of Western colonial institutions and practices (Thornton, Graham & Burgh, 2019, 2021). In this way, place-based education has the potential to not only accommodate Indigenous notions of land as part of experiential learning, but Indigenous perspectives on relations to land can broaden the understanding of place in place-based education and reshape it. Later in this chapter, we look at place in the context of Aboriginal culture in Australia, in which self and community are inextricably linked and emerge out of a place-based understanding of connectedness to country.

At the very least, place-based education broadens students' experiences beyond the classroom and standardised knowledge and testing that permeates education policy. At its best, as Renshaw and Tooth (2018a) explain, it is a pedagogy of embodiment in which a two-way mode of learning can occur 'through the relational activity of the body in place—through walking, touching, shaping, smelling, hearing, sensing in place' (p. 12). Their words reflect those of Dewey's who favoured the coordination of perception between the child and the world, between their habits and their habitat which act in concert, so that they experience being-in-the-world. Eric Anthamatten (2012) expresses it in this way: 'When the philosopher amputates the hands and feet from the process of wisdom she severs herself from the very possibility of loving wisdom and eliminates philosophy's potential for analysis, transformation, and action, thus perilously disconnecting philosophy from life itself' (p. 26). Drawing on the work of Margaret Somerville (2010) and Doreen Massey (2005), Renshaw and Tooth (2018a) also make the connection between human activity and the environment, and propose that 'places are not bounded and stable but continually constructed through relational activities between people across time and space' (p. 3). On this account, place is 'an unfolding event with overlapping and intersecting stories' *so far*, which 'conveys openness to both the past and the future, and frames place as a site of ongoing negotiation between related unfolding and perhaps incompatible stories' (p. 3). These 'unfinished stories' are contestable and can open up dialogue on a collective understanding of place.

> Stories create a range of possible relationships to place, for example, as a site for recreation and physical activity ('look at this place—I could ride my bike right through here'), or as a site for contemplation ('look at this place—I could sit quietly here for hours'), or as a site for scientific inquiry ('look at the ecology of this place'), and so on. Narratives in and

of places are nested in larger cultural and political narratives that shape how we might come to see and understand places, for example, as an economic resource or a threat or sacred site or comfort zone. A pedagogy of place based on storying opens up a myriad of ways of relating to and understanding place.

(p. 13)

Renshaw and Tooth's place-based education is a critical place-based pedagogy that is both place-conscious and place-responsive by focusing on embodiment, storying, and contested stories (pp. 12–14). It is place-conscious because it is committed to understanding 'the cultural and material complexity of place and the ethical responsibility we share to care for local places in order to address global challenges' (p. 2). It is place-responsive because it conveys a sustained consciousness and awareness of place that depends on a relational ontology of place-making through a composite of 'learners, places, stories and all kinds of entities' (Mannion & Lynch, 2016, p. 90). In other words, place is not neutral ground upon which activities take place. Nor is place an object that is made knowable through a union between the knower and the known concerned narrowly with the study of natural ecology. Place is epistemically inhabited, filled with stories of the past and future imaginings. To ignore the multi-voiced narratives is to silence the epistemic landscape, the multiple experiences, and perspectives, and allow the dominant societal ideology to continue to colonise place as the only legitimate narrative. Teachers must, therefore, be advocates for place, otherwise—and Freire's words on neutrality again resonate—they fail to interrupt the dominant narrative, leaving it in peace. However, to be an advocate of place is not to advocate *substantive values*, that is, the universal acceptance of specific ethical prescriptions or environmental values. Rather, it is to advocate *procedures*, which requires teachers to be traitorous to the dominant identity and provide opportunities through practical place-based activities for the other voices to be understood, to allow for the reconstruction of place. Place-responsive pedagogies, therefore, find a natural place in social reconstruction learning. In turn, social reconstruction learning is ecologically embedded through place-responsive approaches to place-based education.

On this view, it makes more sense to think of democracy as ecological democracy. If the community of inquiry is exemplar of democracy in action, a self-corrective process aimed at sustaining multi-voiced dialogue, then it must be responsive to place as the past stories and future imaginings inhabit place in the form of social relationships, institutional structures and practices, cultural values, and ecological relations (human and non-human). Democracy is, therefore, not only an epistemic practice but also a place-based practice. It requires us to be responsive to the embedded epistemologies of place, or to put it another way, government of the people, by the people, for the people is better described as collective governance of embedded narratives of place. We must, that is, have an ecological relationship with democracy— an eco-democracy.[1] In terms of our theoretical framework for democratic education, it is inherently place-based ecological education and, thus, can also be considered as education for sustainability (or sustainability education) in that it connects the social and environmental dimensions of sustainable living (as integral to democracy as mode of associated living). It should be noted, then, that our focus is *not* on environmental advocacy or environmental education, as this implies that civics and citizenship education and environmental education can be conceptually separated. They of course can be, if seen as discrete subjects or areas of learning, but this is exactly what we are trying to avoid. To reiterate, our focus is on education as identity formation, which in a social democracy is a complex relationship between self, community, and ecological identities. Thus, to be a citizen is to be embedded in a particular place, locally, nationally, and globally. Democratic education, therefore, is environmental education and vice versa.

For these reasons, we have not provided a classroom-ready model or blueprint for the creation and implementation of educational programs for civics and citizenship, the studies of environment and society, or sustainability. There are different ways to teach and to organise curriculum, which is dependent also on where the school is located and other educational factors. As accredited members of the teaching profession, teachers have their own pedagogical and curriculum expertise which should be utilised. Teacher educators, educational psychologists, curriculum designers, and other professionals in allied fields of education must also be consulted to develop and implement curriculum, pre-service and in-service programs, and classroom resources. However, the following list of essential characteristics and principles provides a theoretical resource for developing educational programs and classroom practice:

- Democracy is understood primarily, not as a system of government and institutional practices, but as a social democratic mode of associated living that relies on deliberative communication.
- It is essential, then, that democratic education is an exemplar of such a democracy in order to achieve its twofold purpose: the reconstruction of education itself and the broader aim of social reconstruction toward the creation of a self-correcting society.
- Education must, therefore, focus on the ongoing re-organisation or reconstruction of experience that increases student's ability to direct and control their lives through self-correcting communities of inquiry, rather than acting as a preparation for something else (e.g., being job ready or a citizen in the future).
- Teachers need to convert the classroom into a community of inquiry, which requires social reconstruction learning, an approach to teaching that re-introduces Dewey's notion of experiential education by integrating philosophy for children with service learning, with the aim of synthesising curriculum though theory (curriculum content, including traditional subjects) and practice (practical learning as experiential education).

- The specific teaching method is the narrow-sense community of inquiry, which is characterised by stages of inquiry and promotes philosophical discussion and critical discourse.
- To convert the classroom into a community of inquiry, requires more than following the stages of the teaching method; the principles of the wide-sense community of inquiry found in the scholarly communities of inquiry, underpinned by a pragmatist epistemology of fallibilism and self-correcting inquiry, acts as an organisational principle and regulative ideal for the reconstruction of education and provides the pedagogical principles for classroom practice.
- The teacher has the dual role of (1) co-inquirer whose understanding of the wide-sense communities that inform curriculum content and textbooks is greater than that of their students, and (2) facilitator of classroom discussion focused on dialogue and intellectual self-correction through mediation between the narrow-sense and wide-sense communities of inquiry.
- Lucid teaching offers an experiential account of mediating between the narrow-sense and wide-sense communities of inquiry essential for social reconstruction, in which the questioning of reality, and knowledge of that reality induces and sustains perplexity, intellectual curiosity, and awareness of the fallibility of our beliefs, thereby multiplying awareness and experience of the divorce between belief and reality.
- As all learning is connected to place, whether internal or external to the classroom, it is essential that the epistemic community is place conscious; that the teacher and the students are responsive to place and, thus, develop a sense of place that is ecologically embedded.

Place-responsive democratic education develops the interpersonal (intersubjective/social) conditions that satisfy Plumwood's criteria for effective democracy as the capacity for correctiveness essential for promoting democracy and ecology. In doing so, the theoretical framework and pedagogical guidelines for practice provide a solution to the problem that education has failed democracy, and consequently that it has failed to empower citizens. Moreover, we believe that our proposal would satisfy Dewey, Lipman, and proponents of philosophy for children, social reconstruction learning, and place-responsive pedagogies. So, next we explore pedagogical possibilities of place, which, together with the characteristics and principles listed above, are intended to generate ideas for creating and implementing place-based democratic education programs.

Pedagogical possibilities of place

In an educational environment that is increasingly moving toward discourses of accountability and standards-based systems of instruction, assessment, grading, and academic reporting, it is to be expected that teachers and students will be unfamiliar with learning through place pedagogy. Our aim here is to provide a diversity of narratives to illustrate place-responsiveness in education. We do this in three different ways: through (1) pedagogical stories from environmental education centres, (2) Indigenous notions of place, and (3) a case study.

Pedagogical stories from environmental education centres

In collaboration with environmental educators at six environmental education centres across Queensland, Australia, Renshaw and Tooth (2018a) documented the distinctive place-responsive pedagogies designed by the educators who 'drew upon the cultural and material affordances of the environmental education centres at which they worked' (p. 1). They invite readers to 'delve into' the distinctive pedagogical possibilities in each of the places to further understand how place can become imbued with place as: advocacy, story, slow time, walking, sacred, shifting sands, and the edge. Our inclusion of these 'pedagogical possibilities' has the same purpose, but with the additional aim of asking readers to reflect on how these ways of responding to place, which evoked a sense of place for students who visited the centres, can be integrated into place-responsive democratic education suitable for the local conditions in which the school is placed. We hope that these summaries will prompt curiosity to go to the original narratives that appear as chapters in Renshaw and Tooth's edited collection. This is especially pertinent for anyone serious about implementing place-responsive democratic education into their school in collaboration with the school community and local communities, as the place-responsive pedagogies were 'designed by committed environmental educators who were acutely aware of the material and cultural affordances at each of their centres' (p. 1). Each approach is distinctive because '[t]he location of the environmental education centres varied from coastal intertidal zones and mangrove forests to a cloud rainforest and urban-fringe forest remnants. The contrasting materiality of the locations is vital to the diversity of pedagogies that were created' (pp. 1–2).

To attune the reader to the different perspectives requires more than a superficial reading as context is vital to an understanding of place. So, it is important to locate the centres in space/time, in networks of influence, and pedagogically (p. 2). Nevertheless, here we will glean only what it necessary for our purposes in order to provide an overview as a starting point for the reader to commence their own research to create their pedagogies of place. To compensate, we have used extensive quotations to let the stories speak for themselves, as told by those who reported or documented them.

Advocacy pedagogy: Karawatha forest's conservation in the 1990s 'is testament to a local citizens' action group led by Bernice Volz who remains part of the environmental education programs at Pullenvale Environmental Education Centre' (p. 14). The advocacy pedagogy at Karawatha is described by Renshaw and Tooth (2018b) as 'pedagogy with a clear normative agenda for the environment where students learn about environmental advocacy and are asked to consider how they might live more sustainably and become advocates in the future' (pp. 22). The underscoring pedagogical practice of the centre is based on the idea of *dadirri*, an Indigenous practice described by Miriam-Rose Ungunmerr-Baumann (1988, 2002) of the Ngangikurung-kurr people in the Northern Territory as an inner, deep listening and quiet, still awareness. The practice provides opportunities to 'tune in' to others and to nature to evoke experiences that can create a deeper understanding of life. To Ungunmerr-Baumann the practice is for everyone, not only Aboriginal people, which, as Renshaw and Tooth (2018b) explain, provided the inspiration to explicitly incorporate the idea of *dadirri* 'to move students to become environmental advocates by offering them multiple ways of knowing and appreciating the forest, and the many stories it holds' (p. 24).

Pedagogy as story in/of landscape: Pullenvale Environmental Education Centre, situated in what Renshaw and Tooth (2018a) describe as 'merely remnants of the original ecological systems that thrived prior to colonisation in the early nineteenth century', is a place of intersecting and unfinished stories 'of habitat transformation and species loss that remains hidden to the contemporary observer' which are connected through networks of power that have significant local consequences (p. 15). Through imagination and story, the 'students can see the present landscape as the outcome of contested interests that intersected at Pullenvale across time', which is dramatically revealed to them on an excursion upon finding 'a display case of preserved birds that a taxidermist made in the 19th century' (p. 15). The birds became extinct in the region 'primarily because in the late 19th century they were hunted for their colourful feathers that were exported to fashion houses in London and Paris' (p. 15). In this landscape, story is itself pedagogical as the history of the present is revealed and, subsequently, heightens the students' sense of 'responsibility and agency in place' (p. 15).

Slow pedagogy: Noeleen Rowntree and Agatha Gambino reported an episode about a group of young students' who disembarked at Bunyaville 'from the buses that had transported them from their nearby suburban school' (p. 15). They conveyed the story as students passing 'from their familiar time/space of fast-paced and noisy everyday life into the Bunyaville time/space that was slower and quieter', providing 'opportunities for being attentive to the elements of the forest' (p. 15). Time is central to their inquiry-based pedagogy, and slow pedagogy the distinctive affordance of Bunyaville, because '[t]o connect to the forest and notice its intricacies requires relaxation, slowing down, being attentive and an attitude that each activity can take as long as it requires' (pp. 15–16). In other words, slow pedagogy, which was part of the design process, offered a stark contrast between students' everyday experiences (i.e., belief-habits, routines) of 'distracted fast time' and a 'meditative and attentive sense of time' (i.e., disruptive moments) of the forest and its nooks. In this narrative, place itself is pedagogical in concrete and particular ways: 'After trying many sites in the forest, Noeleen and Agatha discovered a particular place where students were prepared to share more heartfelt and significant comments with each other' (p. 16).

Walking pedagogy: For millennia, Barambah has been known through walking. Sue Gibson reported that she found walking and talking on the Barambah tracks (many of them constructed by her co-author Mark Cridland during his holidays over many years) 'a really effective way to engage some reluctant students' (p. 16). Her story conveyed the distinctive Barambah pedagogy as 'walking', which she had already named 'walking-talking pedagogy'; 'an inductive strategy of following-in students' casual conversations rather than providing an expert commentary on the forest' (p. 16). Different tracks meant that students were required to walk in different ways and, thus, they were 'specific places of embodied learning' (p.16). The program 'focuses on an Indigenous culture where walking one's country is regarded as part of custodianship', which provides opportunities to reflect 'on the history of walking the tracks at Barambah for Indigenous and non-Indigenous people' (p. 16).

Sacred pedagogy: Rainforest excursions at Paluma evoke a sense of sacredness due to its 'Indigenous and a non-Indigenous history as a place for healing and spiritual renewal' (p. 17) and the material features, including swirling clouds, shafts of sunlight, and an ancient fig tree with arches and tall hollowed trunk. Linda Venn and Louka Lazaredes deliberately chose this site for student visits to highlight 'the vast age and spectacular beauty of the rainforest and to create a sense of awe as they compared their own (small) size and (young) age to that of the fig tree', thus, as a place-responsive pedagogy, 'the rainforest becomes a text for inquiring into the beauty of nature and reflecting more deeply on the meaning of life' (p. 17). The rainforest is also part of scientific exploration, which is a central aspect of the pedagogy, 'but it is accompanied by questions about the purpose and beauty of life' (p. 17). Whether students express their feelings about the rainforest as related to God or science, or they wonder at the beauty of nature, all responses become part of inquiry 'to keep open for students their particular door into world of the sacred, however they might understand this notion' (p. 17).

Shifting sands pedagogy: The Nudgee Beach environmental education centre is situated near an extensive intertidal zone. The pedagogy is integrally related to shifting sands, as the changing seasons, the daily tide variations, and related events such as submerged roads during king tides and coastal erosion, determine Mary-Ann Pattison's planning of activities and programs. A core part of one program is learning to read the sand. Students 'are guided to pay close attention to the markings and patterns that are imprinted by animals on the sand as the tide recedes' (p. 17). Serendipity also arises 'from the unpredictability of events at the beach and the appearance and disappearance of animal species' (p. 17). Such serendipity 'requires educators to be flexible and opportunistic in their pedagogical practices ... planning necessarily shifts opportunistically', which contrasts 'with current instrumentalist pedagogies and accountability regimes in schools that privilege effectiveness and efficiency' (p. 18).

Edge pedagogy: Aboard the Moreton Bay environmental centre's catamaran, *Inspiration*, a group of primary school students explore the Bay, 'particularly its tidal sandbanks where small hermit crabs and other sea creatures can be observed' (p. 18). From the deck, the view shows that geographically the Bay is on 'the edge of Brisbane, and ecologically it is on the edge in terms of sustainability due to obvious signs of silting and pollution' flowing in from the connected river systems, and the 'intensive commercial and recreational use by local citizens' (p. 18). These material affordances provoke a pedagogy that needs to both confront the ecological challenges and 'evoke a response from students about their own behaviour at the edge' (p. 18). However, edge pedagogy is not only about confronting the destructive human impact. Renshaw and Tooth observed that '[b]eing on Inspiration that day was an enlivening experience of seeing over the horizon and feeling the rhythm of the waves and experiencing the beauty of the hermit crabs with their delicate features and colours' (p. 18). The contrast is crucial in producing the edge pedagogy which provides opportunities to explore 'multiple material and semiotic edges to reveal fragility and beauty simultaneously' (p. 18).

All pedagogies of place described here evoke a sense of place through their ability to be responsive to the materiality and culture of the local landscapes. Place as a site of experience that, through reflective awareness, elicits diverse responses distinguishes these approaches to place-based education from traditional place-based education. In terms of our proposal for democratic education, place-responsiveness is crucial to situating democracy in a locality so that citizenship is ecologically in place—citizenship, not as an abstract notion of the individual as the possessor of liberty and the bearer of rights, but cultural citizenship as learning processes through diverse narratives steeped in place. It is noteworthy, and pertinent, that some of the learning activities described here either implicitly or explicitly drew on Indigenous pedagogies (see Lowan-Trudeau, 2017; Nakata et al., 1971; Wildcat et al., 2014). To extend the conversation, in the next section, we explore Indigenous notions of place.

Indigenous notions of place

Given Western-style democracies were founded on dubious colonial pasts that have seen the desecration of sacred sites, displacement of First Nations people and their culture, and the silencing of their stories, place-responsive pedagogies cannot avoid the stories embedded in the landscapes, which are not only stories of the past but of future imaginings. In Australia, the doctrine of *Terra Nullius* sought to nullify First Nations peoples' cultural and agricultural practices, ontologies, epistemic practices, and methodologies that have developed through connections with the land for more than 60,000 years. Under international law at the time, a country could be settled if it were uninhabited, or *Terra Nullius* meaning no-one's land. However, as Aboriginal peoples had already inhabited the continent for tens of thousands of years, claiming Australia to be *Terra Nullius* was a myth used to justify invasion. As Lloyd (2000) states, the 'idea of terra nullius allowed thought of the sovereignty of Australia to be organized around reassuring ideas of discovery and settlement, rather than more disturbing notions of invasion and conquest' (pp. 31–32). Its repercussions are still felt by Aboriginal and Torres Strait Islander peoples, and the process of recognition, decolonisation, restoration, and reconciliation has shown slow progress, despite increasing public awareness, the High Court of Australia's *Mabo* decision in 1992 regarding 'native title', and an ongoing international struggle for recognition of Indigenous languages, knowledge, and culture.

Education needs to acknowledge the essential role that First Nations people continue to have in social reconstruction and the development of an inclusive democracy and, therefore, in the reconciliation process toward building new relationships between Indigenous and non-Indigenous people. It should be noted that reconciliation can have two meanings and it is important that in the political context we speak of here we are not referring to the 'restoration of friendly relations' but the 'action of making one view or belief compatible with another' through a reconstruction of the dominant narrative, rather than an assimilation of the other. It is not the restoration of friendly relations as the relationship established by first colonisation was a violent one marked by a racist narrative which dehumanised other. As Aileen Moreton-Robinson (2015) writes:

> We were perceived as living in a state of nature that was in opposition to the discourse of white civility. This racist discourse enabled patriarchal white sovereignty to deny Indigenous people their sovereign rights while regulating and disciplining their behavior through legislative and political mechanisms and physical and social measures.
>
> (p. 157)

In other words, it is not the re-establishment of a relationship that is needed, rather it is the fundamental reconstruction of a relationship of domination that is called for. Place-responsive pedagogies can bring together seemingly incommensurable narratives to begin the educational process of epistemic disruption, reconciliation, and decolonisation essential for mitigating epistemic violence towards inquiry as multi-voiced, deliberative dialogue.

Indigenous stories are diverse, complex, and place-oriented in contrast to the dominant reductivist Western narrative that permeates education policy, curriculum, and pedagogy. The stories can contribute to new pedagogies and curriculum design, which is not restricted to Indigenous history and culture or sustainability but can make significant contributions to all subjects across the curriculum (see Pascoe, 2014; Thornton, 1995). For example, *Living Maths* (Thornton, 1995) documents the Garma Maths program that was developed by the Yolngu community at Yirrkala Community School. Using Indigenous place-based pedagogies, it takes formal concepts of Yolngu thought that are found in the Yolngu way of life and reasoning and enhances and adapts them to Western mathematics. In *Dark Emu*, Bruce Pascoe (2014), a Bunurong man, argues that the hunter-gatherer understanding of pre-colonial Aboriginal peoples in Australia needs to be reconsidered.

The evidence he provides shows that Aboriginal peoples across the continent were domesticating plants, sowing, harvesting, irrigating, and storing crops for thousands of years—behaviours inconsistent with hunter-gatherer culture. His book has implications for science, technology, history, geography, and ecological sustainability to name a few.

Our aim here is to illustrate a response to place from an Aboriginal perspective of custodial ethics, which, through Indigenous pedagogies of place, can provide students with a portal to diverse experiences of sense of place so that they develop greater understanding of Indigenous ways of knowing, being, and doing. We draw on the work of Mary Graham,[2] a Kombumerri person (Gold Coast) through her father's heritage and affiliated with Wakka Wakka (South Burnett) through her mother's people (located in the state of Queensland, Australia), which explores traditional Aboriginal ways of knowing, being and doing as philosophy. This understanding is crucial for reconciliation (as explained above), which requires that Indigenous people tell their stories and that they are heard, a necessary process for decolonisation in education (i.e., confronting epistemic violence that occurs through exclusion, silencing, neutrality, and so forth in classroom practice, curriculum subjects, textbooks, and assessment). The following analysis provides the reader with an account of Land[3] as the source of obligation that is central to Aboriginal ethics. Graham compares such an ethic to the familiar liberal philosophy that underpins Western values viewed from her perspective as a First Nations woman. An understanding of her analysis calls for non-Aboriginal teachers to be traitorous to their own identities, which requires being sensitive and responsive to how marginalised peoples see the dominant ideology and a recognition of the teachers place within it.

Graham (1999) observes that from an Aboriginal perspective, separation from nature was the beginnings of a commodification of nature: 'spirit or the sacred has been reified by Westerners as "money": Western behaviour, as we have observed it over the last two hundred years, is consistent with that of a community for whom money is sacred' (p. 8). With the sacralising of money, the relational is reduced to the economic, that which money can buy, and 'everything has a price'; therefore, with enough money nothing is off-limits, and nothing is sacred. Neoliberal laissez-faire economics illustrates this well—potentially everything is reduced to economic value and, thus, of instrumental value only. In this way, the sacralising of money co-exists with an ethic that values only individualism; the right of the individual to freedom and self-realisation, which entails the fundamental right to life, liberty, and property.

As the very nature of the liberal individual is that of an individual human being abstracted from social context and nature, such an ethic does not provide a basis for obligation, only a right to exercise freedom. Following this line of thought, a strange and terrible freedom is obtained; a freedom from ethical limits, precariously restrained only by a self-regulating society of individuals—essentially a minimalist politic of self-interest, in which individuals compete for resources to survive. Graham (2021) describes this as a survivalist ethos,

> a form of self-orientation where the self is placed at a distance from others because all environments—natural, human, and social—are seen as potentially hostile; so, the self has to arm itself psychically and physically to keep 'safe'. Social and technological developments ensue, and then praxis follows which includes the normalisation of competitiveness.
>
> (p. 8)

In *On Liberty*, Mill (1859) articulates a core tenet of liberalism—and, by extension, traditional Western ethics that underpin liberal-democratic political and social institutions. He focuses on the principle of equal consideration of interests, that individuals are free to do as they please provided their actions do not *harm* others (i.e., impinge upon the freedom of other individuals). Thus, Mill's conception of liberty, in which individuals are self-interested, equal, and rational, has self-regarding and other-regarding morality as two sides of the same coin. Thereby, political intervention is limited regarding self-interest, or as Mill put it: 'That the only purpose for which power can be rightfully exercised over any member of a civilized community, against his will, is to prevent harm to others' (p. 223). However, harm, in the traditional liberal sense, means harm only to other humans, hence Richard Sylvan (2009) deems the harm principle to be founded on 'human chauvinism', a prejudicial preference for the human species above all others.

The lack of ethical consideration given to nature means, as Graham concludes, that nature becomes open to 'instrumental use' as defined and regulated by systems other than ethics; primarily legal, economic, and political. Spirituality and the sacred, accordingly, is restricted to religion, usually monotheistic religions that create a Platonic split between earth and spirit. Western religion has traditionally viewed

> the spirituality of place as something to be overcome or drawn into its larger scheme which figures *the value of place accordingly, in the largely instrumental terms* of leading us to a higher, non-earthly place. Historical Christianity, as John Passmore remarks, often saw pagan place and nature reverence as its main enemy, and set itself the task of destroying pagan shrines or absorbing them into its own framework of transcendence.
>
> (Plumwood, 2001, p. 219, *italics* added)

In many cultures around the world, spirit conjures up thoughts of the supernatural, which is neither earth nor human, but greater than or superior to both.

However, Graham explains that in Aboriginal culture spirit emerges from earth and is a part of nature. Accordingly, organisms and the earth are sacred, valued, and relational; based on relationships of respect and understanding learnt over enormous spans of time. The sacred calls forth limitations on acts and, in doing so, extends ethics to nature. Aboriginal ethics are ethics of a particular kind, not strictly deontological rule-based ethics, nor strictly consequentialist, outcome-based tools used to determine the rightness of an act, although they often contain elements of both. In Western philosophical terms, Aboriginal ethics resembles an ethic of flourishing, but one which extends far beyond the Aristotelian sense of 'human flourishing' as life with other people, to include ecological others. Even though Aristotle had greater faith in the earth than Plato, he still delivers us a very human-centred notion of flourishing:

> Aristotle's metaphysic does not develop in a holistic or systemic direction, but stops short at an emphatic form of individualism—a pluralism of discrete biological individuals. The concrete relations in which these individuals stand to one another are entirely external to their identity, and in principle such individuals could be rearranged or reshuffled at will. There is no anticipation here of the concept of ecology, or of the indivisibility of systems.
>
> (Mathews, 1991, p. 109)

Contra Aristotle, Graham (2012) describes Aboriginal ethics as holistic and relational. *Land* is the great teacher, the first value. Land is sacred and the beginning of ethics, as it is the beginning of all things; that which confers responsibility. Value comes from the Land, just as we, the valuers, come from the Land. In this sense, 'Land is the Law' (p. 2). However, Graham points out that the use of the term Law differs to that of Western notions of law. In liberal political theory 'law' refers to the *rule of law*, which is one of the core principles of liberal constitutionalism, aimed at protecting the fundamental rights of individuals, including the security of persons, property (i.e., ownership and contract), and human rights. Laws are supposed to guide the ethical conduct of the individual regarding these fundamental rights, which implies preventing harm to other individuals and their interests (i.e., the application of Mill's harm principle). Conversely, the Aboriginal approach is to locate Law as first principle (i.e., a foundational proposition or assumption that cannot be deduced from other propositions or assumptions), as the sacralised and foundational, relationalist principle of the Land as the source of the Law.

Land, as Graham explains, has created everything including humans, and is seen by Aboriginal peoples as a maternal process (e.g., 'Mother Nature') and inherently spiritual: 'Land is a moral entity with both physical and spiritual attributes manifest in myriad life forms' (p. 2). From this, 'spiritual significance and meaning arises, and more obligations develop with particularised responsibilities according to place/locality' (p. 5). Ethics, then, is not based solely on character, received commands, rules, universal principles, or consequences (although it can certainly take many of these into account), instead, it 'grows in a natural organic way with the deepening of feeling coalesced with stewardship practices' (p. 5). These senses or feelings are reified into socially constructed systems of governance. Through understanding the value of Land and self we become civilised, and in this way '*[e]thics becomes habituated and made valuable, rather than idealised*' (p. 2). Ethics then, becomes a structuring force and a way of dealing with inevitable instability. Instability is a part of the process of the world, a part of living that must be faced and understood for both practical and ethical reasons. On the practical side, understanding the process of flux, of being and becoming, can facilitate flourishing. However, it is necessary to understand in a way that is relational and accounts for the flourishing of other organisms, including ensuring the other's continued existence. Such understanding, as Graham explains, allows for the emergence of a custodial ethic; an obligation to *care for country*, and a necessary condition for the creation of a stable and flourishing society.

In Australian Aboriginal culture, ethics, beginning with Land, is a structuring force that 'lays the foundations for the organising principle that governs the social and political structures, decision-making and conflict management systems developed over an immense period of time, forming the basis of our concept of Sovereignty' (p. 1). Balance and stability are achieved through protocols based on the custodial ethic, that is, '1. the ethical principle of maintaining a respectful, nurturing relationship with Land, Place and Community; 2. the organising principle based on autonomy and identity of Place' (Graham, 2012, p. 5). Such an ethic developed in relationship to Land and others over tens of thousands of years achieving political and environmental stability in part through an appreciation of flux. Stability, in the political sense, does not need to be viewed in opposition to flux as an understanding of flux in itself helps create stability. Protocols were developed through careful observation and detailed communication, aimed at the preservation and reproduction of knowledge tied to the preservation and reproduction of Land. Communication took and continues to take many forms, for example, teaching, conferences, storytelling, painting, dancing, and songlines, the combination of which, as Plumwood (2012) writes,

> function both to impress their meanings cunningly and irresistibly in the memory, and to bind together botanical, experiential, practical and philosophical knowledge, community identity and spiritual practice in a rich and satisfying integration of what we [non-Indigenous people] usually place in opposing groups of life and theory [dualisms].
>
> (p. 27)

These 'opposing groups' form the basis of a Western reductionist worldview. However, as Graham (2012) says of Aboriginal ethics, flourishing is not thought of in terms of the atomistic individual but in terms of the group, which is 'not to say that the group is more important than the individual, nor is it a competition between the group/others and the individual, but rather that the group is the originator of Being; that Being comes from and is shared by and with others' (p. 4) including environments. *Places*, like humans, are autonomous and '[i] n terms of values, the aim of the organis-ing principle is to respect and protect the integrity of Regional, Clan/group and individual values and rights' (p. 5).

To explain this relationship further, Graham introduces the concept of autonomous regard,[4] which she describes as an integral component of an Aboriginal ethic, a way of gazing at each other from a distance. The dis-tance is necessary for respect, for recognition of sovereignty, limits, and the existence of the self in the other, because, although distant, the self is not starkly separate from the self or the other. Autonomous regard also extends to non-human others, hence nature as human, non-human, and land is not seen as starkly other, and the value it holds is not only monetary or instru-mental but sacralised. This relationalist system, emerging from Land and collectively applied in social and political ordering, would manifest as some-thing like a 'Law of Obligation'—a fully relational system. The Law of Obli-gation, then, brings about, what Graham describes as:

> a collective ethical responsibility, to look after Land, family and com-munity, which is vital in transcending the persuasion of advantage at the expense of others. This approach is centred in the significance of Place, a particular locality (or localities) of Land within a particular region. 'Land' includes the landscape and all living things within it, humans, spirits, animals, air, sea, rivers, moon, stars, birds, insects, the wind, lan-guage, dreams etc; with Place the core interest, conscience and spirit of culture. These collective values are the template for looking after the whole society, that is, part of the organising principle of society.
>
> (p. 4)

The custodial ethic is the combination of many laws of obligation—reciproc-ity, sharing, stewardship, looking after relations, etc., with the cultivation of people's qualities of mind, character, and behaviour. These obligatory habits become a tradition which collectively becomes a general law underpinned by the sacralising of land—a process of *becoming* and *being*.

Graham contends that a major problem of atomistic individualism—the basis of Western ethics and politics stemming from liberal theory, which manifests in an ethic of individual freedom and human rights—is that indi-viduals are not bound by claims that are independent of their private inter-ests. Her concern is that this leaves people exposed to a world without the Law of Obligation, open to the threat of collective living without the self-awareness required to live ethical relationships with other, both human and non-human, and earth.

> The Law of Obligation prevents or can prevent a collective 'crossing the Rubicon' or 'point of no return' step into the barbarism of nuclear bombing or invading other people's countries.[5] If primitiveness, mean-ing a kind of end justifies the means rationale, is the path chosen, barba-rism is or becomes the variety of methods utilised to gain the wished-for

outcome. For example, she suggests that if a Law of Obligation was in place and adhered to, it is doubtful that Rio Tinto would have blown-up a 46,000-year-old sacred site[6] or that climate change would be worsening unchecked.

(Thornton, Graham & Burgh, 2021, p. 14)

Place, as land and country, therefore, is pivotal to Aboriginal culture. The land is not just material/physical, treated as property for development. In Graham's (1999) words:

> The land is a sacred entity, not property or real estate; it is the great mother of all humanity. The Dreaming[7] is a combination of meaning (about life and all reality), and an action guide to living. The two most important kinds of relationship in life are, firstly, those between land and people and, secondly, those amongst people themselves, the second being always contingent upon the first. The land, and how we treat it, is what determines our human-ness. Because land is sacred and must be looked after, the relation between people and land becomes the template for society and social relations. Therefore all meaning comes from land.
>
> (p. 106)

Place-responsive approaches to education cannot, then, avoid the meaningfulness of land that provide narratives of place that can be observed though autonomous regard for other (human and non-human that dwell within). To treat place as only historical, geographical, economic, or neutral insofar as it is merely where events occur, such as a location for experiential learning, fails to acknowledge the ancient, the spiritual and other stories as potentialities for the many pedagogies associated with place. It is, therefore, crucial that students develop a sense of place by experiencing place as the interface between Indigenous and non-Indigenous ways of knowing, being, and doing. As Graham writes (1999):

> Accommodation within the education system of programs with activities through which this identity [a collective spiritual identity] is grown in children, activities such as groups caring for particular chosen tracts of land, not only via gardening, but tending, having recreational and ceremonial activities there, creating stories about and artistic expressions of the relevant sites, protecting them from damage, and maintaining continuity with them throughout the formative years of childhood and on into adulthood.
>
> (p. 108)

Place-responsive pedagogies, such as critical Indigenous pedagogies of place, underscore the importance of 'collectively understanding and deconstructing individual and communal narratives of place that influence how we understand our regions and nations' (Lowan-Trudeau, 2017, p. 514). Critical Indigenous pedagogies of place seek 'to decolonize and reinhabit the storied landscape through "reading" the ways in which Indigenous peoples' places and environment have been injured and exploited' (Johnson, 2012, p. 829) as part of a process of unlearning the dominant narrative. Such a reading casts light on the shadow places traditional classrooms create. 'Shadow places' go hand-in-glove with uninterrupted human/nature dualisms, such as social and political institutions divorced from Land; they *cast a shadow* over ethical responsibility and obligation, obscuring our knowledge of the places upon which our existence depends, driving impoverishment and environmental degradation (Plumwood, 1995, p. 139). When we view ourselves as hyper-separated from place, we perpetuate the existence of shadow places and the environmental injustices they create because '[a]s hyper-individuals, we owe nothing to nobody, not to our mothers, let alone to any nebulous earth community' (Plumwood, 2001, p. 91). Attuning our attention to place, then, becomes an ethical matter, in the manner Graham speaks of, and a necessary first step to realising obligations to place. Imaginings of place have the potential to 'replace the consumer-driven narratives of place that mark our lives by different ones that make our ecological relationships visible and accountable' (Plumwood, 2008, n.p.). Because critical Indigenous pedagogies of place are grounded and, thus, reject hyper-separation, they provide an understanding of place as ontological. This is crucial to identity formation in education to mitigate place neutrality, the view of place as just a location in which learning occurs, making place an integral part of the development of personal, community, and political identity. Reconstructing place through Indigenous understandings of place is, therefore, a necessary step toward social reconstruction and the formation of onto-epistemically inclusive social and ecological identities (see Elicor, 2019; Reed-Sandoval, 2014; Thornton, Graham & Burgh, 2019, 2021).

Case study

Recall in Chapter 4 that we drew on the example of an inner-city primary school in Brisbane and the children's experience finding dead fish in their local creek. They identified this discovery as a social and environmental issue and subsequently developed and implemented solutions. However, while attention was on place as a site for exploring and investigating local problems and issues, which included the local history, economy, and ecology, the potential for place as a responsive pedagogy was not considered. Although the use of advocacy pedagogy is apparent, as students were committed to the restoration and preservation of the health of the waterways which involved different levels of community advocacy, attention was not on the potential of the unique features and the inherent value of local site, which can 'imbue students and teachers with a heightened sense of agency and renewed appreciation of the more-than-human world' (Renshaw & Tooth, 2018a, p. 19).

Designing place-responsive pedagogies would require the teachers and students to experience place as stories of the creek and the surrounding areas. For example, the land as sacred is present in the stories of the Turrbal people, whose hunting, agricultural, and aquacultural practices were disrupted by European colonisation and settlement. They are the traditional custodians of the ancient land that the school is built upon, including the creek in which the dead fish were found. Engagement with such a sense of place could be achieved through an extension of the project using pedagogies of sustainability in order to motivate students to act locally for global sustainability. The school had already made connections with a school in Osaka and, thus, was already making global connection regarding healthy waterways. Extending place to develop relationships with and learn from local First Nation custodians would provide students with experiences otherwise hidden from view. A pedagogy of sacredness holds potential for non-Indigenous students to see the problem as more than an issue of scientific experimentation that provides data to improve the health of the waterways in terms of sustainability.

There is, of course, a diversity of ways to be conscious of and responsive to place. However, to pre-empt them is a failure to understand that place-responsive pedagogies require first experiencing place from which pedagogies can then emerge. Our brief case study gives but one example of the myriad of possible ways in which schools can re-evaluate their place-based educational programs.

Democratic education, bureaucracy, and political change

Democratic education, as presented here, is a radical approach to education that places civic literacy and democratic engagement at the core of formal education from which all learning occurs, with the purpose of integrating curriculum, pedagogy, and assessment with practical place-responsive activities aimed at social reconstruction in order to strengthen social democracy as a corrective mechanism for societal change. The truth of such a statement is, of course, a matter for empirical investigation. In terms of the purposes or wider aims of education in a democracy, democratic education may not be fully consistent with the liberal/communitarian conception of politics, but it is well-aligned with and essential for the development of deliberative forms of democracy. Moreover, deliberative practice is necessary for any form of democracy, including liberal and communitarian conceptions, to allow for greater meaningful citizen participation. However, the relationship between education and legitimate forms of power cannot be separated, and it would be naïve to ignore this. Elected representatives have an interest in what is taught in schools and, therefore, it is unlikely that our proposal for education reform will gain support from state education departments and the corporate sector, and if the interests of the elected representatives are identified with the survival or interests of the state, it is unlikely to get widespread support from the voting community.

Given the seemingly insurmountable problems with democracy, it would be foolish to believe that the capacity of education as a catalyst for change will fast ensure any significant changes. However, it would be equally foolish if the extent of social, political, and ecological crises continued to elicit apathy among citizens because we 'have come to the conclusion that it is simply unprofitable and unproductive to engage in reflection about things that cannot be changed anyhow' (Lipman, Sharp & Oscanyan, 1980, p. 31). Ideally, governments should take civics and citizenship education seriously, but like all reforms, changes to education policy and practices will inevitably be slow moving. Education reform, like most political movements, requires working against the perpetual constraints that society constructs to preserve and maintain the existing social and political order, including the tendency to transmit the same cultural practices to each new generation. Historically, these constraints, imposed even by so-called democratic societies, have been complicit in the reinforcement and perpetuation of elitism and social divisions. Unfortunately, from the reformer's viewpoint, much of history has shown that the maintenance of commitment to social reform takes its toll. Political movements can, and do, fall short of their potential as agents of change, or internal power struggles sometimes threaten to destabilise the momentum generated.

Ironically then, one of the major barriers preventing students from participating in educational philosophy is the very education system itself. The contemporary educational system is constrained by bureaucratic rationality, which not only informs the way teachers approach education, but tends to thwart efforts by teachers, parents, and concerned members of the local community who seek democratic reforms. Ideally, it is preferable to eliminate, or, at least, minimise the impact of bureaucracy on the way schools are presently administered (Hunter, 2020; Rizvi, 1989, 1993; Walker, 1990). As Jal Mehta (2013) observes, the problems education faces are artefacts of the very bureaucratic structure that requires reform. He suggests that the wrong question is being asked:

> When reforms don't grow as far or as fast as we hope, we ask, 'What's wrong with the reform?' when instead we should ask, 'What's wrong with the sector?' The root problem is that the educational sector as a whole is organized around a core system that functions as a bureaucracy rather than as a profession; we are trying to solve a problem that requires professional skill and expertise by using bureaucratic levers of requirements and regulations. Many of the specific problems we see today— wide variability in levels of teacher skill from classroom to classroom, failure to bring good practices to scale across sites, the absence of an 'educational infrastructure' to support practice, the failure to capitalize on the knowledge and skill of leading teachers, and the distrustful and unproductive relationships between policy makers and practitioners— are by-products of the form in which the educational sector was cast.
>
> (p. 463)

Currently, education reform is driven by neoliberal educational restructuring that expand 'privatization, standardized testing, and the standardization of knowledge, curriculum, and pedagogy' (Saltman, 2015, p. 7). Rather than approach reform through the democratic discourse of civic engagement, the public interest and shared and contested values, neoliberal restructuring appeals to corporate metaphors such as the 'natural efficiencies of the market' as a solution to the 'inefficiencies of bureaucratic red tape' (see Chubb & Moe, 1990). For education to be relevant to democracy as a mode of associated living, as Dewey intended, education reform requires a reconstruction of bureaucracy, re-cast as a facilitative structure that is consistent with democratic imperatives, comprising teachers, researchers, curriculum designers, and other education professionals engaged in rigorous inquiry, evaluation of alternatives, and experimentation prior to implementation.

However, an upheaval of current institutional practices is difficult to coordinate, as teaching professionals operate in complex, multitask environments determined by education bureaucracy, in which they cannot avoid making trade-offs between the multiple outputs expected of them (Smith & Larimer, 2004). While such conditions prevail, education reform is better served incrementally, as bottom-up reforms are more practical as means to subverting dominant epistemic practices and accompanying social, economic, and political agendas. This approach not only regards reform as a social process, rather than one dictated by government policy that must somehow be implemented, but it also has an educative potential, insofar as it can provide opportunities for increased participation (from parents, teachers, and other professionals in allied fields of education) in formulating educational policy. Moreover, this is a practical approach to the integration of philosophical awareness and procedures in all aspects of curriculum, pedagogy, and assessment. The emergence of philosophy for children in over sixty countries illustrates this well. It indicates a growing willingness of researchers, administrators, teachers, and parents to challenge the institutional practices of the educational system (see Burgh & Thornton, 2016c, 2017, 2019c; Lipman, 2008; Naji & Hashim, 2017). Some educators see the introduction of philosophy in the classroom as a reappraisal of education, others see it as an appealing approach to be integrated into the current curriculum or one which can drive new curriculum innovations, while others realise its potential as an appropriate pedagogy for value inquiry or for the improvement of reasoning skills (Burgh, 2014, p. 24).

Notwithstanding any misgivings about contemporary educational institutions, there is a contrast between the approach of philosophy and that of other disciplines. While it is true that other disciplines, like philosophy, require the use of certain conceptual tools, the discipline of philosophy also prepares students to think in other disciplines. Philosophy, therefore, provides an effective model for the educational process. In one sense, this means simply that educational philosophy can make a fundamental, and much needed, contribution to the present curriculum. Lipman's (1988) vision, however, promises much broader horizons. He envisioned educational philosophy as paradigmatically representing 'the education of the future as a form of life that has not yet been realized and as a kind of praxis' (p. 17). If we take Lipman's words seriously, then we must start somewhere and, thus, the implementation of democratic education requires individual teachers to commit to implementing it in their own classrooms. Indeed, if what we seek is democracy, especially the kind we advocate here, then people are sovereign, which requires individual action that can lead to collaborative strategies to bring about change. But as the history of philosophy for children as an educational movement demonstrates, successful implementation not only requires commitment and support from philosophers, teacher-educators, school principals, parents, and the greater community, but well-constructed and effective pre-service and in-service programs for teachers, as well as institutional and financial support.

If philosophy improves academic performance, and delivers social gains, then there is no good educational reason it should not receive appropriate funding, institutional support, and be allocated a place in the curriculum for the betterment of all students and wider society. However, despite the growing number of studies, by Trickey and Topping and others that provide empirical support that philosophy does produce cognitive gains and provide social benefits, philosophy has not been given priority on the education agenda as it is often seen as irrelevant to modern society. Its ivory tower associations, in a decidedly anti-intellectual political climate, contribute to philosophy suffering 'from an image problem, with it sometimes being thought of as a remote and abstract discipline suitable only for a small number of academically-minded adults' (Millett & Tapper, 2012, pp. 546–547). Thoughts of philosophers conjure images closer to Rodin's *The Thinker*, motionless, introverted, cold, and distant, instead of cognitively able and active members of society. Moreover, within philosophy's most esteemed ranks, Plato himself can be quoted as saying that philosophy is not mere child's play, but rather, serious business. Unfortunately, this attitude is enduring, to which Lipman (1993) attests.

> To the report that very young children almost invariably greeted opportunities to discuss philosophy with joy and delight, the standard reply was that this proved that the children could not be doing philosophy, since the study of philosophy is a serious and difficult matter. The recent career of philosophy in elementary and secondary education has been a matter of overcoming precisely these objections and misconceptions.
>
> (p. 1)

Arguably, the existing curriculum, built around well-established core subjects (or learning areas), already provides what philosophy is said to do, and, therefore, there is no case to be made for expanding it to include philosophy. We take an alternative stance that philosophy, as reflective communal dialogue, is unique in its ability to not only provide students with the knowledge and skills needed to exercise competent autonomy for active and informed citizenship, but that it can promote reflective communal self-correction and, as such, is an exemplar of democracy as a mode of associated living; the kind of deliberative inquiry required for the correction of social and political institutions (Burgh, 2018) needed to face social and environmental crises.[8]

Conclusion

Let's go back to the beginning. Val Plumwood (1995) gave a persuasive argument that it is 'not democracy that has failed ecology, but liberal democracy that has failed both democracy and ecology' (p. 134). Radical inequality perpetuated by liberal theory, which promotes abstract individualism and separation from other and nature, underpins liberal-democracy, and has, therefore, failed democracy and ecology because it lacks the capacity for correctiveness (the ability to correct social and political institutions). Dewey (1956) warned us that social life has 'undergone a thorough and radical change', and it continues to do so, and '[i]f education is to have any meaning for life, it must pass through an equally complete transformation' (p. 49). Liberal-democracy, as we have argued, has also failed education. This prompted us to ask the question: How can education in a democracy best develop civic literacy that increases civic participation and engagement in public affairs?

Our response to this question is the theoretical framework for democratic education we have presented here. We have proposed a theoretical framework for democratic education that emphasises philosophy functioning educationally and recognises the purpose of schooling as social reconstruction in which students have an integral role to play in shaping democracy. It is a form of experiential learning through the community of inquiry and its use of collaborative inquiry-based pedagogical methods that brings together democracy, epistemology, and place-based learning. Its origins are steeped in Lipman's philosophical community of inquiry, but reconstructed through Peirce's understanding of fallibilism, Camus' conception of lucidity, Dewey's theory and practice of connecting curriculum to learning activities that are representative of, or engage with, real-life situations to test understanding and to reconstruct meaning, and Plumwood's strategy of adopting traitorous identities to challenge worldviews. Its educational emphasis is on deliberative awareness of epistemic harms and epistemological privilege present in dominant discourses that colonise education and marginalise or exclude other discourses, and subsequently prevent democratic correctiveness. Pedagogically, focus is on experiences that do not fit the dominant narrative in order to be mindful of prejudices, which becomes a model of inquiry for developing eco-cultural identities and cross-cultural dialogue in a pluralist democracy.

We have argued that it is essential for children and adolescents to develop the capacity for collective self-correction for democratic education to achieve the aim of social reconstruction as the goal of education reform. As much as possible, they should be encouraged to engage in collaborative decision-making about what affects their daily lives, not only in the classroom, but also in the context of the school community and the greater community generally. As educators, we must, therefore, actively support education reforms that promote deliberative communication and civic literacy, while also maintaining a vigilant eye on increasing corporate management policies and test-based accountability of schools which have little educational value. Often, the pursuit of efficiency *per se* has over-shadowed more important social goals. Of vital importance is the facilitation of epistemic inclusiveness and democratic correctiveness, in order to strengthen democracy as a deliberative process for public decision-making, which is essential for ecological flourishing.

Notes

1 There is much literature devoted to eco-democracy by proponents who argue that it is a legitimate form of democracy and by critics who contend that it suffers from the dilemma of prioritising 'green values' over fundamental liberal-democratic values of human freedom and rights. For further discussion, see Cohen (1989), Dryzek (1995), Goodin (1992), and Mathews (1995, 1996). However, the pragmatist approach we take relies on deliberative forms of democracy to provide justification for the legitimacy of democracy. To use Seyla Benhabib's (1994) words, democracy 'is best understood as a form of organizing the collective and public exercise of power in the major institutions of a society on the basis of the principle that decisions affecting the well-being of a collectivity can be viewed as the outcome of a procedure of free and reasoned deliberation among individuals considered as moral and political equals' (p. 27). See also Dryzek (2004), McAfee (2004), Misak (2004), and Talisse (2004). Of course, there are a number of caveats to the validity of this claim, but we have dealt with these here and in previous chapters regarding the nature of individual identity in relation to collective identity, pragmatist epistemology regarding the nature of inquiry and decision-making, and humans as place-embedded beings that share onto-epistemological relationships with ecological others.

2 We would like to thank Mary Graham (Adjunct Associate Professor at the School of Political Sciences and International Relations at The University of Queensland) for the numerous conversations from 2016 to 2021. These conversations and her thoughts published in Graham (1999, 2012, 2014) inform the content of this section. See also Graham (2021), Thornton, Graham & Burgh (2019, 2021).

3 The term Land (capital L) denotes biodiversity, biosphere, nature, the natural world, environment, earth, wildlife, geographical and geological forms, ecosystem, landscape, flora, and fauna.

4 Not to be mistaken for the liberal notion of autonomy as 'individual autonomy', understood as the capacity to be our own person, to be independent of others— to live according to reasons and motives that are our own and not the result of manipulation from external forces.

5 Arguably, mechanistic science was such a moment. As Carolyn Merchant (2012) puts it: 'Technologies and attitudes of domination stemming from the Scientific Revolution have acted as a legitimating framework, enabling humans to threaten nature with deforestation and desertification, chemical pollution, destruction of habitats and species, and ultimately with nuclear fallout, ozone depletion, and global warming' (p. 3).

6 https://www.abc.net.au/religion/stop-destroying-indigenous-sites-and-lives-morgan-brigg-and-mar/12355284.

7 The Dreamtime or the Dreaming is a term used to describe important features of Aboriginal spiritual beliefs and existence. There is no universal Dreamtime; distinct tribes have different beliefs about how the Creator being shaped the world. These diverse stories tell Aboriginal people which places are sacred. Ceremonies and customary songs take place near the sacred sites to please the Ancestral spirits and to keep themselves alive. The terms Dreaming and Dreamtime are Western terms that try to describe a complex system of beliefs and practices and are second best to the multiple Aboriginal terms for these systems.

8 For further discussion on 'why should philosophy be taught in schools?', see Hand (2018). This special issue journal contains articles by Michael Hand, Angela Hobbs, Gilbert Burgh, Philip Cam, Peter Worley, Laura D'Olimpio and Andrew Petersen, and Carrie Winstanley.

References

ACARA (2020). *The shape of the Australian curriculum: Civic and citizenship, version 5.0.* Sydney: Australian Curriculum, Assessment and Reporting Authority.

Anthamatten, E. (2012). The hands and feet of the child: Towards a philosophy of habilitation. *Education and Culture, 28*(2), 26–35.

Anyon, J. (2006). Social class, school knowledge, and the hidden curriculum. In G. Dimitriadis, L. Weis & C. McCarthy (Eds.), *Ideology, curriculum, and the new sociology of education: Revisiting the work of Michael Apple* (pp. 37–45). New York: Routledge.

Arends, R.I. (2012). *Learning to teach.* New York: McGraw-Hill.

Arendt, H. (1958). *The human condition.* Chicago: University of Chicago Press.

Aristotle (1999). *Nicomachean ethics.* T.H. Irwin (Ed./trans.). Indianapolis: Hackett Publishing Co.

Aspin, D. (2000). A clarification of some key terms in values discussions. In M. Leicester, C. Modgil & S. Modgil (Eds.), *Moral education and pluralism: Education, culture and values, Vol. 4* (pp. 171–180). London: Farmer Press.

Australian Bureau of Statistics (2006). *Measures of Australia's progress.* Belconnen: ABS.

Ayim, M. (1988). Violence and domination as metaphors in academic discourse. In T. Govier (Ed.), *Selected issues in logic and communication* (pp. 184–195). Belmont: Wadsworth

Bailey, A (1998). Locating traitorous identities: Toward a view of privilege-cognizant white character. *Hypatia 13*(3), 27–42.

Barber, B. (1984). *Strong democracy: Participatory politics for a new age.* Berkeley: University of California Press.

Barber, B. (1996). Foundationalism and democracy. In S. Benhabib (Ed.), *Democracy and difference: Contesting boundaries of the political* (pp. 348–359). Princeton: Princeton University Press.

BBC (2019). Greta Thunberg quotes: 10 famous lines from teen activist. *Newsround.* https://www.bbc.co.uk/newsround/49812183.

Benda, J. (2007). Where freedom is not a utopia. *People's Voice,* January 9.

Benhabib, S. (1994). Deliberative rationality and models of democratic legitimacy. *Constellations, 1*(1), 26–52.

Bennett, W.J. (1985). Educators in America: The three R's. Speech delivered at the National Press Club, Washington, D.C., March 27, 1985.

Bettelheim, B. (1970). Bruno Bettelheim. In H.H. Hart (Ed.), *Summerhill: For and against* (pp. 99–113). New York: Hart.

Bjereld, U., Ekengren. A-M., & Schierenbeck, I. (2009). Power, identity, modernity: Individualisation and destabilisation in a globalised world. *International Review of Sociology*, *19*(2), 263–272.

Bleazby, J. (2004). Practicality and philosophy for children. *Critical & Creative Thinking: The Australasian Journal of Philosophy in Education*, *12*(2), 33–42.

Bleazby, J. (2006). Autonomy, democratic community, and citizenship in philosophy for children: Dewey and philosophy for children's rejection of the community/individual dualism. *Analytic Teaching*, *26*(1), 30–52.

Bleazby, J. (2011). Overcoming relativism and absolutism: Dewey's ideals of truth and meaning in philosophy for children. *Educational Philosophy and Theory*, *43*(5), 453–466.

Bleazby, J. (2012). Dewey's notion of imagination in philosophy for children. *Education and Culture*, *28*(2), 95–111.

Bleazby, J. (2013). *Social reconstruction learning: Dualism, Dewey and philosophy in schools*. London: Routledge.

Bleazby, J. (2015). Why some school subjects have a higher status than others: The epistemology of the traditional curriculum hierarchy. *Oxford Review of Education*, *41*(5), 671–689.

Bleazby, J., & Slade, C. (2019). Philosophy for children goes to university. In G. Burgh & S. Thornton (Eds.), *Philosophical inquiry with children: The development of an inquiring society in Australia* (pp. 215–232). Abingdon; New York: Routledge.

Bloom, B.S. (1968). Learning for mastery. Instruction and curriculum. Regional Education Laboratory for the Carolinas and Virginia, Topical Papers and Reprints, Number 1, 1–12. Reprint from *Evaluation Comment*, *1*(2), May 1968.

Brubaker, N.D. (2016). Cultivating democratically-minded teachers: A pedagogical journey. In J. Kitchen, D. Tidwell & L. Fitzgerald (Eds.), *Self-study and diversity II: Inclusive teacher education for a diverse world* (pp. 173–191). Rotterdam: Sense Publishers.

Burgh, G. (2003a). Philosophy in schools: Education for democracy or democratic education? *Critical & Creative Thinking: The Australasian Journal of Philosophy in Schools*, *11*(2), 18–30.

Burgh, G. (2003b). Democratic education: Aligning curriculum, pedagogy, assessment and school governance. In P. Cam (Ed.), *Philosophy, democracy and education* (pp. 102–120). Seoul: Korean National Commission for UNESCO.

Burgh, G. (2005). From Socrates to Lipman: Making philosophy relevant. In D. Shepherd (Ed.), *Creative engagements: Thinking with children, Vol. 31* (pp. 25–31). Oxford: Inter-Disciplinary Press.

Burgh, G. (2009). Reconstruction in philosophy education: The community of inquiry as a basis for knowledge and learning. In *Proceedings of the Philosophy of Education Society of Australasia 2008 Conference: The ownership and dissemination of knowledge*. 36th Annual Conference of the Philosophy of Education Society of Australasia, Queensland University of Technology, Brisbane, Australia (pp. 65-1–65-12). December 4–7, 2008.

Burgh, G. (2010). Citizenship as a learning process: Democratic education without foundationalism. In D.R.J. Macer & S. Saad-Zoy (Eds.), *Asian-Arab philosophical dialogues on globalization, democracy and human rights* (pp. 59–69). Bangkok: UNESCO, Regional Unit for Social and Human Sciences in Asia and the Pacific.

Burgh, G. (2014). Democratic pedagogy. *Journal of Philosophy in Schools, 1*(1), 22–44.

Burgh, G. (2018). The need for philosophy in promoting democracy: A case for philosophy in the curriculum. *Journal of Philosophy in Schools, 5*(1), 38–58.

Burgh, G., Field, T., & Freakley, M. (2006). *Ethics and the community of inquiry: Education for deliberative democracy.* South Melbourne: Thomson.

Burgh, G., & Nichols, K. (2012). The parallels between philosophical inquiry and scientific inquiry: Implications for science education. *Educational Philosophy and Theory, 44*(10), 1045–1059.

Burgh, G., & Thornton, S. (2016a). Inoculation against wonder: Finding an antidote in Camus, pragmatism and the community of inquiry, *Educational Philosophy and Theory, 48*(9), 884–898.

Burgh, G., & Thornton, S. (2016b). Lucid education: Resisting resistance to inquiry. *Oxford Review of Education, 42*(2), 165–177.

Burgh, G., & Thornton, S. (2016c). Philosophy goes to school in Australia: A history 1982–2016. *Journal of Philosophy in Schools, 3*(1), 59–83.

Burgh, G., & Thornton, S. (2017). From *Harry* to *Philosophy Park*: The development of philosophy for children resources in Australia. In M.R. Gregory, J. Haynes & K. Murris (Eds.), *The Routledge international handbook of philosophy for children* (pp. 163–170). Abingdon: Routledge.

Burgh, G., & Thornton, S. (2019a). The philosophical classroom: An Australian story. In G. Burgh & S. Thornton (Eds.), *Philosophical inquiry with children: The development of an inquiring society in Australia* (pp. 1–5). Abingdon; New York: Routledge.

Burgh, G., & Thornton, S. (2019b). Ecosocial citizenship education: Facilitating interconnective, deliberative practice and corrective methodology for epistemic accountability. *Childhood & Philosophy, 15,* 43–61.

Burgh, G., & Thornton, S. (Eds.). (2019c), *Philosophical inquiry with children: The development of an inquiring society in Australia.* Abingdon; New York: Routledge.

Burgh, G., Thornton, S., & Fynes-Clinton, L. (2018). 'Do not block the way of inquiry': Cultivating collective doubt through sustained deep reflective thinking. In E. Duthie, F.G. Moriyón & R.R. Loro (Eds.), *Parecidos de familia: Propuestas actuales en filosofía para niños / Family resemblances: Current trends in philosophy for children* (pp. 47–61). Madrid: Anaya.

Burgh, G., & Yorshansky, M. (2011). Communities of inquiry: Politics, power and group dynamics. *Educational Philosophy and Theory, 43,* 436–452.

Cam, P. (Ed.) (1993). *Thinking stories 1: Philosophical inquiry for children and teacher resource/activity book.* Sydney: Hale & Iremonger.

Cam, P. (Ed.) (1994). *Thinking stories 2: Philosophical inquiry for children and teacher resource/activity book.* Sydney: Hale & Iremonger.

Cam, P. (1995). *Thinking together: Philosophical inquiry for the classroom.* Sydney: Hale & Iremonger/Primary English Teaching Association.

Cam, P. (1997). *Thinking stories 3: Philosophical inquiry for children and teacher resource/activity book.* Sydney: Hale & Iremonger.

Cam, P. (2000). Philosophy, democracy and education: Reconstructing Dewey. In I-S. Cha (Ed.), *Teaching philosophy for democracy* (pp. 158–181). Seoul: Seoul University Press.

Cam, P. (2006). *Twenty thinking tools: Collaborative inquiry for the classroom.* Melbourne: ACER.

Cam P. (2008). Dewey, Lipman and the tradition of reflective education. In M. Taylor, P. Ghiraldelli Jr. & H. Schreier (Eds.), *Pragmatism, education and children* (pp. 163–181). Amsterdam: Rodopi Press.

Cam, P. (2015). On the philosophical narrative for children. *Childhood & Philosophy*, *11*(21), 37–53.

Cam, P. (2017). P4C stories: Different approaches and similar applications? In S. Naji & R. Hashim (Eds.), *History, theory and practices of philosophy for children: International perspectives* (pp. 128). London: Routledge.

Cam, P., Fynes-Clinton, L., Harrison, K., Hinton, L., Scholl, R., & Vaseo, S. (2007). *Philosophy with young children: A classroom handbook.* Deakin West: Australian Curriculum Studies Association.

Camus, A. (1977 [1955]). *The myth of Sisyphus.* London: Penguin Books.

Camus, A. (1960). *The stranger.* New York: Knopf.

Camus, A. (1991). *The rebel.* New York: Vintage International.

Camus, A. (2001 [1948]). Democracy is an exercise in modesty. A. van den Hoven (trans.). *Sartre Studies International*, *7*(2), 12–14.

Carson, L., & Martin, B. (1999). *Random selection in politics.* Westport: Praeger.

Çayır, A. (2018). Philosophy for children in teacher education: Effects, difficulties, and recommendations. *International Electronic Journal of Elementary Education*, *11*(2), 173–180.

Checkoway, B., & Aldana, A. (2013). Four forms of youth civic engagement for diverse democracy. *Children and Youth Services Review*, *35*(11), 1894–1899.

Chetty, D. (2014). The elephant in the room: Picturebooks, philosophy for children and racism. *Childhood & philosophy*, *10*(19), 11–31.

Chetty, D., & Suissa, J. (2017). 'No go areas': Racism and discomfort in the community of inquiry. In M.R. Gregory, J. Haynes & K. Murris (Eds.), *The Routledge international handbook of philosophy for children* (pp. 11–18). Abingdon: Routledge.

Chubb, J., & Moe, T. (1990). *Politics, markets, and America's schools.* Washington D.C.: Brookings Institute.

Clabaugh, G.K. (2008). Second thoughts about democratic classrooms. *Educational Horizons*, *87*(1), 2025.

Clarke, J., Coll, K., Dagnino, E., & Neveu, C. (2014). *Disputing citizenship.* Bristol: Policy Press.

Code, L. (1991). *What can she know? Feminist theory and the construction of knowledge.* Ithaca: Cornell University Press.

Cohen, J. (1989). Deliberation and democratic legitimacy. In A. Hamlin & P. Pettit (Eds.), *The good polity: Normative analysis of the state* (pp. 17–34). New York: Blackwell.

Cole, D.R., & Somerville, M. (2020). The affect(s) of literacy learning in the mud. *Discourse: Studies in the Cultural Politics of Education*, 1–17.

Cole, M., & Cole, S.R. (1989). *The development of children.* New York: Scientific American.

Cox, E. (1988). Explicit and implicit moral education. *Journal of Moral Education*, *17*, 92–97.

Cragg, C.E., Plotnikoff, R.C., Hugo, K., & Casey, A. (2001). Perspective transformation in RN-to-BSN distance education. *Journal of Nursing Education*, *40*(7), 317–322.

Craig, R. (1981). Some problems with values clarification. *Educational Considerations*, *8*(4), 13–14.

Crain, W.C. (2010). *Theories of development: Concepts and applications*, sixth edition. Denver: Pearson.

Cranton, P. (2002). Teaching for transformation. *New Directions of Adult and Continuing Education*, *93*, 63–71.

Cravey, M., & Petit, A. (2012). A critical pedagogy of place: Learning through the body. *Feminist Formations*, *24*(2), 100–119.

Credit Suisse Research Institute (2020). *Global wealth report 2020*. Authors: A. Shorrocks, J. Davies & R. Lluberas. Credit Suisse Research Institute.

Croall, J. (1983). *All the best, Neill: Letters from Summerhill*. London: Andre Deutsch.

Curzon-Hobson, A. (2003). Between exile and the kingdom: Albert Camus and empowering classroom relationships. *Educational Philosophy and Theory*, *35*(4), 367–380.

Curzon-Hobson, A. (2013). Confronting the absurd: An educational reading of Camus' *The Stranger*. *Educational Philosophy and Theory*, *45*(4), 873–887.

Curzon-Hobson, A. (2017). The experience of strangeness in education: Camus, Jean-Baptiste Clamence and the little ease. *Educational Philosophy and Theory*, *49*, 264–272.

Curzon-Hobson, A. (2014). Extending the contribution of Albert Camus to educational thought: An analysis of *The Rebel*. *Educational Philosophy and Theory*, *46*(10), 1098–1110.

Dahl, R.A. (1996). Democratic theory and democratic experience. In S. Benhabib (Ed.), *Democracy and difference: Contesting boundaries of the political* (pp. 336–339). Princeton: Princeton University Press.

Daniel, M-F. (1998). P4C in preservice teacher education: Difficulties and successes encountered in two research projects. *Analytic Teaching*, *19*(1), 15–28.

Davey Chesters, S. (2012). *The Socratic classroom: Reflective thinking through collaborative inquiry*. Rotterdam: Sense Publishers.

Davey Chesters, S., Fynes-Clinton, L., Hinton, L., & Scholl, R. (2013). *Philosophical and ethical inquiry for students in the middle years and beyond*. Deakin West: Australian Curriculum Studies Association.

Davey Chesters, S., & Hinton, L. (2017). What's philosophy got to do with it? Achieving synergy between philosophy and education in teacher preparation. In M.R. Gregory, J. Haynes & K. Murris (Eds.), *The Routledge international handbook of philosophy for children* (pp. 208–215). Abingdon: Routledge.

Davies, I., Mizuyama, M., & Thompson, G.H. (2010). Citizenship education in Japan. *Citizenship, Social and Economics Education*, *9*(3), 170–178.

Davis, M. (2003). What's wrong with character education? *American Journal of Education*, *110*(1), 32–57.

de Bono, E. (1990). *Six thinking hats*. London: Penguin.

de Bono, E. (1994). *Parallel thinking: From Socratic thinking to de Bono thinking*. London: Viking.

DEEWR. (2005). *National framework for values education in Australian schools*. Canberra: Department of Education, Employment and Workplace Relations.

DEEWR (2010). *Civics & citizenship education professional learning package*. Canberra: Department of Education, Employment and Workplace Relations.

Delanty, G. (2000). *Citizenship in a global age: Society, culture, politics*. Philadelphia: Open University Press.

Delanty, G. (2003). Citizenship as a learning process: Disciplinary citizenship versus cultural citizenship. *International Journal of Lifelong Education*, *22*(6), 597–605.

Del Nevo, M. (Ed.) (2002). *The continental community of inquiry*. Sheffield: International Society for Philosophers.

De Marzio, D.M. (2011). What happens in philosophical texts: Matthew Lipman's theory and practice of the philosophical text as model. *Childhood & Philosophy, 7*(13), 29–47.

Denton, D. (1963). *Albert Camus and the moral dimensions of education*. ProQuest Dissertations and Theses.

Denton, D.E. (1964). Albert Camus: Philosopher of moral concern. *Educational Theory, 14*, 99–127.

Denton, D.E. (1967). *Camus: A critical analysis*. Boston: Prime Publishers.

Denzin, N.K., & Lincoln, Y.S. (2008). Introduction: Critical methodologies and Indigenous inquiry. In N.K. Denzin, Y.S. Lincoln & L.T. Smith (Eds.). *Handbook of critical and Indigenous methodologies*. London; Los Angeles: SAGE.

Dewey, J. (1897). My pedagogic creed. *School Journal, 54*, 77–80.

Dewey, J. (1900). Psychology of occupations. *The Elementary School Record, 3*, 108–111.

Dewey, J. (1910). Science as subject-matter and as method. *Science, 31*(787), 121–127.

Dewey, J. (1916). *Democracy and education: An introduction to the philosophy of education*. New York: Macmillan.

Dewey, J. (1933). *How we think*. Boston: Heath.

Dewey, J. (1934). *Art as experience*. New York: Capricorn Books.

Dewey, J. (1936). The theory of the Chicago experiment. In K.C. Mayhew & A.C. Edwards, *The Dewey School: The Laboratory School of the University of Chicago, 1896–1903*, Appendix II (pp. 462–477). New York: Appleton-Century.

Dewey, J. (1937). The challenge of democracy to education. In J.A. Boydston (Ed.), *The later works, 1925–1953, Vol. II:1935–1937* (pp. 181–190). Carbondale: Southern Illinois University Press.

Dewey, J. (1938). *Experience in education*. New York: Collier Books.

Dewey, J. (1956 [1899]). *The school and society*, second revised edition. Chicago: University of Chicago Press.

Dewey, J. (1970 [1920]). *Reconstruction in philosophy*, enlarged edition with new introduction. Boston: Beacon Press.

Dewey, J. (1981 [1896]). The reflex arc concept in psychology. In J.J. McDermott (Ed.), *The philosophy of John Dewey* (pp. 137–138). Chicago: University of Chicago Press.

Dewey, J. (1988). Creative democracy: The task before us. In J.A. Boydston (Ed.), *The later works of John Dewey, Vol. 14*. Carbondale, IL: Southern Illinois University Press.

Dewey, J. (2010). The need for a philosophy of education (1934). *Schools: Studies in Education, 7*(2), 244–245.

Dewey, J. (2012). Education and democracy in the world of today (1938). *Schools: Studies in Education, 9*(1), 96–100.

Dombayci, M.A. (2014). Philosophy for children and social inquiry: An example of education for democratic citizenship through political philosophy. *Cumhuriyet International Journal of Education, 3*(2), 85–101.

Dotson, K. (2011). Tracking epistemic violence, tracking practices of silencing. *Hypatia, 26*(2), 236–257.

Dryzek, J.S. (1995). Political and ecological communication. *Environment Politics, 4*(4), 13–30.

Dryzek, J.S. (2004). Pragmatism and democracy: In search of deliberative publics. *The Journal of Speculative Philosophy, 18*(1), 72–79.

Dune, J. (1997). *A critique of research evaluating moral education interventions.* San Luis Obispo: California Polytechnic State University.

Durst, A. (2010). *Women educators in the progressive era: The women behind Dewey's laboratory school.* New York: Palgrave Macmillan.

Echeverria, E., & Hannam, P. (2017). The community of philosophical inquiry (P4C): A pedagogical proposal for advancing democracy. In M.R. Gregory, J. Haynes & K. Murris (Eds.), *Routledge international handbook of philosophy for children* (pp. 3–10). Abingdon: Routledge.

Elicor, P.P. (2019). Philosophical inquiry with indigenous children: An attempt to integrate indigenous forms of knowledge in philosophy for/with children. *Childhood & Philosophy, 15,* 23–42.

Elicor, P.P. (2021). I am keeping my cultural hat on: Exploring a 'culture-enabling' philosophy for/with children practice. *Childhood & Philosophy, 17,* pp. 1–18.

Elliot, J. (1971). The concept of the neutral teacher. *Cambridge Journal of Education, 1*(2), 60–67.

Englund, T. (2000) Rethinking democracy and education: Towards and education of deliberative citizens. *Journal of Curriculum Studies, 32*(2), 305–313.

Erikson, E.H. (1968). *Identity: Youth and crisis.* New York: Norton.

Fabes, R.A., Fultz, J., Eisenberg, N., May-Plumlee, T., & Christopher, F.S. (1989). Effects of rewards on children's prosocial motivation: A socialization study. *Developmental Psychology, 25*(4), 509–515.

Field, T. (1995). Philosophy for children and the feminist critique of reason. *Critical & Creative Thinking: The Australasian Journal of Philosophy for Children, 3*(1), 9–12.

Field, T. (1997). Feminist epistemology and philosophy for children. *Thinking: The Journal of Philosophy for Children, 13*(1), 17–22.

Filmer, R. (1680). *Patriarcha, or, The natural power of kings.* London: Walter Davis.

Fisher, P. (1998). *Wonder, the rainbow, and the aesthetics of pure experiences.* *Cambridge*; London: Harvard University Press.

Flum, H., & Kaplan, A. (2012). Identity formation in educational settings: A contextualized view of theory and research in practice. *Contemporary Educational Psychology, 37,* 240–245.

Ford, S.M. (2010). Reconceptualizing the public/private distinction in the age of information technology. *Information, Communication & Society, 14*(4), 550–567.

Fountain, S. (1999). *Peace education in UNICEF.* New York: UNICEF.

Freakley, M., Burgh, G., & Tilt MacSporran, L. (2008). *Values education in schools: A resource book for student inquiry.* Camberwell: Australian Council for Educational Research.

Freire, P. (1970). *Pedagogy of the oppressed.* London: Continuum.

Fricker, M. (2007). *Epistemic injustice power and the ethics of knowing.* Oxford; New York: Oxford University Press.

Furlong, J.J., & Carroll, W.J. (1990). Teacher neutrality and teaching of ethical issues. *The Educational Forum, 54*(2), 157–168.

Furlong, M., & Morrison, G. (2000). The school in school violence: Definitions and facts. *Journal of Emotional and Behavioral Disorders, 8*(2), 71–82.

Fynes-Clinton, L. (2015). Genuine doubt, fallibilism and collaborative philosophical inquiry. Paper presented at *Identity and philosophical inquiry in an age of diversity,* XVII International Council for Philosophical Inquiry with Children (ICPIC)

Conference, The University of British Columbia, Vancouver, Canada. June 25–27, 2015.

Galtung, J. (1969). Violence, peace and peace research. *Journal of Peace Research*, 6(3), 167–191.

Gaard, G. (2011). Ecofeminism revisited: Rejecting essentialism and re-placing species in a materialist feminist environmentalism. *Feminist Formations*, 23(2), 26–53.

Gadamer, H.G. (2004). *Truth and method*, second revised edition. London; New York: Continuum.

Galbraith, R.E., & Jones, T.M. (1975). Teaching strategies for moral dilemmas: An application of Kohlberg's theory of moral development to the social studies classroom. *Social Education*, 39(1), 16–22.

Gallop, J. (1992). *Feminism and psychoanalysis: The daughter's seduction*. London: Macmillan.

Garcia-Moriyon, F., Robello, I., & Colom, R. (2005). Evaluating philosophy for children: A meta-analysis. *Thinking: The Journal of Philosophy for Children*, 17(4), 14–22.

Gatens, M. (1996). *Imaginary bodies: Ethics, power and corporeality*. London; New York: Routledge.

Gazzard, A. (2012). Do you need to know philosophy to teach philosophy to children? A comparison of two approaches. *Analytic Teaching and Philosophical Practice*, 33(1), 45–53.

Gibbons, A. (2013a). Like a stone: A happy death and the search for knowledge. *Educational Philosophy and Theory*, 45, 1092–1103.

Gibbons, A. (2013b). Beyond education: Meursault and being ordinary. *Educational Philosophy and Theory*, 45, 1104–1115.

Gibbons, A. (2013c). The teaching of tragedy: Narrative and education. *Educational Philosophy and Theory*, 45, 1150–1161.

Gibbons, A. (2013d). Tragedy and teaching: The education of narrative. *Educational Philosophy and Theory*, 45, 1162–1174.

Gilbert, R. (2004). Elements of values education. *The Social Educator*, 22(4), 8–14.

Giles, D.E. Jr., & Eyler, J. (1994). The theoretical roots of service-learning in John Dewey: Toward a theory of service learning. *Michigan Journal of Community Service Learning*, 1(1), 77–85.

Gilligan, C. (1982). *In a different voice: Psychological theory and women's development*. Cambridge: Harvard University Press.

Gilligan, C. (1987). Moral orientation and moral development. In E. Feder & D. Meyers (Eds.), *Women and moral theory* (pp. 19–33). Totowa: Rowman & Littlefield.

Glaser, J. (1994). Reasoning as dialogical inquiry: A model for the liberation of women. *Thinking: The Journal of Philosophy for Children*, 11(3&4), 14–17.

Glaser, J. (2007). Educating for citizenship and social justice. In D. Camhy (Ed.), *Philosophical foundations of innovative learning* (pp. 16–25). Sankt Augustin: Academia Verlag.

Glaser, J. (2019). 'What's so special about a story?': Revisiting the IAPC text-as-story paradigm. In G. Burgh & S. Thornton (Eds.), *Philosophical inquiry with children: The development of an inquiring society in Australia* (pp. 87–95). Abingdon; New York: Routledge.

Glassman, M. (2001). Dewey and Vygotsky: Society, experience, and inquiry in educational practice. *Educational Researcher*, 30(4), 3–14.

Goad, P. (2010). A chrome yellow blackboard with blue chalk: New education and the new architecture: modernism at Koornong School. *History of Education*, 39(6), 731–748.

Goodin, R.E. (1992). *Green political theory*. Cambridge: Polity.

Goralnik, L., Dobson, T., & Nelson, M.P. (2014). Place-based care ethics: A field philosophy pedagogy. *Canadian Journal of Environmental Education, 19*, 180–196.

Gorur, R. (2016). Governments need to look beyond education rankings and focus on inequities in the system. *The Conversation* (Dec 5). Available from http://the-conversation.com/governments-need-to-look-beyond-education-rankings-and-focus-on-inequities-in-the-system-69715.

Götz, I.L. (1987). Camus and the art of teaching. *Educational Theory, 37*, 265–276.

Gould, C.C. (1988). *Rethinking democracy: Freedom and social cooperation in politics, economy, and society*. Cambridge: Cambridge University Press.

Graham, M. (1999). Some thoughts about philosophical underpinnings of Aboriginal world views. *Worldviews: Global Religions, Culture and Ecology, 3*(2), 105–118.

Graham, M. (2012). The concept of ethics in Australian Aboriginal systems of thought. *Custodial Navigator*, 1–12. Retrieved from: http://www.indigenouss-overeigntyaustralia.com.au/wp-content/uploads/2013/06/CustodialNavigator.pdf.

Graham, M. (2014). Place and spirit – Spirit and place. *EarthSong, 2*(7), 5–7.

Graham, M. (2021). Aboriginal ethics: Australia becoming, Australia dreaming. Unpublished manuscript.

Greene, M. (1973). *Teacher as stranger: Educational philosophy for the modern age*. Belmont: Wadsworth.

Greenwood, D. (2014). A critical theory of place-conscious education. In R. Stevenson, M. Brody, J. Dillon & A. Wals (Eds.), *International handbook of research on environmental education* (pp. 93–100). New York: Routledge.

Gregory, M.R. (2002). Constructivism, standards, and the classroom community of inquiry. *Educational Theory, 52*(4), 397–408.

Gregory, M. (2004). Practicing democracy: Social intelligence and philosophical practice. *International Journal of Applied Philosophy, 18*(2), 161–174.

Gregory, M. (2005). Conflict, inquiry and education for peace. In S.N. Chattopadhyay (Ed.), *World peace: Problems of global understanding and prospect of harmony* (pp. 265–278). Kolkata: Punthi Pustak.

Gregory, M. (2006). Normative dialogue types in philosophy for children. *Gifted Education International, 2*(3), 160–171.

Gregory, M.R. (2007). A framework for facilitating classroom dialogue. *Teaching Philosophy, 30*(1), 59–84.

Gregory, M. (2008). Philosophy in schools: Ideals, challenges and opportunities. *Critical & Creative Thinking: The Australasian Journal of Philosophy in Education, 16*(1), 5–22.

Gregory, M.R., Haynes, J., & Murris, K. (Eds.) (2017). *The Routledge international handbook of philosophy for children*. Abingdon: Routledge.

Gregory, M., & Granger, D. (2012). Introduction: John Dewey on philosophy and childhood. *Education and Culture, 28*(2), 1–25.

Grimshaw, J. (1987). Philosophy and aggression. *Radical Philosophy, 47*, 18–20.

Gruenewald, D. (2003a). The best of both worlds: A critical pedagogy of place. *Educational Researcher, 32*(4), 3–12.

Gruenewald, D. (2003b). Framework for place-conscious education. *American Educational Research Journal, 40*(3), 619–654.

Gutmann, A. (1987). *Democratic education*. Princeton: Princeton University Press.

Gutmann, A. (1996). Democracy, philosophy, and justification. In S. Benhabib (Ed.), *Democracy and difference: Contesting the boundaries of the political* (pp. 340–347). Princeton: Princeton University Press.

Habermas, J. (1996). *Between facts and norms: Contributions to a discourse theory of law and democracy*. Cambridge: Polity.

Halstead, J. M. (1996). Values and values education in schools. In J. M. Halstead & M. J. Taylor (Eds.), *Values in education and education in values* (pp. 3–14). London: The Falmer Press.

Hand, M. (Ed.). (2018) Why should philosophy be taught in schools? [Special issue], *Journal of Philosophy in Schools, 5*(1).

Harding, S., & Hintikka, M.B. (1983). *Discovering reality: Feminist perspectives on epistemology, metaphysics, methodology, and philosophy of science*. Dordrecht: D. Reidel.

Harding, S. (1991). *Whose science? Whose knowledge?: Thinking from women's lives*. Ithaca: Cornell University Press.

Haynes, J. (2008). *Children as philosophers: Learning through enquiry and dialogue in the primary school*, second edition. London: Routledge.

Haynes, J., & Murris, K. (2012). *Picturebooks, pedagogy and philosophy*. New York: Routledge.

Hechinger, F.M. (1970). Fred M. Hechinger. In H.H. Hart (Ed.), *Summerhill: For and against* (pp. 34–43). New York: Hart.

Heraud, R. (2013). The stranger: Adventures at zero point. *Educational Philosophy and Theory, 45*, 1116–1132.

Hicks, D. (1987). Education for peace: Principles into practice. *Cambridge Journal of Education, 17*(1), 3–12.

Hicks, D. (2004). Teaching for tomorrow: How can futures studies contribute to peace education? *Journal of Peace Education, 1*(2), 165–178.

Hildebrand, D.L. (1996). Genuine doubt and the community in Peirce's theory of inquiry. *Southwest Philosophy Review, 12*, 33–43.

Hildebrand, D.L. (2018). John Dewey. In E.N. Zalta (Ed.), *The Stanford Encyclopedia of Philosophy*. Stanford: Center for the Study of Language and Information (CSLI), Stanford University.

Hilferty, F. (2001). Subject teaching associations and the professional representation of teachers in New South Wales. In *Education Futures and New Citizenships, Proceedings of the 10th National Bicentennial Conference of the Australian Curriculum Studies Association*, Australian National University, Canberra, Australia (pp. 1–14). September 29 to October 1, 2001.

Hinton, L. (2003). Reinventing a school. *Critical & Creative Thinking: The Australasian Journal of Philosophy for Schools, 11*(2), 47–60.

Hinton, L., & Davey Chesters, S. (2013). A whole school approach to philosophy in schools: Outcomes and observations. In S. Goering, N. Shudak & T. Wartenberg (Eds.), *Philosophy in schools: An introduction for philosophers and teachers* (pp. 266–276). Abingdon: Routledge.

Hobbes, T. (1973 [1651]). *Leviathan*. K.R. Minogue (introduction). London: Everyman's Library.

Hobson, A. (2017a). *Albert Camus and education*. Rotterdam: Sense Publishers.

Hobson, A. (2017b). Camus and education. In M. Peters (Ed.), *Encyclopedia of educational philosophy and theory* (pp. 1–5). Singapore: Springer.

Hodgson, C. (2004). *Absurd limits: Camus, Dewey and metaphysics* (M.A. thesis). http://repository.tamu.edu/handle/1969.1/ETD-TAMU-2004-THESIS-H63.

Hunter, I. (2020). *Rethinking the school: Subjectivity, bureaucracy, criticism.* Abingdon: Routledge.

Hyde, D. (2016). *Veronica Brady: A most curious theist.* Veronica Brady Symposium, UWA, February 2016.

IPCC (2018). *Global Warming of 1.5°C: An IPCC special report.* Intergovernmental Panel on Climate Change (IPCC).

Irigaray, L. (1985 [1977]). *This sex which is not one.* C. Porter & C. Burke (trans.). Ithaca: Cornell University Press.

Jäger, U. (2014). Peace education and conflict transformation. In *Berghof handbook for conflict transformation* (pp. 3–18). Berlin: Berghof Foundation.

Jaggar, A.M. (1983). *Feminist politics and human nature.* Totowa: Rowman & Littlefield.

Jaggar, A.M. (1989). Love and knowledge: Emotion in feminist epistemology. In A.M. Jaggar & S.R. Bordo (Eds.), *Gender/body/knowledge: Feminist reconstructions of being and knowing* (pp. 145–171). New Brunswick: Rutgers University Press.

Jarrett, J.L. (1991). *The teaching of values.* London: Routledge.

Johnson, A.P. (2010). *Making connections in elementary and middle school social studies,* second edition. Thousand Oaks: SAGE.

Johnson, J.T. (2012). Place-based learning and knowing: Critical pedagogies grounded in Indigeneity. *GeoJournal, 75*(1), 829–836.

Kapai, P. (2012). Developing capacities for inclusive citizenship in multicultural societies: The role of deliberative theory and citizenship education. *Public Organization Review: A Global Journal, 12*(3), 277–298.

Kaplan, A., & Flum, H. (2012). Identity formation in educational settings: A critical focus for education in the 21st century. *Contemporary Educational Psychology, 37*(3), 171–175.

Kelly, A.V. (1995) *Education and democracy: Principles and practices,* London: Paul Chapman.

Kennedy, D. (1995). Philosophy for children and school reform: Dewey, Lipman, and the community of inquiry. In J.P. Portelli & R.F. Reed (Eds.), *Children, philosophy, and democracy* (pp. 159–177). Calgary: Detselig Enterprises.

Kennedy, D. (1998). Reconstructing childhood. *Thinking: The Journal of Philosophy for Children, 14*(1), 29–37.

Kennedy, D. (2006). *The well of being: Childhood, subjectivity, and education.* Albany: State University of New York Press.

Kennedy, D. (2012). Lipman, Dewey, and the community of philosophical inquiry. *Education and Culture, 28*(2), 36–53.

Kennedy, D. (2017). Anarchism, schooling, and democratic sensibility. *Studies in Philosophy and Education, 36,* 551–568.

Kirschenbaum, H. (1976). Clarifying values clarification: Some theoretical issues and a review of research. In D. Purpel & K. Ryan (Eds.), *Moral education: It comes with the territory* (pp. 99–116). Berkeley: McCutchan Publishing.

Kizel, A. (2021). The facilitator as self-liberator and enabler: Ethical responsibility in communities of philosophical inquiry. *Childhood & Philosophy, 17,* 1–20.

Knapp, C.E. (2005). The 'I-thou' relationship, place-based education, and Aldo Leopold. *The Journal of Experiential Education, 27*(3), 277–285.

Knoll, M. (2016). John Dewey's laboratory school: Theory versus practice. Paper presented at ISCHE 38, International Standing Conference for the History of Education, Loyola University Chicago (p. 1–4). August 17–20, 2016.

Kohan, W. (1995). The origin, nature and aim of philosophy in relation to philosophy for children. *Thinking: The Journal of Philosophy for Children*, *12*(2), 25–30.

Kohan, W.O. (2018). Paulo Freire and philosophy for children: A critical dialogue. *Studies in Philosophy and Education*, *37*(6), 615–629.

Kohan, W.O., & Costa Carvalho, M. (2019). Finding treasures: Is the community of philosophical inquiry a methodology? *Studies in Philosophy and Education*, *38*(3), 275–289.

Kohan, W.O., Santi, M., & Wozniak, J.T. (2017). Philosophy for teachers: Between ignorance, invention and improvisation. In M.R. Gregory, J. Haynes & K. Murris (Eds.), *The Routledge international handbook of philosophy for children* (pp. 253–259). Abingdon: Routledge.

Kohlberg, L. (1981). *The philosophy of moral development*. San Francisco: Harper and Row.

Kohlberg, L. (1985). The just community approach to moral education in theory and practice. In M.W. Berkowitz & F. Oser (Eds.), *Moral education: Theory and application* (pp. 27–88). Hillsdale: Earlbaum.

Kourany, J. (2009). Why are women only 21% of philosophy?: Introduction to the panel presentations. *American Philosophical Association Newsletter on Feminism and Philosophy*, *8*(2), 9–10. Available at: http://www.apaonline.org/publications/newsletters/v08n2_Femini sm_07.aspx.

Krueger, J. (2014). Dewey's rejection of the emotion expression distinction. In T. Solymosi & J.R. Shook (Eds.), *Neuroscience, neurophilosophy and pragmatism: Brains at work with the world* (pp. 140–161). Basingstoke; New York: Palgrave Macmillan.

Kudryavtsev, A., Stedman, R.C., & Krasny, M.E. (2012). Sense of place in environmental education. *Environmental Education Research*, *18*(2), 229–250.

Langer-Buchwald, J. (2010). Reception of Arthur Sutherland Neill's pedagogical concept and his Summerhill School in Hungarian and German pedagogical literature and press. *US-China Education Review*, *7*(10), 114–119.

Laverty, M.J. (1994). Putting ethics at the center. *Thinking: The Journal of Philosophy for Children*, *11*(3&4), 73–74.

Laverty, M.J. (2014). Philosophy in schools: Then and now (with commentary). *Journal of Philosophy in Schools*, *1*(1), 107–130.

Laverty, M., & Gregory, M. (2007). Evaluating classroom dialogue: Reconciling internal and external accountability. *Theory and Research in Education*, *5*(3), 281–308.

Lefrançois, D., & Ethier, M.A. (2010). Translating the ideal of deliberative democracy into democratic education: Pure utopia? *Educational Philosophy and Theory*, *42*(3), 271–292.

Legg, C. (2008). Letting reality bite. *Transactions of the Charles S. Peirce Society*, *44*(2), 208–212.

Legg, C. (2014). Charles Peirce's limit concept of truth. *Philosophy Compass*, *9*(3), 204–213.

Lenz, M. (2020). The adversarial culture in philosophy does not serve the truth. *Aeon*. https://aeon.co/ideas/the-adversarial-culture-in-philosophy-does-not-serve-the-truth.

Leonardo, Z., & Porter, R.K. (2010). Pedagogy of fear: Toward a Fanonian theory of 'safety' in race dialogue. *Race, Ethnicity and Education, 13*(2), 139–157.

Lickona, T. (2004). *Character matters*. New York: Touchstone.

Lipman, M. (1971). *Harry Stottlemeier's Discovery*. Upper Montclair: Institute for the Advancement of Philosophy for Children.

Lipman, M. (1981). *Pixie*. Upper Montclair: Institute for the Advancement of Philosophy for Children.

Lipman, M. (1982). *Kio and Gus*. Upper Montclair: Institute for the Advancement of Philosophy for Children.

Lipman, M. (1987). Preparing teachers to teach for thinking. *Philosophy Today, 31*(1), 90–96.

Lipman, M. (1988). *Philosophy goes to school*. Philadelphia: Temple University Press.

Lipman, M. (1991). *Thinking in education*. New York: Cambridge University Press.

Lipman, M. (1993). The educational role of philosophy. *Critical & Creative Thinking: The Australasian Journal of Philosophy for Children, 1*(1), 1–9.

Lipman, M. (1998). The contributions of philosophy to deliberative democracy. In D. Evans & I. Kuçuradi (Eds.), *Teaching philosophy on the eve of the twenty-first century* (pp. 6–29). Ankara: International Federation of Philosophical Societies.

Lipman, M. (2003). *Thinking in education*, second edition. Cambridge: Cambridge University Press.

Lipman, M. (2004). Philosophy for children's debt to John Dewey. *Critical & Creative Thinking: The Australasian Journal of Philosophy in Education, 12*(1), 1–8.

Lipman, M. (2008). *A life teaching thinking*. Monclair: IAPC, Montclair University.

Lipman, M. (2014). The educational role of philosophy (with a new commentary by Philip Cam). *Journal of Philosophy in Schools, 1*(1), 4–14.

Lipman M. & Sharp A.M. (1978). Some educational presuppositions of philosophy for children. *Oxford Review of Education, 4*(1), 85–90.

Lipman, M., Sharp, A.M., & Oscanyan, F.S. (1980). *Philosophy in the classroom*, second edition. Philadelphia: Temple University Press.

Lloyd, G. (1984). *The man of reason: 'Male' and 'female' in western philosophy*. London: Methuen.

Lloyd, G. (2000). No one's land: Australia and the philosophical imagination. *Hypatia, 15*(2), 26–39.

Locke, J. (1965 [1689/90]). *Two treatises of government*. P. Laslett (introduction). New York: Mentor.

London, S. (2021). The politics of education: An interview with Benjamin Barber. Adapted from the radio program *Afternoon Insights*, WYSO-FM, December 14, 1992. http://scott.london/interviews/barber.html.

Lourenço, O. (2012). Piaget and Vygotsky: Many resemblances, and a crucial difference. *New Ideas in Psychology, 30*(3), 281–295.

Lowan-Trudeau, G. (2017). Narrating a critical Indigenous pedagogy of place: A literary métissage. *Educational Theory, 67*(4), 509–525.

Luke, A. (2018). Curriculum, ethics, metanarrative: Teaching and learning beyond the nation. *Educational policy, narrative and discourse* (pp. 139–152). New York: Routledge.

Luntley, M. (2016). What's the problem with Dewey? *European Journal of Pragmatism and American Philosophy, VIII*(1), 1–21.

MacColl, S. (1994). Opening philosophy. *Thinking: The Journal of Philosophy for Children, 11*(3&4), 5–9.

MacIntyre, A. (1988). *Whose justice? Which rationality?* Notre Dame: University of Notre Dame Press.

Macintyre, S. (1995). Teaching citizenship. In L. Yates (Ed.), *Citizenship and education Australia*. Carlton: La Trobe University Press.

Mackenzie, C. (2014). Feminist philosophy. In G. Oppy & N.N. Trakakis (Eds.), *History of philosophy in Australia and New Zealand* (pp. 593–635). Dordrech: Springer.

MacKinnon, C.A. (1989). *Toward a feminist theory of the state*. Cambridge: Harvard University Press.

Maitles, H. (1997). Teaching political literacy. Paper presented at the Scottish Educational Research Association Annual Conference, University of Dundee. September 18–20, 1997.

Makaiau, A.S., Wang, J.C-S., Ragoonaden, K., & Leng, L. (2017). Empowering global P4C research and practice through self-study: The philosophy for children Hawai'i international journaling and self-study project. In M.R. Gregory, J. Haynes & K. Murris (Eds.), *The Routledge international handbook of philosophy for children* (pp. 227–235). Abingdon: Routledge.

Mallory, C. (2009). Val Plumwood and ecofeminist political solidarity: standing with the natural other. *Ethics and the Environment, 14*(2), 3–21.

Mannion, G., Fenwick, A., & Lynch, J. (2013). Place-responsive pedagogy: Learning from teachers' experiences of excursions in nature. *Environmental Education Research, 19*(6), 792–809.

Mannion, G., & Lynch, J. (2016). Primacy of place in education in outdoor settings. In. B. Humberstone, H. Prince & K. Hendersen (Eds.), *Routledge international handbook of outdoor studies* (pp. 85–94). Abingdon: Routledge.

Mansbridge, J., & Okin, S.M. (1993). Feminism. In R. Goodin & P. Pettit (Eds), *A companion to contemporary political philosophy* (pp. 269–290). Oxford: Blackwell.

Markauskaite, L., & Goodyear, P. (2017). *Epistemic fluency and professional education innovation, knowledgeable action and actionable knowledge*. Dordrecht: Springer.

Marshall, J.D. (2007). Philosophy, polemics, education, *Studies in Philosophy and Education, 26*, 97–109.

Marshall, J. (2008). Philosophy as literature. *Educational Philosophy and Theory, 40*, 383–393.

Martin, J. (1983). What should we do with a hidden curriculum when we find one? In H. Giroux & D. Purpel (Eds.), *The hidden curriculum and moral education* (pp. 122–139). Berkeley: McCutchan Publishing Corporation.

Mascall, B., & Rolheiser, C. (2006). Pedagogical synergy: Linking assessment, curriculum, and instruction. *Brock Education Journal, 16*(1), 45–61.

Massey, D. (2005). *For space*. London: Sage.

Mathews, F. (1991). *The ecological self*. London: Routledge.

Mathews, F. (1995). Community and the ecological self. *Environmental Politics, 4*(4), 66–100.

Mathews, F. (1996). *Ecology and democracy*. Portland: Frank Cass.

Mathews, F. (2004). Letting the world do the doing. *Australian Humanities Review*, 1–10.

Matthews, G. (1980). *Philosophy and the young child*. Cambridge: Harvard University Press.

Matthews, G. (1984). *Dialogues with children*. Cambridge: Harvard University Press.

Mayer, S.J. (2008). Dewey's dynamic integration of Vygotsky and Piaget. *Education and Culture, 24*(2), 6–24.

McAfee, N. (2004). Three models of democratic deliberation. *The Journal of Speculative Philosophy, 18*(1), 44–59.

McKinnon, R. (2016). Epistemic injustice. *Philosophy Compass, 11*(8), 437–446.

Mehta, J. (2013). From bureaucracy to profession: Remaking the educational sector for the twenty-first century. *Harvard Educational Review, 83*(3), 463–543.

Mellor, S., Meiers, M., & Knight, P. (2010). The Digest edition 2010/8: Civics and citizenship education. *Research Digest.* https://research.acer.edu.au/digest/7.

Merchant, C. (2012). Women and nature: Responding to the call. In J. Bowersox & K. Arabas (Eds.), *Is nature calling?* (pp. 1–13). Santa Rosa: Polebridge Press.

Mesquita, G.R. (2012). Vygotsky and the theories of emotions: In search of a possible dialogue. *Psicologia: Reflexão e Crítica, 25*(4), 809–816.

Mezirow, J. (1997). Transformative learning: Theory to practice. *New Directions for Adult and Continuing Education, 74*, 5–12.

Mill, J.S. (1859). *On liberty.* London: John W. Parker & Sons.

Miller, J.P. (2010). *Whole child education.* Toronto: University of Toronto Press.

Millett, S., Scholl, R., & Tapper, A. (2019). Australian research into the benefits of philosophy for children. In G. Burgh & S. Thornton (Eds.), *Philosophical inquiry with children: The development of an inquiring society in Australia* (pp. 199–214). Abingdon; New York: Routledge.

Millett, S., & Tapper, A. (2012). Benefits of collaborative philosophical inquiry in schools. *Educational Philosophy and Theory 44*(5), 546–567.

Misak, C.J. (2004). Making disagreement matter: Pragmatism and deliberative democracy. *The Journal of Speculative Philosophy, 18*(1), 9–22.

Mitchell, J. (1974). *Psychoanalysis and feminism.* London: Allan Lane.

Moreton-Robinson, A. (2015). *The white possessive: Property, power, and indigenous sovereignty.* Minneapolis: University of Minnesota Press.

Morrell, A., & O'Connor, M. (2002). Introduction. In E. O'Sullivan, A. Morrell & M. O'Connor (Eds.), *Expanding the boundaries of transformative learning: Essays on theory and praxis* (pp. xv–xx). New York: Palgrave Macmillan.

Morrison, K.A. (2008). Democratic classrooms: Promises and challenges of student voice and choice, Part One. *Educational Horizons, 87*(1), 50–60.

Moulton, J. (1983). A paradigm of philosophy: The adversary method. In S. Harding & M.B. Hintikka (Eds.), *Discovering reality. Feminist perspectives on epistemology, metaphysics, methodology and philosophy of science* (pp. 149–164). Dordrecht: D. Reidel.

Murphy, J.P. (1990) *Pragmatism: From Peirce to Davidson.* Boulder: Westview Press.

Murris, K.S. (2008). Philosophy with children, the stingray and the educative value of disequilibrium. *Journal of Philosophy of Education, 42*, 667–685.

Murris, K. (2013). The epistemic challenge of hearing child's voice. *Studies in Philosophy and Education, 32*(3), 245–259.

Murris, K. (2015). Listening-as-usual: A response to Michael Hand. *Studies in Philosophy and Education, 34*(3), 331–335.

Murris, K. (2016a). The philosophy for children curriculum: Resisting 'teacher proof' texts and the formation of the ideal philosopher child. *Studies in Philosophy and Education, 35*, 63–78.

Murris, K. (2016b). *The Posthuman Child: Educational transformation through philosophy with picturebooks.* Abingdon. Routledge.

Naji, S., & Hashim, R. (Eds.) (2017). *History, theory and practices of philosophy for children: International perspectives* (pp. 157–166). London: Routledge.

Nakata, N.M., Nakata, V., Keech, S., & Bolt, R. (2012). Decolonial goals and pedagogies for Indigenous studies. *Decolonization: Indigeneity, Education & Society*, *1*(1), 120–140.

Nash, K. (1997). The feminist critique of liberal individualism as masculinist. *Journal of Political Ideologies*, *2*(1), 13–28.

Neill, A.S. (1960a). *Summerhill*. New York: Hart.

Neill, A.S. (1960b). *Summerhill: A radical approach to child rearing, foreword by Erich Fromm*. New York: Hart.

Neill, A.S. (1992). *The new Summerhill*, A. Lamb (Ed.). New Delhi: Penguin.

Nelson, L. (1965). *Socratic method and critical philosophy: Selected essays*. Thomas K. Brown III (trans.). New York: Dover.

Neoh, J.Y. (2017). Neoliberal education? Comparing character and citizenship education in Singapore and civics and citizenship education in Australia. *Journal of Social Science Education*, *16*(3), 29–39.

Nichols. K., Burgh, G., & Fynes-Clinton, L. (2017a). Reconstruction of thinking across the curriculum through the community of inquiry. In M.R. Gregory, J. Haynes & K. Murris (Eds.), *The Routledge international handbook of philosophy for children* (pp. 245–252). Abingdon: Routledge.

Nichols, K., Burgh, G., & Kennedy, C. (2017b). Comparing two inquiry professional development interventions in science on primary students' questioning and other inquiry behaviours. *Research in Science Education*, *47*(1), 1–24.

Nord, W. (1995). *Religion & American education*. Chapel Hill: University of North Carolina Press.

Nussbaum, M. (2010). *Not for profit: Why democracy needs the humanities*. Princeton: Princeton University Press.

Nxumalo, F., & Cedillo, S. (2017). Decolonizing place in early childhood studies: Thinking with Indigenous onto-epistemologies and Black feminist geographies. *Global Studies in Childhood*, *72*(2), 99–112.

Ó Gallchóir, C., & McGarr, O. (2021). An Irish perspective on initial teacher education: How teacher educators can respond to an awareness of the 'absurd'. *Educational Philosophy and Theory* (early online), 1–9.

Okin, S.M. (1979). *Women in western political thought*. Princeton: Princeton University Press.

Oliver, T. (1973). Camus, man, and education. *Educational Theory*, *23*, 224–229.

Olsson, L., Opondo, M., Tschakert, P., Agrawal, A., Eriksen, S.H., Ma, S., Perch, L.N., & Zakieldeen, S.A. (2014). Livelihoods and poverty. In C.B. Field, V.R. Barros, D.J. Dokken, K.J. Mach, M.D. Mastrandrea, T.E. Bilir, M. Chatterjee, K.L. Ebi, Y.O. Estrada, R.C. Genova, B. Girma, E.S. Kissel, A.N. Levy, S. MacCracken, P.R. Mastrandrea & L.L. White (Eds.), *Climate change 2014: Impacts, adaptation, and vulnerability. Part A: Global and sectoral aspects. Contribution of working group II to the fifth assessment report of the Intergovernmental Panel on Climate Change* (pp. 793–832). Cambridge; New York: Cambridge University Press.

Orr, D. (1992). *Ecological literacy: Education and the transition to a postmodern world*. Albany: State University of New York Press.

Pardales, M.J., & Girod, M. (2006) Community of inquiry: Its past and present future. *Educational Philosophy and Theory*, *38*(3), 299–309.

Pascoe, B. (2014). *Dark Emu: Black seeds agriculture or accident?* Broome: Magabala Books.

Pateman, C. (1988). *The sexual contract*. Cambridge: Polity Press.

Pateman, C. (1989). *The disorder of women: Democracy, feminism and political theory.* Cambridge: Polity Press.

Peirce, C.S. (1868). Some consequences of four incapacities. *The Journal of Speculative Philosophy, 2*(3), 140–157.

Peirce, C.S. (1877). The fixation of belief. *Popular Science Monthly, 12,* 1–15.

Peirce, C.S. (1878). How to make our ideas clear. *Popular Science Monthly, 12,* 286–302.

Peirce, C.S. (1899). First rule of logic. In Peirce Edition Project (Ed.), *The essential Peirce: Selected philosophical writings, Volume 2 (1893–1913)* (pp. 42–56). Bloomington; Indianapolis: Indiana University Press.

Peirce C.S. (1960). *Collected papers of Charles Sanders Peirce, Vols 1–6.* C. Hartshorne & P. Weiss (Eds.), Cambridge: The Belknap Press of Harvard University Press.

Peters, R.S. (1966). *Ethics and education.* London: Allen & Unwin.

Phillips, R. (1994). A sincere word for the devil's advocate. *Critical & Creative Thinking: The Australasian Journal of Philosophy for Children, 2*(1), 15–20.

Piaget, J. (1936). *Origins of intelligence in the child.* London: Routledge & Kegan Paul.

Plato (1961). *Meno.* B. Jowett (trans.). Cambridge: Cambridge University Press.

Plumwood, V. (1993). *Feminism and the mastery of nature. London;* New York: Routledge.

Plumwood, V. (1995). Has democracy failed ecology? An ecofeminist perspective. *Environmental Politics, 4*(4), 134–168.

Plumwood, V. (1999). Being prey. In D. Rothenberg & M. Ulvaeus, *The new earth reader: The best of Terra Nova* (pp. 76–92). Canberra: ANU Press.

Plumwood, V. (2001). Nature as agency and the prospects for a progressive naturalism. *Capitalism Nature Socialism, 12*(4), 3–32.

Plumwood, V. (2002). *Environmental culture: The ecological crisis of reason. London;* New York: Routledge.

Plumwood, V. (2008). Tasteless: Towards a food-based approach to death. *Environmental Values, 17*(3), 323–330.

Plumwood, V. (2012). *The eye of the crocodile.* L. Shannon (Ed.). ACT: ANU E Press.

Postman, N., & Weingartner, C. (1969). *Teaching as a subversive activity.* New York: Delacorte.

Poulton, J. (2019). Teacher education and professional development. In G. Burgh & S. Thornton (Eds.), *Philosophical inquiry with children: The development of an inquiring society in Australia* (pp. 145–155). Abingdon; New York: Routledge.

Punch, M. (1976). The Summerhill way: A critique of A.S. Neill's notion of freedom. *Amsterdams Sociologisch Tijdschrift, 2*(4), 31–45.

Powell, T.C. (2001). Fallibilism and organizational research: The third epistemology. *Journal of Management Research, 4,* 201–219.

Pritchard, M. (1985). *Philosophical adventures with children.* Lanham: University Press of America.

Prior, S., & Wilks, S. (2019). Philosophy in public and other educational spaces. In G. Burgh & S. Thornton (Eds.), *Philosophical inquiry with children: The development of an inquiring society in Australia* (pp. 185–198). Abingdon; New York: Routledge.

Rainville, H. (2001). Philosophy for children in native America: A post-colonial critique. *Analytic Teaching, 21*(1), 65–77.

Raths, L.E., Harmin, M., & Simon, S.B. (1966). *Values and teaching.* Columbus: Charles E. Merrill.

Razfar, A. (2013). Dewey and Vygotsky: Incommensurability, intersections, and the empirical possibilities of metaphysical consciousness. *Human Development, 56,* 128–133.

Reed-Sandoval, A. (2014). The Oaxaca philosophy for children initiative as place-based philosophy: Why context matters in philosophy for children. *American Philosophical Association Newsletter on Hispanic/Latino Issues in Philosophy, 14*(1), 9–12.

Reed-Sandoval, A., & Sykes, A.C. (2017). Who talks? Who listens? Taking positionality seriously in philosophy for children. In M.R. Gregory, J. Haynes & K. Murris (Eds.), *The Routledge international handbook of philosophy for children* (pp. 219–226). Abingdon: Routledge.

Renshaw, P., & Tooth, R. (2018a). Diverse place-responsive pedagogies Historical, professional and theoretical threads. In R. Renshaw & R. Tooth (Eds.), *Diverse pedagogies of place: Educating students in and for local and global environments* (pp. 2–21). Abingdon: Routledge.

Renshaw, P., & Tooth, R. (2018b). Pedagogy as advocacy in and for place. In R. Renshaw & R. Tooth (Eds.), *Diverse pedagogies of place: Educating students in and for local and global environments* (pp. 22–44). Abingdon: Routledge.

Reznitskaya, A., & Gregory, M. (2013). Student thought and classroom language: Examinating the mechanisms of change and dialogic teaching. *Educational Psychologist, 48*(2), 114–133.

Ripple, W., Wolf, C., Newsome, T., Barnard, P., & Moomaw, W. (2020). World scientists' warning of a climate emergency. *Bioscience, 70*(1), 8–12.

Rivage-Seul, M. (1987). Critical thought or domestication? In F. Estes & T. Haute (Eds.), *Philosophical studies in education: proceedings of the annual (1987-1988) meeting of the Ohio Valley Philosophy of Education Society* (pp. 230–246). Indiana: OVPES.

Rizvi, F. (1989). Bureaucratic rationality and the promise of democratic schooling. In W. Carr (Ed.), *Quality in teaching* (pp. 55–75). London: Falmer Press.

Rizvi, F. (1993). Contrasting perceptions of devolution. *Professional Magazine, 11*(1), 1–5.

Roberts, P. (2008a). Teaching, learning and ethical dilemmas: lessons from Albert Camus. *Cambridge Journal of Education, 38,* 529–542.

Roberts, P. (2008b). Bridging literary and philosophical genres: Judgement, reflection and education in Camus' *The Fall. Educational Philosophy and Theory, 40,* 873–887.

Roberts, P. (2013a). Education and the face of the other: Levinas, Camus and (mis) understanding. *Educational Philosophy and Theory, 45,* 1133–1149.

Roberts, P. (2013b). Acceptance, resistance and educational transformation: A Taoist reading of *The First Man. Educational Philosophy and Theory, 45,* 1175–1189.

Roberts, P., Gibbons, A., & Heraud, R. (2013). Introduction: Camus and education. *Educational Philosophy and Theory, 45,* 1085–1091.

Rockström, J., & Stern, N. (2020). Science, society and a sustainable future. In C. Henry, J. Rockström & N. Stern (Eds.), *Standing up for a sustainable world: Voices of change* (pp. 3–9). Cheltenham: Edward Elgar Publishing.

Rooney, P. (2010). Philosophy, adversarial argumentation, and embattled reason. *Informal Logic, 30*(3), 203–234.

Rooney, P. (2012). When philosophical argumentation impedes social and political progress. *Journal of Social Philosophy, 43*(3), 317–333.

Rorty, R. (1996). Idealizations, foundations, and social practices. In S. Benhabib (Ed.), *Democracy and difference: Contesting boundaries of the political* (pp. 333–335). Princeton: Princeton University Press.

Ross, D., Oppegaard, B., & Willerton, R. (2019). Principles of place: Developing a place-based ethic for discussing, debating, and anticipating technical communication concerns. *IEEE Transactions on Professional Communications, 99*, 1–23.

Rousseau, J-J. (1909). *The social contract, or, principles of political right*, third edition. London: Swan, Sonnenschein & Co.

Rousseau, J-J. (1979 [1762]). *Emile; or, On education*. A. Bloom (introduction, trans., and notes). New York: Basic Books.

Russell, C.L. & Bell, A.C. (1996). A politicized ethic of care: Environmental education from an ecofeminist perspective. In K. Warren (Ed.), *Women's voices in experiential education* (pp. 172–181). Dubuque: Kendall/Hunt Publishing Company.

Russell, D. (1980). *The Tamarisk tree: Vol. 2 My school and the years of war*. London: Virago.

Sagi, A. (2002). *Albert Camus and the philosophy of the absurd*. Amsterdam: Rodopi.

Saint, E. (2019). Democratic education: A theoretical review (2006–2017). *Review of Educational Research, 89*(5), 655–696.

Saito, N. (2006) Philosophy as education and education as philosophy: Democracy and education from Dewey to Cavell. *Journal of Philosophy of Education, 40*, 345–356.

Saltman, K.J. (2015). Democratic education against corporate school reform: The new market bureaucracy in U.S. public schooling. In J.M. Paraskeva & T. LaVallee (Eds.), *Transformative researcher and educators for democracy: Dartmouth dialogues* (pp. 7–22). Rotterdam: Sense Publishing.

Sameroff, A. (2009). The transactional model. In A. Sameroff (Ed.), *The transactional model of development: How children and contexts shape each other* (pp. 3–21). Washington: American Psychological Association.

Sanderse, W. (2013). The meaning of role modelling in moral and character education. *Journal of Moral Education, 42*(1), 28–42.

Santrock, J.W. (2004). *Educational psychology*, second edition. Boston: McGraw-Hill.

SBS News (2019). US commentator slammed after comparing Greta Thunberg to Nazi propaganda (updated 23/09/2019). http://www.sbs.com.au/news/us-commentator-slammed-after-comparing-greta-thunberg-to-nazi-propaganda.

Scholl, R., Nichols, K., & Burgh, G. (2009). Philosophy for children: Towards pedagogical transformation. In *Teacher education crossing borders: Cultures, contexts, communities and curriculum*. Annual Conference of the Australian Teacher Education Association (ATEA), Albury, Australia (pp. 1–15). June 28 to July 1, 2009.

Scholl, R., Nichols, K., & Burgh, G. (2014). Transforming pedagogy through philosophical inquiry. *International Journal of Pedagogies and Learning, 9*(3), 253–272.

Scholl, R., Nichols, K., & Burgh, G. (2016). Connecting learning to the world beyond the classroom through collaborative philosophical inquiry. *Asia-Pacific Journal of Teacher Education, 44*(5), 436–454.

Scholz, S.J. (2013). Political solidarity and the more-than-human world. *Ethics and the Environment, 18*(2), 81–99.

Schreiber, J.B., & Moss, C.M. (2002). A Peircean view of teacher beliefs and genuine doubt. *Teaching and Learning: The Journal of Natural Inquiry and Reflective Practice, 17*(1), 25–42.

Schwartzman, L.H. (2006). *Challenging liberalism: Feminism as political critique.* University Park: Pennsylvania State University Press.

Seixas, P. (1993). The community of inquiry as a basis for knowledge and learning: The case of history. *American Educational Research Journal, 30*(2), 305–324.

Shanley, M.L., & Pateman, C. (Eds.) (1991). *Feminist interpretations and political theory.* Cambridge: Polity Press.

Sharp, A.M. (1991). The community of inquiry: Education for democracy. *Thinking: The Journal of Philosophy for Children, 9*(2), 31–37.

Sharp, A.M. (1993). Peirce, feminism, and philosophy for children. *Analytic Teaching, 14*(1), 51–62.

Sharp, A.M. (2017a). Philosophical novel. In S. Naji & R. Hashim (Eds.), *History, theory and practices of philosophy for children: International perspectives* (pp. 18–29). London: Routledge.

Sharp, A.M. (2017b). Philosophy in the school curriculum. In S. Naji & R. Hashim (Eds.), *History, theory and practices of philosophy for children: International perspectives* (pp. 39–42). London: Routledge.

Shaull, R. (1970). Foreword. In P. Freire, *Pedagogy of the oppressed* (pp. 3–34). London: Continuum.

Sherwin, S. (1989). Philosophical methodology and feminist methodology: Are they compatible? In A. Garry & M. Pearsall (Eds.), *Women, knowledge, and reality: Explorations in feminist philosophy* (pp. 21–35). Boston: Unwin Hyman.

Shor, I., & Freire, P. (1987). *A pedagogy for liberation.* South Hadley: Bergin & Garvey Publishers.

Simon, S.B. (1976). Values clarification vs. indoctrination. In D. Purpel & K. Ryan (Eds.), *Moral education: It comes with the territory* (pp. 126–135). Berkeley: McCutchan Publishing.

Simon, S.B., Howe, L.W., & Kirschenbaum, H. (1972). *Values clarification: A handbook of practical strategies for teachers and students.* New York: Hart.

Simpson, E.L. (1974). Moral development research: A case study of scientific cultural bias. *Human Development, 17,* 81–106.

Slade, C. (1994). Harryspeak and the conversation with girls. *Thinking : The Journal of Philosophy for Children, 11*(3–4), 29–32.

Slattery, L. (1995). Sophie meets Socrates. *The Australian Magazine,* 20–24.

Slavich, G.M., & Zimbardo. P.G. (2012). Transformational teaching: Theoretical underpinnings, basic principles, and core methods. *Educational Psychology Review, 24,* 569–608.

Slavin, R.E. (2012). *Educational psychology: Theory and practice,* tenth edition. Boston: Pearson.

Smith, G. (2002). Place-based education: Learning to be where we are. *Phi Delta Kappan, 83*(8), 584–594.

Smith, K.B., & Larimer, C.W. (2004). A mixed relationship: Bureaucracy and school performance. *Public Administration Review, 64*(6), 728–736.

Smith, L.T. (2012). *Decolonizing methodologies: Research and indigenous peoples,* second edition. London: Zed Books.

Smith, L.T., Tuck, E., & Yang, K.W. (Eds.) (2019). *Indigenous and decolonizing studies in education: Mapping the long view.* New York: Routledge.

Snarey, J.R., Reimer, J., & Kohlberg, L. (1985). Development of social-moral reasoning among Kibbutz adolescents: A longitudinal cross-cultural study. *Developmental Psychology, 21*(1), 3–17.

Sobel, D. (2004). *Place-based education: Connecting classrooms and communities.* Great Barrington: Orion Press.

Social and Character Development Research Consortium (2010). *Efficacy of school-wide programs to promote social and character development and reduce problem behavior in elementary school children (NCER 2011-2001).* Washington, DC: National Center for Education Research, Institute of Education Sciences, U.S. Department of Education.

Somerville, M. (2010). A place pedagogy for 'global contemporaneity'. *Educational Philosophy and Theory, 42*(3), 326–344.

Spivak, G.C. (2003). Can the subaltern speak? *Die Philosophin, 14*(27), 42–58.

Spelman, E. (1982). Woman as body: Ancient and contemporary views. *Feminist Studies, 8*(1), 109–131.

Splitter, L.J. (1987). Educational reform through philosophy for children. *Thinking: The Journal of Philosophy for Children, 7*(2), 33–39.

Splitter, L.J. (1991a). *How low can you go?: The case for integrating (critical) thinking into early childhood education.* A paper presented at the Second National Conference on Reasoning, Flinders University, Adelaide, Australia (pp. 1–16). October 1991.

Splitter, L. (1991b). Critical thinking: What, why, when and how. *Educational Philosophy and Theory, 23*(1), 89–109.

Splitter, L. (1993). Peace, violence, discrimination and the classroom community of inquiry. *Ethos P-6*, 8–19.

Splitter, L.J. (2003). Transforming how teachers teach and how students learn. *Critical & Creative Thinking: The Australasian Journal of Philosophy in Schools, 11*(2), 31–46.

Splitter, L.J. (2014). Preparing teachers to 'teach' philosophy for children. *Journal of Philosophy in Schools, 1*(1), 89–106.

Splitter, L.J. (2019). 'Memo to Harry Stottlemeier and friends: You are not wanted here!: Reflections on the idea of a philosophical curriculum in Australia. In G. Burgh & S. Thornton (Eds.), *Philosophical inquiry with children: The development of an inquiring society in Australia* (pp. 73–86). Abingdon; New York: Routledge.

Splitter, L.J., & Sharp, A.M. (1995). *Teaching for better thinking: The classroom community of inquiry.* Melbourne: Australian Council for Educational Research.

Sprod, T. (2001). *Philosophical discussion in moral education: The community of ethical inquiry.* London; New York: Routledge.

Starkey, H. (2018). Fundamental British values and citizenship education: Tensions between national and global perspectives. *Geografiska Annaler: Series B, Human Geography, 100*(2), 149–162.

Stenhouse, L. (1971). The humanities curriculum project: The rationale. *Theory into Practice, 10*(3), 154–162.

Stewart, J.S. (1975). Clarifying values clarification: A critique. *The Phi Delta Kappan, 56*(10), 684–688.

Stone, A. (2004). Essentialism and anti-essentialism in feminist philosophy. *Journal of Moral Philosophy, 1*, 135–153.

Strandbrink, P. (2017). *Civic education and liberal democracy: Making post-normative citizens in normative political spaces.* Cham: Springer.

Sylvan, R. (2009). Is there a need for a new, an environmental, ethic? In J.B. Callicott & R. Frodeman (Eds.), *Encyclopedia of environmental ethics and philosophy* (Vol. 2, pp. 484– 489). Macmillan Reference USA.

Svensson, F. (1979). Liberal democracy and group rights: The legacy of individualism and its impact on American Indian tribes. *Political Studies, 27*(3), 421–439.

Talisse, R.B. (2004). Introduction: Pragmatism and deliberative politics. *The Journal of Speculative Philosophy, 18*(1), 1–8.

Tanner, L.N. (1991). The meaning of curriculum in Dewey's Laboratory School (1896–1904). *Journal of Curriculum Studies, 23*(2), 101–117.

Tanner, L.N. (1997). *Dewey's Laboratory School: Lessons for today.* New York: Teachers College Press.

Taylor, C. (1994). *Multiculturalism: Examining the politics of recognition.* Princeton: Princeton University Press.

Taylor, E.W. (1998). *The theory and practice of transformative learning: A critical review.* Information Series No. 374. Columbus: ERIC Clearinghouse on Adult, Career, and Vocational Education, Center on Education and Training for Employment, College of Education, Ohio State University.

Taylor, E.W. (2001). Transformative learning theory: A neurobiological perspective of the role of emotions and unconscious ways of knowing. *International Journal of Lifelong Education, 20*(3), 218–236.

ten Dam, G., & Volman, M. (2004). Critical thinking as a citizenship competence: Teaching strategies. *Learning and Instruction, 14*(4), 359–379.

Theobald, P. (1997). *Teaching the Commons: Place, pride, and the renewal of community.* Boulder: Westview Press.

Theobald, P., & Curtiss, J. (2000). Communities as curricula. *Forum for Applied Research and Public Policy, 15*(1), 106–111.

Thomas, R.M. (2000). *Comparing theories of child development*, fifth edition. Belmont: Wadsworth Thomson Learning.

Thornton, M.B. (1995). *Living maths.* The book of the videos based on the thought, research and development of the Yolngu community. Northern Territory: Boulder Valley Films production company for Yirrkala Community School.

Thornton, S. (2019). The educational cost of philosophical suicide: What it means to be lucid. *Educational Philosophy and Theory, 51*(6), 608–618.

Thornton, S. (2022, forthcoming). *Education in a time of environmental crisis: A philosophy of eco-rational education.* Abingdon; New York: Routledge. [Page numbers refer to: Thornton, S. (2019). Disruptive philosophies: Eco-rational education and the epistemology of place. PhD Thesis. Brisbane: School of Historical and Philosophical Inquiry, The University of Queensland. DOI: 10.14264/uql.2019.534].

Thornton, S., & Burgh, G. (2017). Making peace education everyone's business. In C-C. Lin & L. Sequeira (Eds.), *Inclusion, diversity and intercultural dialogue in young people's philosophical inquiry* (pp. 55–65). Rotterdam: Sense Publishers.

Thornton, S., & Burgh, G. (2019). Growing up with philosophy in Australia: Philosophy as cultural discourse. In G. Burgh & S. Thornton (Eds.), *Philosophical Inquiry with Children: The development of an inquiring society in Australia* (pp. 235–249). Abingdon; New York: Routledge.

Thornton, S., Graham, M., & Burgh, G. (2019). Reflecting on place: Environmental education as decolonisation. *Australian Journal of Environmental Education, 35*(3), 239–249.

Thornton, S., Graham, M., & Burgh, G. (2021). Place-based philosophical education: Reconstructing 'place', reconstructing ethics. *Childhood & Philosophy, 17*, 1–29.

Tooth, R., & Renshaw, P. (2009). Reflections on pedagogy and place: A journey into learning for sustainability through environmental narrative and deep attentive reflection. *Australian Journal of Environmental Education, 25*, 95–104.

Topping, K.J., & Trickey, S. (2007a). Collaborative philosophical enquiry for school children: Cognitive gains at two-year follow-up. *British Journal of Educational Psychology*, *77*(4), 787–796.

Topping, K.J., & Trickey, S. (2007b). Impact of philosophical enquiry on school students' interactive behaviour. *Thinking Skills and Creativity*, *2*(2), 73–84.

Topping, K.J., & Trickey, S. (2007c). Collaborative philosophical enquiry for school children: Cognitive effects at 10–12 years. *British Journal of Educational Psychology*, *77*(2), 271–288.

Toulmin, S. (1994). Wonder, puzzlement, and perplexity. In M. Lipman & A.M. Sharp, *Growing up with philosophy* (pp. 77–84). Dubuque: Kendall/Hunt Publishing Company.

Trickey, S., & Topping, K.J. (2004). Philosophy for children: A systematic review. *Research Papers in Education*, *19*(3), 365–380.

Trickey, S., & Topping, K.J. (2006). Collaborative philosophical enquiry for school children: Socio-emotional effects at 10–12 Years. *School Psychology International*, *27*(5), 599–614.

Trickey, S., & Topping, K.J. (2007). Collaborative philosophical enquiry for school children: Participant evaluation at 11–12 years. *Thinking: The Journal of Philosophy for Children*, *18*(3), 23–34.

Tudball, L., & Henderson, D.J. (2014). Contested notions of civics and citizenship education as national education in the Australian curriculum. *Curriculum and Teaching*, *29*(2), 5–24.

Turgeon, W. (1998). The reluctant philosopher: Causes and cures. *Critical & Creative Thinking: The Australian Journal of Philosophy for Children*, *6*(2), 9–17.

UNESCO (2007). *Philosophy, a school of freedom: Teaching Philosophy and Learning to Philosophize: Status and Prospects*. Paris: UNESCO.

Ungunmerr-Baumann, M-R. (1988). Dadirri. *Compass Theology Review*, *22*, 9–11.

Ungunmerr-Baumann, M-R. (2002). *Dadirri: A reflection by Miriam-Rose Ungunmerr Baumann*. Retrieved from http://nextwave.org.au/wp-content/uploads/Dadirri-Inner-Deep-Listening-M-R-Ungunmerr-Bauman-Refl.pdf.

United Nations (UN) (1999). *General Assembly, UN documents*. Retrieved from http://www.un-documents.net/a53r243a.htm.

UN News (2018). *Special Coverage of COP24, the UN Climate Change Conference*. https://news.un.org/en/events/cop24.

Venter, W., & Higgs, L.G. (2014). Philosophy for children in a democratic classroom. *Journal of Social Sciences*, *41*(1), 11–16.

Veugelers, W. (1995). *Teachers, value stimulation, and critical thinking*. Paper presented the Annual Meeting of the American Educational Research Association, San Francisco, CA (April 18–22, 1995), 1–16.

Vicuna Navarro, A.M. (1998). Ethical education through philosophical discussion. *Thinking: The Journal of Philosophy for Children*, *14*(2), 23–26.

Vygotsky, L.S. (1962). *Thought and language*. Cambridge: MIT Press.

Vygotsky, L.S. (1978). *Mind in society: The development of higher psychological processes*. Cambridge: Harvard University Press.

Walker, J.C. (1990). Functional decentralization and democratic control. In J.D. Chapman (Ed.), *School-based decision making and management* (pp. 83–100). London: Falmer Press.

Walker, J.C. (1992). Education for democracy: The representative/participation dualism. *Educational Theory*, *42*(3), 315–330.

Walsh, M.B. (2012). Private and public dilemmas: Rawls on the family. *Polity, 44*(3), 426–445.

Was, C.A., Woltz, D.J., & Drew, C. (2006). Evaluating character education programs and missing the target: A critique of existing research. *Educational Research Review, 1*(2), 148–156.

Watson, I. (2011). Aboriginal(ising) international law and other centres of power. *Griffith Law Review, 20*(3), 619–640.

Watson, I. (2014). Re-centring first nations knowledge and places in a terra nullius space. *AlterNative: An International Journal of Indigenous Peoples, 10*(5), 508–520.

Wattchow, B., & Brown, M. (2011). *A pedagogy of place: Outdoor education for a changing world.* Clayton: Monash University Publishing.

Weddington, H.S. (2007). The education of Sisyphus: Absurdity, educative transformation, and suicide. *Journal of Transformative Education, 5,* 119–133.

Weinbaum, A.E. (2019). *The afterlife of reproductive slavery: Biocapitalism and black feminism's philosophy of history.* Durham: Duke University Press.

Weinstein, M. (1991). Critical thinking and education for democracy. *Educational Philosophy and Theory, 23*(2), 9–29.

Westbrook, R.B. (1996). Public schooling and American democracy. In R. Soder (Ed.), *Democracy, education, and the schools* (pp. 125–150). San Francisco: Jossey-Bass.

White, K.K., with Fynes-Clinton, L., Hinton, L., Howells, J., Skoutas, E., Smith, D., & Wills, M. (2019). Philosophy in schools across Australia. In G. Burgh & S. Thornton (Eds.), *Philosophical inquiry with children: The development of an inquiring society in Australia* (pp. 172–184). Abingdon; New York: Routledge.

Wildcat, M., McDonald, M., Irlbacher-Fox, S., & Coulthard, G. (2014). Learning from the land: Indigenous land based pedagogy and decolonization. *Decolonization: Indigeneity, Education & Society, 3*(3), i–xv.

Wilks, S. (2019). Resourceful teachers and teacher resources. In G. Burgh & S. Thornton (Eds.), *Philosophical inquiry with children: The development of an inquiring society in Australia* (pp. 96–108). Abingdon; New York: Routledge.

Wolfe, P. (2006). Settler colonialism and the elimination of the native. *Journal of Genocide Research, 8*(4), 387–409.

Wollstonecraft, M. (1975 [1792]). *A Vindication of the rights of woman.* C.H. Poston (Ed.). London; New York: Norton.

Wringe, C. (1984). *Democracy, schooling and political education.* London: G. Allen & Unwin.

Yu, Tianlong (2004). *In the name of morality: Character education and political control.* Bern: Peter Lang.

Index

Page numbers followed by n indicate notes.

Printed in the United States
by Baker & Taylor Publisher Services